Contemporary Architecture and the Digital Design Process

Bilbao looks like my drawings. When I saw it I couldn't believe it.
(Frank Gehry, 2003)

To the parishioners of St. Paraskeva and those of The Precession,
Lytovyzh, Volyn, Ukraine.

Contemporary Architecture and the Digital Design Process

Peter Szalapaj

AMSTERDAM • BOSTON • HEIDELBERG • LONDON • NEW YORK • OXFORD
PARIS • SAN DIEGO • SAN FRANCISCO • SINGAPORE • SYDNEY • TOKYO

Architectural Press is an imprint of Elsevier

ELSEVIER

Architectural
Press

Architectural Press
An imprint of Elsevier
Linacre House, Jordan Hill, Oxford OX2 8DP
30 Corporate Drive, Burlington, MA 01803

First published 2005

British Library Cataloguing in Publication Data
A catalogue record for this book is available from the British Library

Library of Congress Cataloguing in Publication Data
A catalogue record for this book is available from the Library of Congress

ISBN 0 7506 5716 2

For information on all Architectural Press publications
visit our website at www.architecturalpress.com

Printed and bound in The Netherlands

Contents

Foreword   viii

Preface   x

Acknowledgements   xii

PART I: Digital Technology

Chapter 1: Introduction   3

1.1   Digital Representation in Architectural Design Practice   6
1.2   Digital Expression   10
1.3   Digital Integration   17
1.4   Computational Modelling the Building Construction Process   20
1.5   Digital Organisation   24
1.6   Integrating CAD into the Manufacturing Process   29
1.7   A Digital Design Case Study   30

Chapter 2: Simple Visualisation of Complex Forms   35

2.1   What you see is what you get   36
2.2   Sketching prior to Digital Modelling   37
2.3   Visualisation Supporting Designers' Perceptions   41
2.4   The Role of Physical Modelling   42

Chapter 3: Pure Form: Solidifying Mathematics   47

3.1   Fractal Geometry   48
3.2   Logarithmic Spirals   49
3.3   Hubner's Stammheim Church   51
3.4   Dynamic Symmetry   52
3.5   Form Constrained by Environment   56

Chapter 4: Parametric Form: Variations on a Theme   59

4.1   The Design of the British Museum Great Court Roof   60
4.2   The Optimisation of Shape and Topology   62
4.3   Shape Optimisation through Parametric Geometry   64
4.4   Structural Materials   71
4.5   Design Constraints   74
4.6   Detailing   78
4.7   The Physical Node   80
4.8   Robotic Manufacture   82
4.9   Computing the Construction Process   83
4.10   Stress, Strain, and Tensors   84
4.11   Hyperspaces and Hypersurfaces   85

Chapter 5: Express Vision: The Changing Face of Architecture   87
    5.1   Modelling the Kunsthaus, Graz   91
    5.2   Planning in 3-D   100
    5.3   Media Facade   103
    5.4   Interactive Surfaces   106
    5.5   Topological Relationships   108
    5.6   Perella's Hypersurfaces   109

PART II: Digital Practice   111

Chapter 6: The Well-Tempered Vision: Client as Patron, Quality on Demand   113
    6.1   Rethinking Construction   118
    6.2   Design Stages   120
    6.3   Feasibility   122
        6.3.1   Feasibility Study for InfoLab 21   122
        6.3.2   Feasibility Analysis Sketches   123
        6.3.3   Key Relationships   124
        6.3.4   Concept Design at Feasibility Stage   128
        6.3.5   Programme and Phasing   129
    6.4   Tender   130
        6.4.1   Value Management   130
        6.4.2   Design Team Management   131
        6.4.3   CAD Massing Models   132
        6.4.4   Site Analysis   134
        6.4.5   View Analysis   135
        6.12   Analysis of Circulation   136
    6.5   Briefing   138
        6.5.1   The Briefing Process   138
        6.5.2   Managing Value   139
    6.6   Concept Design   140
        6.6.1   Early Concept Design   140
        6.6.2   Testing Ideas   141
        6.6.3   Developing the Brief   144
        6.6.4   Environmental Analysis   146
        6.6.5   CAD-Generated Massing Model Studies   148
        6.6.6   CAD Presentation Models   150
        6.6.7   Strategic Massing   151
    6.7   Scheme Design   152
        6.7.1   Structural Analysis   152
        6.7.2   Environmental Services   153
        6.7.3   External Expression   154
    6.8   Summary   157

Chapter 7: Visionary Integration: This Blessed Plot   159
    7.1   Key Issues in the Digital Representation of the Eden Project   160

7.2	The Site	162
7.3	Site Work	164
7.4	Geodesic Geometry	166
7.5	Positioning the Buildings	168
7.6	Structural Form	172
7.7	The *Hex-tri-hex* Structural Form	174
7.8	Structural Analysis	179
7.9	Cladding Design	182
7.10	The Cladding System	184
7.11	Environmental Loads	186
7.12	Thermal Performance of the Biome Environment	190
7.13	Landscape and Construction	192
7.14	Future Use and Maintenance	195
7.15	Architectural Qualities of the Biome Form	197
7.16	CAD/CAM Technology	198
7.17	Procurement Process	199
7.18	Geodesic Domes	200
7.19	Unfolding Geodesic Spheres	201
7.20	Tensegrity	202
7.21	Summary	205

Chapter 8: The Exuberant Vision: Throwing off the Bowlines   207

8.1	The Importance of the Sketch	211
8.2	The Realisation of the Sketch	212
8.3	The Ray and Maria Stata Center at MIT	215
8.4	The Laboratory for Computer Science (LCS)	216
8.5	Artificial Intelligence Laboratory (AI Lab)	217
8.6	Laboratory for Information and Decision Systems (LIDS)	218
8.7	Department of Linguistics and Philosophy	219
8.8	The Role of Physical Models	220
8.9	Value Engineering	224
8.10	Gaussian Analysis	225
8.11	Architectural Planning	232
8.12	Dialogues with Jim Glymph	234
8.13	Creative Expression in CAD Environments	240
8.14	Human-Computer Interaction	242
8.15	Digital Sketching	243
8.16	From Sketches to Models	246
8.17	Developable Surfaces	248
8.18	Modelling with NURBS surfaces, phantom surfaces and directrices	250
8.19	Rapid Prototyping	254
8.20	Summary	255

Chapter 9: Conclusions   257

Bibliography

Index

Foreword

Only recently has the architectural profession become aware of a subtle but important change taking place within design studios in recent years. We have begun to see for the first time an emerging generation of young architects who are true children of the digital age. Their immersion since childhood in a world of computer hardware and software has given them a natural ease with digital technology. And unlike the generation before them who have had to live through a period of adjustment, perceiving technology as interference to their work, the new generation has an expectation of ubiquitous technology. This generation views technology as an *enabler*, rather than a disabler, helping the creation, realisation and communication of their ideas.

For many years now the use of Computer Aided Design has been the established norm within any architectural office or studio. Ironically this new technology has been used primarily to enhance drafting work, a very important but nontheless mundane task. But over recent years a gradual change has crept up on architectural designers. We are beginning now to see the use of digital technology as a tool to help enable the exploration of new possibilities of form linked importantly with the communication of that form to fabricators and constructors.

I witness these changes in my own work daily. For example, the ease with which sophisticated 3-D CAD modelling techniques have helped to model geometrically complex indoor ski slopes has enabled us to innovate and push forward the design of such building types. Equally, the increasing accuracy and confidence with which these complex geometries can be communicated to both other designers and to fabricators should not be underestimated. So this twin pattern of digital enabler and digital communicator is beginning to leave a recognisable legacy.

Managing the expectation of clients has been always been a central issue for the architectural profession, and there is an increased belief amongst experienced clients that digital representation of design proposals is essential to close the gap between their understanding of the conceptual ideas and the realised finished form.

I am also optimistic by the extent to which this new 'digital' generation of architects is comfortable with technology, and that they perceive it as one of many tools available within the architect's inventory to help realise and communicate ideas. Whilst some in the profession advocate the replacement of old technologies, I am personally encouraged by the fact that immensely powerful tools such as a piece of tracing paper and a felt pen can sit comfortably alongside a computer running CAD software. In fact our practice has actively sought to retain drawing boards and tracing paper alongside computers and plotters. The digital upbringing of this new generation enables them to move easily between one medium and another with no apparent shift in consciousness. This is powerfully demonstrated by young architects who manipulate complex geometrical design ideas with ease using digital 3-D modelling tools transferring very quickly from sketches at their drawing board to digital representations.

Architectural history, like all art history, reflects upon the past and identifies the many links between new technologies and step changes in art or design. One only has to look at the impact of steel frame technology for the creation of high rise structures, or the use of ETFE foil technology to create super-translucent lightweight canopies, to see how strong the causal link is between technology and art. Similar parallels can be identified in the fine arts, such as with the invention of photography.

Over the last few decades there has also been an increasing expectation within architecture and construction that the time allocated to design and construction of new buildings should continue to reduce year on year. One consequence of this trend is that young architectural designers are not able to experience a period of 'apprenticeship' within a practice environment to hone their skills with tools and techniques of the profession. But if this new generation is to realise the potential benefits of digital technology to architectural design, then 'Contemporary Architecture and the Digital Design Process' is an important work which should be recommended to any young architect starting his career.

The impact of digital technology on architectural design is only just beginning to emerge in a powerful way and this new work by Peter Szalapaj is an important indication of its breadth demonstrated through practical examples.

Andrew Kane
Partner
FaulknerBrowns Architects

Preface

Perhaps a less pretentious title might have been *some contemporary architecture and bits of the digital design process*. The problem is always where to start, and how to develop key ideas. This book is rooted in my own experience of teaching computer aided design in a school of architecture in such a way as to generate enthusiasm beyond the limited resources of pseudo-corporate academia, and to give design students insights into the forces that drive design practice, with particular emphasis on the role of digital technologies. I have tried to choose case studies that illustrate some of the dynamic and expressive ways in which computer-based design processes are currently being used in contemporary design practice. These range from innovative applications in office organisation through to the computer modelling of mathematically complex forms.

There really does appear to be a sea-change in the ways in which digital processes are being applied in design practice. It is not just the sophistication and complexity of modelling techniques that are being exploited. Digital models are now forming the basis of fabrication and construction processes by presenting contractors with digital information instead of conventional drawings and textual descriptions. The case studies also aim to show that the digital design process is not a substitute for creative design thinking, but fully supports it. According to Lindsey:

> . . . *the building process [is] never disconnected from the aesthetic tension that the architect pursues or the digital methods at times used to pursue it; a combination of craft and knowledge* . . .
> (Lindsey, 2001, p. 7).

In all of the case studies, whichever design medium is being used, it is effective expression that enables development of design ideas. This expression or externalisation of ideas is a constant phenomenon which occurs throughout design formulation. Architectural designers are continually trying to make the technology work for them, to fit technological developments to their own design practices, to make connections between disparate software developments in specialist areas. The experience gained by designers in the application of computing technology to real design projects has now reached a position in which it is entirely feasible for an architectural practice to control projects involving complex architectural form, requiring difficult and varied cycles of analysis and testing, right through to the construction stage. This control cycle involves knowing not simply how to apply CAD techniques, but when to apply them, in a design process that is responsive to the constantly changing demands and idiosyncrasies of individual designers and design practices. I believe that it is now possible for diverse design practices to configure their own integrated CAD environments in response to the kind of architecture they want to produce, and the analytical procedures they need to make it happen. I hope that this book will attract the interest of practicing architects and design oriented engineers, as well as others in different design fields.

My intention was to make the book accessible to students and designers, and to avoid the jargon and the technicalities of software use. This book may be used as a coursebook for students of CAD in general, even though the many examples and illustrations are predominantly architectural. Some basic design theory is assumed, as well as some basic computing concepts, but no previous experience of the use of particular CAD software is required in order to understand the main issues.

Parts of the book should have some relevance for all design disciplines. Design professionals of various backgrounds are under pressure to adopt new technology and are in urgent need of help in identifying relevance to themselves. The book also aims to be relevant for undergraduate and postgraduate students, and professionals in specialist courses. This book is intended to give students in architectural schools, and designers in architectural practice, some insights into the use of CAD in architectural design practice. It may also be of interest to engineering students seeking to gain more of an insight into CAD in architectural design. The case studies upon which most of the key ideas are based have been presented with minimal reference to particular CAD software systems. Instead, the emphasis is on the functionalities within software that enables designers to design and offices to organise their work. I have taken the liberty of indicating and sometimes addressing related issues within the case study descriptions. Once the reader has understood the ways in which CAD functionalities are being exploited in architectural design projects, it should then be easier for them to appreciate how their own design intentions can potentially be supported computationally. Issues of functionality are introduced in **Part I**, and the constraints that these technological issues meet in design practice are described through more detailed case studies in **Part II**. I have made use of the following symbols in referring to some of the key issues:

KEY

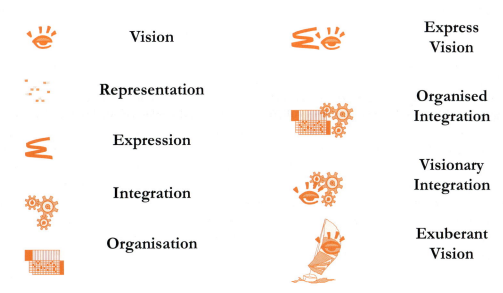

Vision		Express Vision	
Representation		Organised Integration	
Expression		Visionary Integration	
Integration		Exuberant Vision	
Organisation			

Acknowledgements

I have tried to bring together in this book a range of case studies in the use of CAD in practice that I have been familiar with, interested in, or inspired by, for a number of years now, believing that there are valuable lessons to be learned from each of them about the changing nature of CAD in contemporary architectural practice. As is often the case, the greatest help and support comes from where one would least expect it. I would first of all like to thank the students that I have had the pleasure of teaching and working with; in particular to Enver Enronen who modelled the Hongkong Shanghai Bank; to Lutz Atitie who translated material on Szyskowitz-Kowalski and suggested titles for this book. Thanks also to Kurt Arlt of the Astrophysikalisches Institut Potsdam for letting me use Eric Mendelsohn's sketches.

I am also grateful to fellow researchers in this field. These include Professor Mark Burry, Andrew Maher and Peter Wood, from RMIT, Australia, who provided information on the computer modelling of the SIAL Project. The Shoal Fly By sculpture is by the artists Cat Macleod and Michael Bellemo, and the SIAL summer students were Lee-Anne Khor and Rebecca Naughtin.

Next is a substantial group of design practitioners that I would like to thank: Anthony Hunt and several members of his Cirencester office, including Alan Jones, for information on the Eden Project; Stephen Brown of Buro Happold and Chris Williams of the Architecture and Civil Engineering Department, University of Bath for information on the computer modelling of the Great Court Roof at the British Museum; Keith Mendenhall of Frank O. Gehry Associates for CAD-generated images of the Walt Disney Concert Hall and of the the MIT Stata Center; Jim Glymph for his valuable insights into the workings of Frank Gehry's office; Karla Kowalska of Szyskowitz-Kowalski; Peter Hubner for material on the Stammheim church; Gernot Stangl of the Arge Kunsthaus, and to Colin Fournier for information about the Kunsthaus, Graz; Jan Edler of realities:united, Berlin, for information on the BIX media facade; Andrew Kane and Eldred Godson of FaulknerBrowns Architects, Newcastle, for information on the InfoLab 21 project at Lancaster University. Andrew was also kind enough to write the foreword to this book.

I would also like to thank Jim Hall for sharing his architectural knowledge, his constructive suggestions, inspiration and encouragement. Finally, to the people at the Architectural Press including Liz Whiting, Alison Yates, Catharine Steers, Debbie Clark and Pauline Sones for being patient with me regarding lapsed deadlines. I humbly apologise to anyone whose name I may have omitted.

I would like to acknowledge at this point the fact that many different CAD systems were used in the generation of CAD model images, either by myself, or by those contributing model data. These included Autocad, Catia, Microstation, Rhino, Vectorworks and Allplan by Nemetschek AG. Thanks also to Jeff Tupper of Pedagoguery Software Inc. for the polyhedral modelling stuff, and to Uberto Barbini for the Fractal Forge software.

PART I: Digital Technology

The first part of the book will look at several kinds of digital techniques available to architects, together with illustrations of the types of architecture that these techniques have been applied to. CAD visualisation techniques such as walkthroughs and flyovers enable the resolution of sketch design ideas simply by moving around 3-D digital models and recognising potential physical conflicts and circulation problems. The ability to express geometric relationships within digital environments is inceasingly feasible, initially through the user-definition and modification of parameterised parts of objects, and increasingly through the expression of functional relationships between different geometric objects. There is also an emerging field of digital technology that is concerned with constraining geometry through mathematically-expressible physical properties.

Some introductory case studies are described, such as the computer modelling of the Great Court roof, for example. In the second part of the book, although the focus is still on the digital design process, the context of the architectural practices within which digital techniques are being applied will take on a more important role.

Chapter 1: Introduction

This book is concerned with digital design processes in contemporary architectural practice, and tries to illustrate the ways in which some design practices use and exploit the potential of new computing technologies in a wide range of areas and applications. A few years ago I published a book entitled *CAD Principles for Architectural Design* (Szalapaj, 2001) which was targeted primarily at architectural design students with the aim of showing basic CAD modelling ideas. In the latter stages of that book, I began to connect some of those ideas with real-world building projects such as Kansai airport, Waterloo Terminal, and the Guggenheim Museum, Bilbao. The focus was on the modelling of form, but it became obvious that formal modelling aspects needed to be considered within the contexts of the working practices of the architectural and engineering offices in which they were carried out. The contextualisation works both ways. Understanding office practice and digital technology are equally important in order to avoid confusion and misrepresentation of this rapidly expanding discipline. For example, consider the following observation:

> *Apparently models remain a key part of Gehry's design process from early to late. He made countless little models of the famous kitchen window in his own house, a kind of sub-building within the building, at war with the host. By the time we get to the Guggenheim Museum in Bilbao of 1993-7, the scale and purpose of the project have changed dramatically, but we are told that it too began with rudimentary sketches and a series of models.*
>
> *Then at some point these constructions are transferred to computer and manipulated on a three-dimensional modelling program which determines dimensions of cladding elements and spacings of the structural frame. At this point the word fractal first appears to describe the odd curves of the external skin. It has been said that you couldn't work out how to build this design without the help of computers, but how can this be so? Isn't it rather that the computer has been given the boring bits?* (Harbison, 2000, p. 230).

Harbison distances himself from familiarity with Gehry's design process without showing a similar reticence in relation to the role of computing. It is only through looking in detail at case studies of specific projects that it becomes possible to gain insight into the nature of digital technology within contemporary office practice. This book will attempt to show that the boring bits are indeed interesting and exciting.

A central thesis of this book is that technology follows design demand, rather than design adjusting to available new technology. Some might find this a contentious thesis, but the alternative view would be to argue that design practice has merely become the passive recipient of prescribed computing tools and techniques. This seems hard to reconcile with the great number of exciting contemporary architecture projects that depend upon detailed technological and organisational input for their success. Consider the following comments by Frank Gehry, for example:

> *Since we discovered the CATIA software program we've worked with Dassault Systemes in France, who makes* (sic) *it. In the last few years they've been working on making the system fit our way of working. So they now have a new enhanced CATIA that they're going to install here, which backs us up even more and allows us to control the architectural processes to within seven decimal points of accuracy. That's what I like about it. They're tuned in to understanding that this can change the way architecture is practiced and can make new buildings possible – more exciting sculptural shapes in the landscape instead of just plain boxes. So they're excited about that. I told them that I'm going to be perverse now and start doing boxes.*
>
> *Bernard Charles, the President of Dassault Systemes, has said that the way we're working has changed their way of thinking about their system, which is now having an impact on the way planes are designed. We're actually helping them in the aircraft and automobile industries.* (Gehry, 1999, p. 51)

I firmly believe that contemporary architectural design is moving in a direction in which CAD becomes the central practical representational means for designing buildings. It seems increasingly to be the case that design practices are now developing their own CAD abilities to a level of dexterity comparable to that of designers fluent in the intuitive use of traditional techniques. The book will investigate what is possible in contemporary architectural practice, and will introduce a range of CAD and computing issues based upon the work of several creative architectural and engineering design practices. These include the offices of Frank O. Gehry, Peter Hubner, Peter Cook and Colin Fournier, Szyskowitz-Kowalski, Anthony Hunt Associates and FaulknerBrowns Architects.

Design intentions often stem from the central analytical aspects of design schemes which subsequently drive the development of the building form. At all stages of design formulation, the interaction and prominence of such analytical criteria constantly change. What is important is the recognition that design activity incorporates both intuitive/intangible and formal/tangible analysis in a manner which is transparent to the designer. An important concern of this book is the identification of pragmatic uses of computational tools that have positively supported the generation of innovative and exciting contemporary architecture. If this can be achieved, it should enrich and enliven the investigation of more philosophical issues surrounding the promises and limitations of information technology in architectural practice.

Digital design technologies have progressed rapidly over recent years, and the range and extent of CAD-related applications in architectural practice have increased beyond the old-fashioned perception of CAD as merely a production tool. The case studies that will be investigated in the book should indicate how much contemporary architectural practice has moved on from this limited, though still important area of application. Steele's observations that *'Many architects only use computers for tedious, repetitive tasks, . . .'* (Steele, 2001, p. 76), and *'. . . for mechanistic, repetitive tasks, for hardlining graphically defined concepts.'* (op. cit., p. 65), will be seen to be dated, if not inaccurate. He does refer to other contemporary computing buzzword approaches such as *cyberspace*, *virtual reality*, *genetic algorithms* and *liquid architecture*, for example, each ostensibly illustrated with unexplained, iconic images from practice. Occasionally, he will judge some projects to be somehow *'less fundamental'*, in terms of the technology used to implement them, than others (e.g. with reference to the Eden Project compared to other practices (op. cit., p. 107)). It is questionable whether such judgments should be made without first describing the details of projects together with the computing techniques that supported their development. We need to know how design schemes are represented and manipulated *throughout* their design lifespans before reaching any conclusions. Images of the end-products of design processes are not enough to gain insight and understanding into the nature of those processes themselves.

Design is a subject that requires not only the creation and development of design ideas, but also increasingly in contemporary architectural practice, the effective *expression* of these ideas within computing environments by *people*. The implications of CAD representations are extremely important in their relationship to design intentions, since the expression of design ideas in architectural practice is carried out and controlled by designers, and not by automated computer algorithms magically generating previously unimagined virtual architecture.

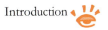

The development of architectural form in the real world is still very much concerned with the resolution of functional issues, whilst taking into account structural and constructional problems and the limitations of materials. It is in these areas that CAD is beginning to play an increasingly important and integrative role, particularly in the relationships between design and engineering. According to Robbin:

> *Enhancing the possibilities for future structures is the recent wide use of computers, which allow for the development of extraordinarily complex building systems. Computers enable interactive design and analysis, giving designers immediate feedback on the structural qualities of prospective shapes. Computer programs are being written to find the optimal shapes for domes and membranes. The greatest value of computers may lie, however, in their ability to make visible the exotic geometric shapes that otherwise are intuited only by mathematicians who devote their lives to such studies. One school of though in the engineering community holds that the new geometries generated by computers are the key to future structures. Not just mathematicians but computer scientists, physicists, and zoologists have information useful to "structural morphology" engineers, who specialize in the geometry of structures.* (Robbin, 1996, p. 6)

This book aims to show not only how particular forms and structures are produced, but also the further implications of the increasingly integrative and organisational role of CAD in design practice.

Each of the case studies will show ways in which particular architectural practices apply their organisational and technological skills, including the use of advanced CAD technologies, to the resolution of complex architectural projects. For example, one of these is the ability to exploit contemporary computer programming environments, an important contemporary example of which is the work done by Buro-Happold engineers for the roof of the Great Court at the British Museum in London. Examples such as this indicate that there is no reason for designers in practice to fear the emerging object-oriented modelling and computer programming environments. These are becoming increasingly accessible through visual user-interfaces that make it feasible for job architects and engineers to exploit them. Paul Goldberger, architecture critic of the New York Times, writing in 1978 and reporting on a convention of the American Institute of Architects, quotes as follows:

> *Mr Pelli, a designer of sleek glass structures, agreed with the notion of postmodernists, as the younger architects are often called, that the modern movement's belief in romanticizing technology was no longer valid. But he did not see conventional, old-fashioned materials and the use of historical styles as an answer. "If the myth of technology is gone, that doesn't make the reality of it disappear," he said. "We must learn to use whatever appropriate technology exists. I feel as if you are sometimes walking east on a plane that is flying west – and the plane is the new technology."* (Goldberger, 1983, p. 10)

The current new technology is the ability of the computer to aid us with our sketches and ideas, to develop the themes, to facilitate the production drawings, to rationalise the environmental controls and to speed the building process. It does not usurp the act of creation: it is not the deus ex machina of the theatre that is architecture.

1.1   Digital Representation in Architectural Design Practice

> *We continue to live in a world of machines, but now for the first time architectural culture seems capable of distinguishing between the methods of science and that form of knowledge necessary to successfully express the experience of life lived among machines.* (Macrae-Gibson, 1985, p. X).

The purpose of this book is to provide a contemporary understanding of how information technologies (IT), and computer-aided design (CAD) in particular, are being used in architectural design practice. The description of the detailed case studies will show the extent to which computer systems support and enable the progression and development of individual practices' design visions during the course of their design processes. The impact of IT on architectural design practice is expanding at an ever-increasing rate, as practices realise the benefits of using IT to support wide-ranging aspects of complex design processes. Three core aspects of the application of information technologies to design practice are as follows:

- digital *expression* of building form
- digital *integration* of specialist design information
- digital *organisation* of office practice

The digital expression of building form concerns ways in which methods of expression such as conventional *sketching* and physical *modelling* can be transferred into digital environments. Digital representation occurs whenever designers use the medium of computing environments to produce objects such as drawings and models that can either be used for analysis or for presentation.

The digital integration of specialist design information is concerned with how environmental aspects can be modelled and supported digitally, such that environmental and physical *analysis* can be carried out upon digital expressions such as 3-D models, for example. In addition to structural and environmental analysis, the other important issue that needs to be investigated here, is the extent to which digital information is integrated into the processes of *fabrication* and *construction*.

The digital organisation of office practice concerns issues of *presentation* and *communication* of information to various design partners and clients throughout the different design stages. In the real world of design practice, responses need to be made to human demands on a daily basis. These demands are often client-driven, constrained by professional bodies and standards, and reflective of the attitudes and design philosophies of the practices themselves.

The interaction and prominence of particular design criteria are constantly changing in the design process, and it is sometimes difficult to determine which criterion takes priority at which stage. There is a continual cyclical process of model generation (**figure 1.1**), in which successive models, both physical and computational, are produced. In some design practices, CAD models frequently alternate with physical models in taking on an analytical role. In other practices, such as that of Frank O. Gehry, CAD models and physical models have clearly defined roles to play at particular stages in the design process (see **chapter 8**). In *CAD Principles* (Szalapaj, 2001), I tried to emphasise the ways in which design activity incorporated both intuitive (intangible) and formal (tangible) analysis in a manner which is transparent to the designer. My emphasis then was particularly on the *analytical* aspects of design, whereas here, more emphasis is placed upon the *expression* of design ideas, whether through sketching or through modelling, both conventionally and computationally.

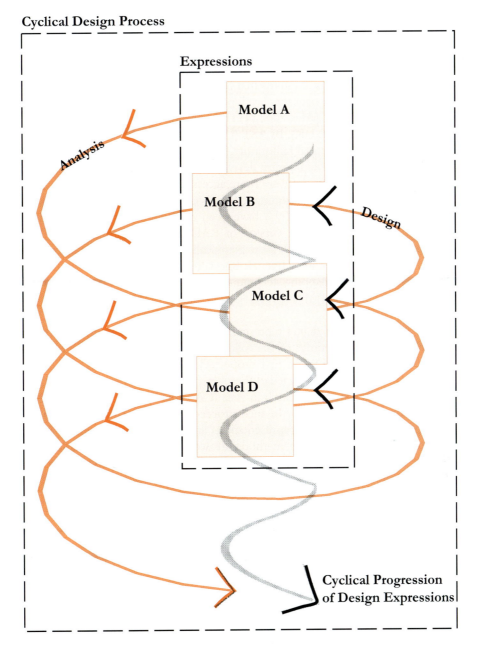

Figure 1.1: The Cyclical Process of Model Development.

Expression and analysis are two aspects of what McKim would call the ETC cycle, where E is the expression of design ideas, T is the testing or evaluation, and C is the cycle in which alternative design strategies are generated (McKim, 1980, p. 135). According to this view, the basic process of design generation is to first express, then to test, and then to cycle until a design idea is fully conceived, at which point the final act is yet another expression.

However, computational support for the formal analytical aspects of the design process has traditionally focused on environmental simulation techniques, with applications in energy, lighting, ventilation and acoustics, for example. Simulation software has tended to be numerically based, with awkward and counterintuitive methods of interaction that have prevented their widespread use in the initial stages of the design process. They have had limited application as tools for validating finalised design schemes. Systems that focus on energy analysis include ESP-r (research version of the energy simulation package developed at the Energy Systems Research Unit at the University of Strathclyde, UK) (Clarke, 2002), HTB2 (developed at the Welsh School of Architecture, University of Wales, Cardiff, UK), BLAST (University of Illinois, Urbana-Champaign, USA), DOE-2 (Lawrence Berkeley National Laboratory, USA) and LT (developed at the Martin Centre, Cambridge University, UK). Contemporary developments in graphical user-interfaces, however, are making environmental analysis software more accessible to designers. Systems such as ECO-TECT (energy analysis based on the admittance method, combined with lighting, solar shading, acoustics and cost analysis) (Marsh, 1997) have been developed to provide visual feedback at conceptual design stages. The current version of RADIANCE (lighting analysis based on ray tracing algorithms) (Ward, 1994) is much more graphically oriented than its precursors. Early stage ventilation analysis software includes Htvent1. Specialised software for the simulation of urban noise levels based on noise mapping techniques currently includes SoundPLAN, Cadna/A (computer aided noise abatement) (DataKustik Gmbh, 2004), LIMA, and Mithra.

Much academic research on the digital representation of architecture continues to focus on the technology itself (c.f. the proceedings of the followings conferences: Education and Research in Computer Aided Architectural Design in Europe (eCAADe), Association of Computer Aided Design in Architecture (ACADIA), Sociedad Iberoamericana de Grafica Digital (SIGraDi), Computer Aided Architectural Design Research in Asia (CAADRIA) and Computer Aided Architectural Design Futures (CAADFutures)). In such proceedings, state-of-the-art digital methods are described that generate both abstract representations and realistic models within design research and teaching contexts. Although such methods are worthy attempts to enhance spatial design experience, they are typically based upon theoretical frameworks detached from the prescient pressures of the architectural profession.

In contrast, this book is concerned with modes of architectural conception that have very direct relationships with realised buildings. It is this directness that is encouraged and supported in professional practice. Emerging trends in the architectural profession, driven as it is by commercial pressures, are transforming the use and application of digital representation techniques, and providing radically new methods for architects to design buildings. These new, integrative methods, relate to refining what was traditionally a long process of design and construction – a step change in what Peters refers to as *technological thought* (Peters, 1996).

The computer-aided architectural design of buildings in practice is increasingly concerned with the creation of three-dimensional objects in space. 2-D drawings are inadequate in fully conveying the conceptual ideas of spatial arrangements. To eliminate misinterpretations of design schemes, 3-D physical and virtual prototypes at various scales and levels of detail can be developed. These allow the exploration of spatial experience and the examination of potential design problems. Computer models are increasingly capable of generating the information needed to produce both virtual and physical prototypes that demonstrate key properties of design schemes. Here I agree with Lynn's observations on the use of the term *virtual*:

*The term **virtual** has recently been so debased that it often simply refers to the digital space of computer-aided design. It is often used interchangeably with the term simulation. Simulation, unlike virtuality, is not intended as a diagram for a future possible concrete assemblage but is instead a visual substitute. 'Virtual reality' might describe architectural design but as it is used to describe a simulated environment it would be better replaced by 'simulated reality' or 'substitute reality'. Thus, use of the term virtual here refers to an abstract scheme that has the possibility of becoming actualized, often in a variety of possible configurations. Since architects produce drawings of buildings and not buildings themselves, architecture, more than any other discipline, is involved with the production of virtual descriptions.* (Lynn, 1999, p. 10)

I agree with the need to repossess the virtual in architecture, but part company with Lynn in the last sentence, since contemporary architects do much more than he gives them credit for. They are often responsible for the integration of digital information into the construction process, and increasingly so when the building form has a complex character. Furthermore, digital representations in architecture are increasingly three-dimensional and not drawing-based. The expression of design ideas through sketching, however, is still fundamentally important, and digital support for this part of the design process is also a subject for further investigation. There are of course more speculative approaches in which designers are no longer in control of design processes, and instead abrogate design responsibilities to computers, from which models evolve in automated ways. Such approaches, although interesting from a theoretical point of view, bear no relation to architectural practice. According to Lynn:

. . . genetic processes should not be equated with either intelligence or nature. The computer is not a brain. Machine intelligence might best be described as that of mindless connections. When connecting multiple variables, the computer simply connects them, it does not think critically about how it connects. The present limits of connectionism are staggeringly complex, and the directness with which multiple entities can be related challenges human sensibility. The response has been to attempt to develop a commensurate sensibility in the machines themselves; but the failures of artificial intelligence suggest a need to develop a systematic human intuition about the connective medium, rather than attempting to build criticality into the machine. (Lynn, 1999, p. 19)

In the real world of architectural practice, permeated as it now is with digital technology, it is the designers that are responsible for connectivity in all its forms. In Coosje van Bruggen's account of Frank Gehry's scheme for the Guggenheim Museum in Bilbao, she made the following observation:

Initially, Gehry was resistant to using the computer in his design process. The program seemed to limit architecture to symmetries, mirror imagery, and "simple Euclidean geometries," as Glymph put it, but questions of how to visualize gestural moves resulting in sculptural three-dimensional forms while retaining the immediacy of a sketch, or how to translate them into a very large scale, were unresolved. "I just didn't like the images of the computer," Gehry said, "but as soon as I found a way to use it to build, then I connected." (van Bruggen, 1997, p. 136)

The recognition by Gehry of the potential to integrate several functions in his practice, not only removed the barriers between what were considered to be distinct parts of the traditional design process, but has since led to the development of a holistic digital design process in which design flair and digital representation go hand in hand. Digital models have the capacity to become reflections and representations of architects' design thinking, and are not merely the static forms developed through CAD modelling techniques. They also have dynamic qualities as a consequence of their roles and functions within the context of the integrative processes of office practice.

1.2   Digital expression

> Q. *form follows function in the digital environment?*
> A.. *form follows means, means follow tools, tools yield to desires,*
>   *and desire is everything.* (Hani Rashid, designboom interview, New York, 2002)

Common understandings of digital expression in architecture relate to ways in which computer modelling systems can be used to manipulate shape during the design process. Computer modelling systems support digital expressions that give rise to wireframe models, surfaces, solids and non-manifold forms (Lee, 1999, p. 102). Digital expressions are those operations that generate more complex forms from simpler initial objects, such as extrusion, sweeping, and Boolean operations, for example (Szalapaj, 2001). Those familiar with digital design processes can accept the following observation:

> *The shapes that are formed in computer-aided design are the result of decisions made using parameters.*
> (Lynn, 1999, p. 25)

Lynn takes the notion of parameterisation further by taking into account not only geometric properties, but also environmental ones such as temperature, gravity, and other forces. According to Lynn:

> *Numerical parameters can be keyframed and dynamically linked through expressions to alter the shape*
> *of objects.* (op. cit.)

It is beyond the scope of this book to discuss the philosophy of expression such as the account given in Collingwood's *The Principles of Art* (Collingwood, 1938) in which emphasis is placed on the internal representations that exist in people's minds. However, it is possible to look at the external manifestations of expression in the form of architecture, the materials from which that architecture is made, and the tools with which the form is produced. In David Hockney's book '*Secret Knowledge*' (Hockney, 2001), in which he gives a revelatory account of how optics were used as tools of painting as far back as the fifteenth century, he notes that:

> *. . . these things could only have been seen by an artist, a mark-maker, who is not as far from practice,*
> *or from science, as an art historian. After all, I'm only saying that artists once knew how to use a tool,*
> *and that this knowledge was lost.* (op. cit.)

The secret, if there is such a thing, with digital tools in architectural practice, lies in the way they support connections between the design of complex sculptural forms and the rational methods of fabrication and construction that are needed to realise them. Complex sculptural forms are nothing new. Morris and Blier's study of the sculptural mud architecture of west Africa shows that structures such as the great mosque of Djenne in Mali (**figure 1.2**) and the Timbuktu mosque are particularly ancient (Morris and Blier, 2003). According to Glancey:

> *What these magnificent mosques prove is that mud buildings can be far more sophisticated than many*
> *people living in a world of concrete and steel might want to believe. Mud is not just a material for*
> *shaping pots, but for temples, palaces and even, as so many west African towns demonstrate, the*
> *framing of entire communities. The very fluidity, or viscosity, of the material allows the architects who*
> *use it to create dynamic and sensual forms.* (Glancey, 2003).

Figure 1.2: The sculptural form of the Djenne mosque, Mali.

These sculptural forms affect not only the architecture, but also the surrounding spatial environments. Archer gives a detailed analysis of the Nabdam compounds of northern Ghana, in which groups of mud huts are in turn organised into villages that reflect social hierarchies (Archer, 1971). Gaudi's unfinished Colonia Guell Chapel has been considered by many, including Calitrava, to be the most interesting of Gaudi's structures. According to Sweeney and Sert:

> *There all the forms employed are determined by structural requirements. They are not, however, merely a product of mathematics, but of mathematics and Gaudi's deep sculptural sensibility combined . . . It is curious to note that Gaudi always designed taking into consideration the practical methods by which his plans could be carried out. He chose warped surfaces because model makers and masons can construct them easily, as both the hyperboloids and the hyperbolic paraboloids are ruled surfaces which can be easily reinforced by straight steel rods, thus providing a considerable economy . . .* (Sweeney and Sert, 1960, p. 78)

Just as Gaudi exploited the mathematics of ruled surfaces in the construction of many of his forms, contemporary digital modelling tools are enabling a wide range of sculptural sensibilities to be expressed. Frank Gehry has demonstrated an acute awareness of this phenomenon, and exploited it within a modelling context in his scheme for the Walt Disney Concert Hall (**figure 1.3**). Some of his more recent projects have taken digital expression into the fabrication and construction processes. According to Gehry:

> *Drawing is a tool. So is the model. Everything is a tool. The building is the only thing that means anything – the finished building.* (van Bruggen, 1997, p. 40)

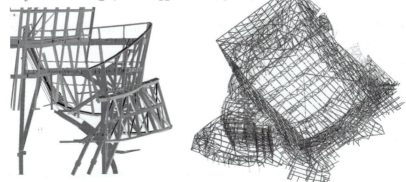

Figure 1.3: The sculptural nature of Gehry's CAD-generated models of the Walt Disney Concert Hall, Los Angeles.

In the 20th century, Erich Mendelsohn envisaged a new form of architectural dynamism which only became buildable several decades later with the emergence of advanced concrete structures. He sketched many curvilinear structures, the most famous of which was the Einstein Tower in Potsdam. Some of Mendelsohn's sketches for the latter are shown in **figures 1.4–1.12**. Contemporary architects such as Frank Gehry have begun to exploit available computing technologies in order realise his own fluid and dynamic design forms. What distinguishes the wild sculptural expressions of Mendelsohn's contemporaries (e.g. Hermann Finsterlin) from those of architects such as Gehry, is the knowledge that, given due planning of the fabrication and construction processes, these crazy forms are now eminently realisable. The expressionists' architectural visions are becoming reality almost a century after they were first imagined. Less well-known members of the expressionist group such as the Luckhardt brothers insisted that an essential element of architectural composition should be that of *movement*. This idea has been taken up again in recent years by a number of architectural practices. According to Wassily Luckhardt:

I can imagine that in a building freely set in nature the masses do not remain quiescent next to each other but push against and through each other with powerful dynamic movements, and that various lines of motion intersect each other or conflict. This occurs, however, in such a way – and this seems important to me – that nevertheless in the end everything is balanced, and equilibrium is maintained; that is to say that every movement is met by an equally strong countermovement, so that no section of the building might threaten to overturn another. Perhaps the result would be that such buildings will have an ideal centre of gravity. (Conrads and Sperlich, 1960, p. 144).

Figure 1.4: Volumetric sketch.

Figure 1.5: Volumetric sketch.

Figure 1.6: Sculptural sketch.

Figure 1.7:Sculptural sketch.

Figure 1.8: Sculptural sketch.

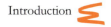

The Einsteinturm (Einstein Tower) was the first important building designed by the architect Erich Mendelsohn. It was planned and built in the years 1919 to 1924, the main part was finished in 1921. The Einstein Tower is a functional building, a solar observatory and until the Second World War the most prominent research institution of its kind in Europe. The tower is therefore also an example of relationships between science and art, as Mendelsohn fulfilled the conditions for the scientific use as well as his own concepts of form. Due to Mendelsohn's interest in Einstein's work, some the spirit of the exciting developments in modern physics is also captured in the building. Today the Einstein tower is a part of the Astrophysical Institute Potsdam, most of the remaining area of the Telegraph Hill is used by the Geological Research Centre, Potsdam and other institutes of climate research and geology.

The tower is often referred to as the icon of architectural *expressionism*, but the sketches in **figures 1.4–1.12** are also recognisable as iconic modern architectural drawings.

Its purpose is not rationally expressed in its structure, but symbolically in its form. (Tietz, 1999, p. 26).

The intention was to exploit the plasticity of the relatively new material of reinforced concrete. The vision was to demonstrate the sculptural qualities of this material in terms of the interaction of convex and concave elements. Because of technical problems of making suitable formwork for the curved elements, the walls above the plinth were constructed in conventional brickwork and then plastered over. Despite or even because of this failure of realisation, this icon of sketching and of expressionist architecture is also a suitable modern-day icon for the application of digital techniques to the design, fabrication and construction of contemporary architecture. The relationship between the architectural vision and its technical realisation will be a recurring theme in some of the case studies presented later.

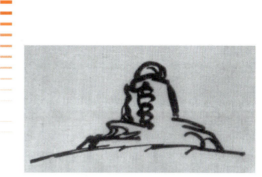

Figure 1.9: Sculptural sketch.

Figure 1.10: Dynamic sketch.

Figure 1.11: Dynamic sketch.

Figure 1.12: Detailed sketch.

Whilst emphasising the role of form and the three-dimensional expression of advanced structural ideas, the following quote is highly relevant to the integration of architectural vision and technical realisation:

In iron, the building material of our time, the revolutionary play of the forces of tension and compression elicits movements which are always astonishing for the professional and still totally incomprehensible for the layman.

It is our task to find the architectural expression for these dynamic forces, to express through architectural configuration the adjustment of these stresses, to master the vitality of the forces which are pressing internally toward actual movement . . .

Just as when dealing with dynamics, so when defining 'function', there are several points of departure. The reduction of all outward forms to their simplest geometric basis is, properly speaking, the primary requirement for an original beginning. Knowledge of the elements has always been the prerequisite of creativity . . .

If, however, this two-dimensional knowledge is transferred to space without a vital relation to the third dimension of depth, which is necessary to create a spatial organism out of the elemental spatial forms of cube, sphere, and cylinder, the peril of a purely intellectual construction arises immediately. The danger of uncontrolled temperament in dynamics here corresponds to the equally great danger of too conscious an abstraction. Full bloodedness and bloodlessness are both areas of danger for vital creation. If the principle is considered to be an end in itself ... Then 'the form per se' does not mean architecture. This is a law for all times, not only for Expressionism and Constructivism . . . (Mendelsohn, 1923).

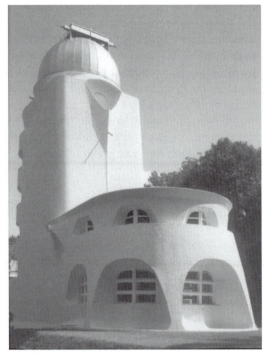

Figure 1.13: The Einstein Tower as built.

The similarities between the expressionists and contemporary architectural practices that exploit digital tools for the development of architecturally expressive sculptural forms are striking. One can find increasingly many contemporary architectural projects in which the expression of new structural ideas has been associated with wonderful architectural visions and aspirations, leading to the production of new building types or radical reinventions of existing ones. Some of these, along with the technologies used in their realisation, will be described in later case studies. The following quote referring to the work of Frank Gehry, for example, would be equally applicable to Mendelsohn's design thinking:

Perspective illusion and perspective contradiction are used throughout Gehry's house, and many of his other projects, to prevent the formation of an intellectual picture that might destroy the continual immediacy of perceptual shock. When nothing is at right angles, nothing seems to vanish to the same point. This results in an ambiguous space that is enhanced by the reflections one sees at strange angles in tilted panes of glass, . . . (Macrae-Gibson, 1985, p. 12).

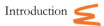

The downfall of expressionist ambitions was that the expressions themselves were detached from techniques of analysis and construction. According to Peters:

> *There were also many architects of the early modern movement and expressionism who attempted to develop forms expressing monolithic structure. Erich Mendelsohn's Einstein Tower (1919-1920) was built in brick and stucco, . . . What had begun as an experiment in structure and method sometimes regressed into formal play.* (Peters, 1996, p. 387).

The ability to express structural forms through design sketches and models, and then to move on to detailed structural analyses of these forms came much later. The analysis of monolithic structural forms, however, resulted in a greater confidence of expression:

> *But it was only with the acceptance of new theories of monolithic structural behaviour, their methods of analysis and dimensioning, . . . , that the profession really began to appreciate and use with confidence the material-, weight-, and labor-saving advantages of contiguous structure. New forms gradually emerged based on this confidence, appearing first in the work of contractors, engineers, and architects with a special interest in structure.* (Peters, 1996, p. 78).

The interrelationship between architectural expression and an engineering approach to analysis is a debate that has continued until the present day. According to Cecil Balmond:

> *. . . it's important to keep the conceptual up front, because in time it will get diluted – pragmatism comes in, you can't keep that pure concept.* (Balmond, 2003)

What seems to distinguish good architect-engineers or engineer-architects is that they are able to resolve the conceptual with the pragmatic in satisfying ways.

> *(Calatrava's) argument is that the languages of structure and geometry are of similar importance in his thinking about design – together with the nature of materials and of nature.* (Lyall, 2002, p. 23)

In contemporary digital design processes, there is less conflict between conceptual and pragmatic issues. What the later case studies will demonstrate is that there are smooth transitions between the digital expression of design proposals and their analytical evaluations.

> *Wright saw no essential conflict between engineering and architectural design; rather, he saw that the converse is true: new aesthetics are the inescapable consequence of new engineering techniques. Wright claimed that if the ancient Greeks had developed steel and glass, they would have made "modern" architecture back then. He expressed loathing for those who clung to an architectural style when there was no functional or structural reason to do so.* (Robbin, 1996, p. 1)

Particularly in early design stages, therefore, there is a need to move between design generation to structural analysis and then to redesign. This cycle of design proposal and structural testing makes it absolutely necessary to manage revisions to CAD models and their associated drawings in a flexible yet organised way.

The realisation of the Einstein Tower, therefore, fell short of Mendelsohn's own expectations of the construction technology of the time .

> . . . *In an illustrated magazine I saw a picture of the Einstein Tower after its completion, but I really do not like it very much; the preliminary sketches were, in my opinion, much more interesting than the executed building. Especially the placement of the windows with their thick crossbars seems to me too affected and not straightforward enough, as indeed, I find altogether too much affectation in this architecture* . . . (Oud, 1921).

Although the sketches in **figures 1.4–1.12** give the impression that the focus was on the external form alone, it is important to bear in mind that Mendelsohn's view of architecture was rooted in architectonic ideas, and that planning issues were equally important (**figure 1.14**). He observed:

> *Spatial geometry, the theory of the control and interrelationship of spaces, of the disposition of bodies and of the layout of space includes all configurations: the simple equations from cube to sphere, the highly complicated ones for any celestial curvature.* (Mendelsohn, 1914-17).

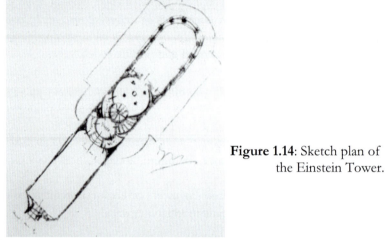

Figure 1.14: Sketch plan of the Einstein Tower.

In other words, the resolution of architectural planning problems happens whatever the design emphasis, whether it be the external form, environmental issues, structural systems etc. Furthermore, responses to these problems require artistic as well as technical sensibilities. Consider Mendelsohn's own view on the split in Dutch architecture in 1919 between architects such as Oud (a member of the De Stijl movement based in Rotterdam) and the Amsterdam school (Wendingen):

> *Oud is functional, so as to talk with Gropius. Amsterdam is dynamic* . . . *The first sets ratio before everything: perception through analysis. The second sets perception through vision. Analytical Rotterdam refuses vision; visionary Amsterdam does not understand cold objectivity. Certainly the primary element is function; but function without sensibility remains mere construction. More than ever I stand by my reconciliatory programme. Both are necessary, and both must find each other* ... *Otherwise, Rotterdam will pursue the way of mere construction with deathly chill in its veins, and Amsterdam will be destroyed by the fire of its own dynamicism. Functional dynamics is the postulate.* (Whittick, 1956, p. 65).

The importance of resolving planning problems alongside the development of building form is an issue that reoccurs in several of the later case studies. The next section on integration will emphasise the functional approach and its implications for digital technology.

1.3   Digital Integration

The integrative role of CAD in contemporary architectural practice concerns the ways in which CAD environments bring together different analytical aspects of design schemes. Of particular importance is the architecture/structure/construction relationship, since all of these relate in direct ways to the building form. A particularly direct relationship between architectural form and construction can occur when architects take the construction process itself into consideration in the design stages. An early exponent of this approach was Louis Kahn, who dimensioned prefabricated concrete parts in relation to the radius of action of a builder's crane – *the extension of the human arm* (Tietz, 1999, p. 71).

'Love for the expression of method' seems to animate all Kahn's work and almost take over from other concerns. (Jencks, 1973, p. 232).

Kahn suggested that architectural drawing should reflect the process of construction, i.e. that it should be a bottom-up approach. This objective is much easier to achieve in CAD systems than on paper, since not only can objects be modelled on numbered *layers* or *levels*, but sub-objects within layers can also be logically grouped (e.g. into *classes, blocks, symbols, cells,* and other mechanisms), which can then also be processed in ordered ways either for presentation purposes, or for further processing in an integrated environment.

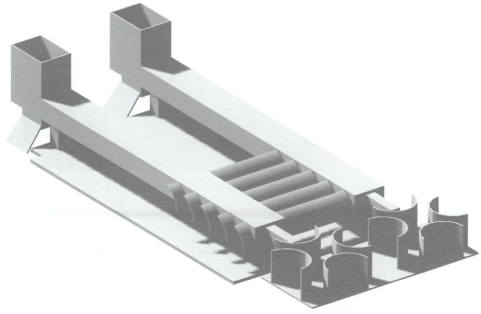

Figure 1.15: CAD model based on Kahn's axonometric drawing of the Salk Institute showing service stacks, service ducts, and study rooms.

The division of buildings into *served and servant spaces* (**figure 1.15**) also formed a prominent part of Kahn's architecture. Pushing services to the outside affects the lifespan of mechanical equipment. In this way, mechanical and electrical equipment can be changed according to the demands of any new development. Services become easily accessible and can be altered or replaced with minimum disruption.

Kahn's ideas had a profound influence on Norman Foster in his student days at Yale. In Foster's design for the 180-metre-tall Hongkong Shanghai Bank, the basic concept was that of *phased generation*, giving rise to the idea of the tower as a multi-storey extendable bridge. Initial sketches conveyed the idea of a *laminated* plan with four bays (reduced to three in the final scheme), suspended from large trusses at varying heights (35, 47 and 28 storeys), with double height spaces at each truss level. The services and vertical circulation allow the floors to be completely unobstructed. The simple idea of *served and servant spaces* and *laminated plan* offered great spatial potential.

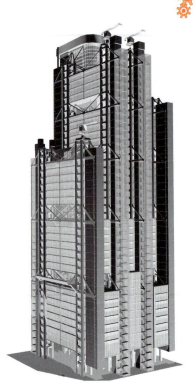

Figure 1.16: CAD isometric view.

By moving the conventional service core to the sides of the building, Foster opened up the plan to panoramic views, and the internal space became a continuation of the landscape. As the design progressed, the introduction of raised floors was further developed, along with the invention of a unique system of circulation combining lifts and escalators. Foster's earliest concepts are always as much technical as spatial and formal, including the technical means by which the building might be constructed. Initial sketches showed detailed explorations of technical as well as visual implications of design decisions (Pawley, 1999, p. 77). The building was conceived as an assembly of components fitted together in precise dimensional relationships, and sketches indicated the importance of the production phase of building components.

The scheme also offered flexibility in section. This flexibility was needed to meet strict shading regulations. Omitted floors left space for large garden terraces situated within holes left in the building. There was also a huge top lit atrium. Ordinary vertical structural elements were later to be replaced by massive, composite steel masts emphasising the bridge-like nature of the building structure. A structural system with double trusses between each bay clearly permitted the bays to rise to different heights. The competition scheme also exhibited a revolutionary system of circulation with escalators, which gave further flexibility to the section.

Figure 1.17: CAD isometric view.

The chevron-shaped structural system gave spatial flexibility by allowing the removal of almost any floor section, thus giving varieties of layered and interlocking spaces. Fosters constructional preference was for a *kit-of-parts*, consisting of accurate, prefabricated metal and glass components, which could be speedily assembled on site.

> *Occasionally, in the biggest projects, the collaboration between architect and product designer is formalized. The best example of this is Norman Foster's HongkongBank Headquarters in which all the main elements of the building, including the curtain wall, structure cladding, service modules, floors, ceilings, partitions, and furniture, were designed, developed, and tested by architect and manufacturer working together.* (Davies, 1988, p. 7)

The structural engineers Ove Arup & Partners designed eight masts to support the whole building. The Vierendeel structure, which is a composite system with four subcolumns was arranged in a square and linked together by rigid horizontal elements at regular storey heights.

Foster Associates set up a Hong Kong office in January 1980 in order to work through details of the scheme. After almost one-year of development work, the final scheme consisted of a steel suspension structure, a lift/escalator circulation system, plug-in pods on the floor, underfloor services, a light scoop, with prefabricated components throughout.

> *Above the banking hall is the building's most dramatic internal feature, a soaring 52-meter[sic]-high atrium that reaches up through ten stories to the inner reflecting mirror of the building's 'sun scoop', a computer-controlled array of mirrors that adjusts to the solar calendar and reflects light into the atrium and down through the glass ceiling to the plaza below.* (Pawley, 1999, p. 78)

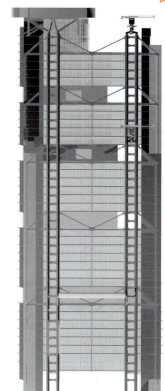

Figure 1.18: CAD elevation view.

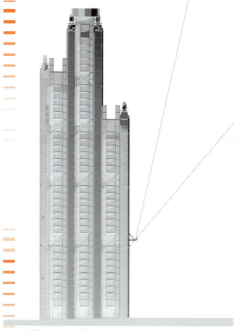

Figure 1.19: CAD elevation view indicating light function.

1.4 Computer Modelling the Building Construction Process.

The CAD modelling process can be used to represent the process of construction in buildings of this nature. Modular components can be modelled in accordance with their construction sequence. The construction of the Eiffel Tower was an early example of a modular approach to construction. Eiffel was acutely aware of the structural potential of wrought-iron, and the original temporary exhibit of the tower became more permanent than he had intended. Eiffel

. . . clearly did use some form of logically ordered thinking process. As a result, he developed a simple yet sophisticated catalog of wrought-iron parts and connection rules that he used to build the complex, nonorthogonal Garabit Bridge and his tower. . . . His kit-of-parts approach to construction simplified the job for steel bridge and high-rise builders.
(Peters, 1996, pp. 350–351)

Figure 1.20: Eiffel Tower.

Likewise, the main structural components of the HongKong Shanghai bank can be modelled in terms of surface forms associated with layers, which in turn correspond to the phased generation of primary construction elements.

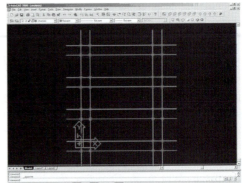

Figure 1.21: Grid setup.

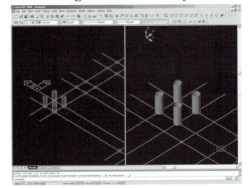

Figure 1.22: Extruding component sections.

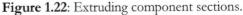

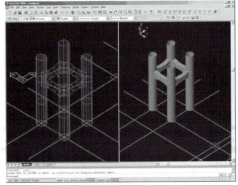

Figure 1.23: Beam insertion.

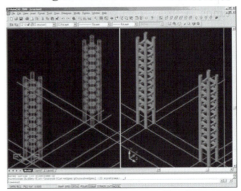

Figure 1.24: Mast replication.

As modelling proceeds, changes in model viewpoints can assist in checking the developing form in 3-D. Solids can be subtracted or added through the use of Boolean operations, but in most proprietary CAD software, solids are represented in terms of surface geometry. The geometric forms in this case are simple enough, but as some of the later case studies will show, more interesting modelling issues arise when these forms are represented in terms of NURBS (non-uniform rational B-spline) surfaces. NURBS surfaces allow the description and modification of surfaces in terms of control points.

Once the base of the model is defined by an accurate grid (**figure 1.21**), it is possible to extrude circles to form hollow sections (**figure 1.22**). For the Hongkong Shanghai Bank, these circles can be extruded 500 units (100 units = 1 m), which is roughly the height of each floor in the building (496 in reality). The beams in **figure 1.23** are formed by extruding a curved shape in elevation, and then duplicating an initial beam element three times. Mast structures are formed by stacking column and beam units, and then replicating completed masts on the grid as in **figure 1.24**.

Composite graphical elements can if necessary be defined as discrete graphical *symbols*, which allow composite objects to have a holistic representation. They can be dismantled into their component parts if needed. Representing objects with many surfaces in terms of symbols often minimises the overall sizes of digital files compared to representation without the use of symbols. Columns, beams, masts and trusses are all potential candidates for representation as symbols. Trusses are introduced in **figures 1.25** and **1.26**, and stacking of composite mast/truss elements is shown in **figure 1.27**.

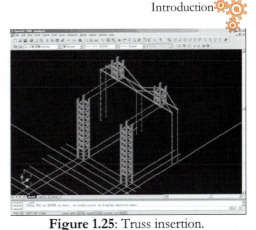

Figure 1.25: Truss insertion.

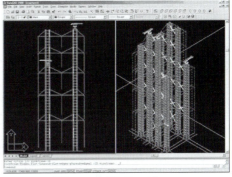

Figure 1.26: Truss replication.

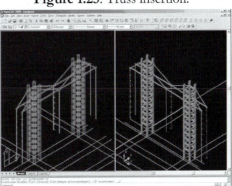

Figure 1.27: Stacking

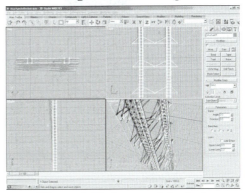

Figure 1.28: Structural Analysis.

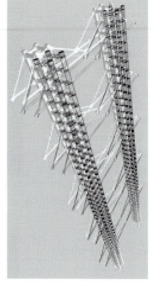

Figure 1.29: Deflection analysis.

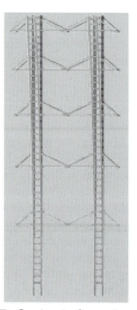

An advantage of dealing with visual feedback from what are essentially numerical analyses is the speed of interpretation. In **figures 1.29–1.31**, deflections arising from the application of advanced engineering calculations are presented visually. 3-D visualisations of the results of structural analyses within CAD systems can minimise design time while producing understandable visual feedback. This is preferable to interpreting huge amounts of numerical data. There are many structural analysis software systems currently available for various stages of design detail. Software utilising structural optimisation techniques, in which design functions such as stiffness, fabrication, weight, and often cost can be analysed. These applications are only available in novel workstation environments and they are optimised for structural constraints (bending and shear stresses). Therefore, a visually coupled design process, involving a 3-D visual content rather than 2-D drafts, can help designers to understand and express basic behaviours and concepts efficiently while increasing control over the working environment.

Figure 1.30: Deflection in front view.

Figure 1.31: Deflection in side view.

Figure 1.32: Structural CAD model.

Figure 1.33: CAD model showing effect of sun scoop in directing sunlight into the building.

1.5 Digital Organisation

Given the wish of some designers to be able to digitally express form and to integrate their expressions into a process of analysis, what then happens to these design intentions in the context of office practice? One would expect creative design practices to exploit emerging digital technologies in imaginative ways that support the realisation of their design visions. On the other hand, it is evident that offices of a more corporate nature are more readily influenced by administrative diktat and managerial doctrine and guidance. Sir Michael Latham's report, *Constructing the Team* (Latham, 1994), aimed to provide guidelines for the organisation of the construction industry in the United Kingdom. It defined the responsibilities of designers, clients and contractors in terms of deliverable outcomes (**figure 1.34**). The report also commented upon pertinent issues in the construction industry ranging from the role of clients through to tendering procedures, contracts, and resolving disputes, particularly in relation to payments. At various points in the report, comments in turn led to firmer recommendations on specific topics. It is evident that the Latham Report has already had a significant effect on working practices in the UK construction industry. A flavour of its effect on design practice can be gleaned by looking at some of its observations and aspirations in more detail:

> *3.11 Once a prospective client has decided that a project should proceed in principle, and roughly how much risk and direct involvement to accept, the projects and design briefs can be prepared. The client who knows exactly what is required can instruct the intended provider. That may involve appointing a Project Manager, or a client's representative to liaise with the designers, or a lead designer, or a contractor for direct design and build procurement.* (op.cit.)

It could be argued that clients today have a better appreciation of quality than they may have had prior to the Latham Report. Some clients realise that the panache of projects is invariably design driven, and see architects as capable of managing projects themselves. Do project managers inhibit this design impetus?

> *4.1 Effective management of the design process is crucial for the success of the project. It should involve:*
> *1. A lead manager.*
> *2. The co-ordination of the consultants, including an interlocking matrix of their appointment documents which should also should also have a clear relationship with the construction contract.*
> *3. A detailed check list of the design requirements in the appointment documents of consultants. This should also be set out in the main contract documentation.*
> *4. Ensuring the client fully understands the design proposals.*
> *5. Particular care over the integration of building services design, and the avoidance of 'fuzzy edges' between consultants and specialist engineering contractors.*
> *6. The use of Co-ordinated Project Information.*
> *7. Signing off the various stages of design when they have been achieved, but with sufficient flexibility to accommodate the commercial wishes of clients.* (op.cit.)

Some of these points begin to linearise and compartmentalise the cyclical qualities of designing that were referred to in section **1.1**. They also emphasise documentation and commercial exploitation.

> *4.7 The design leader must ensure that the client fully understands the design proposals, and agrees that they meet its objectives. It is rarely satisfactory for clients to be shown conceptual drawings, still less outline plans of rooms. The design team must offer the client a vision of the project in a form which it can understand and change in time.* (op.cit.)

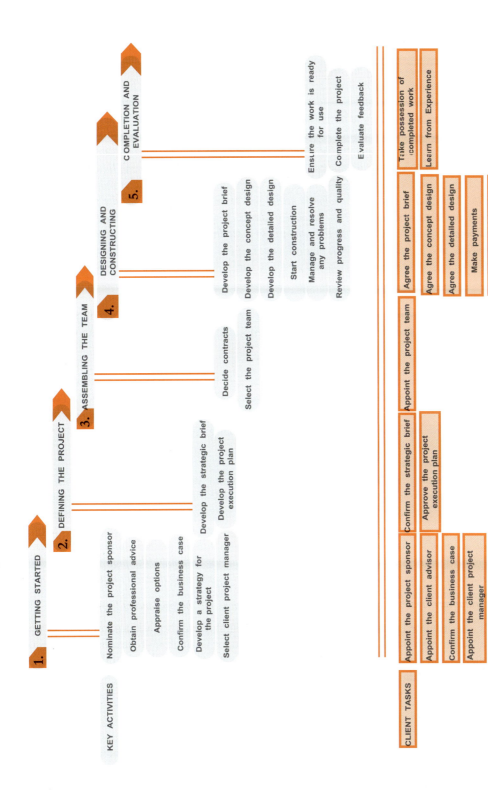

KEY ACTIVITIES

1. GETTING STARTED	2. DEFINING THE PROJECT	3. ASSEMBLING THE TEAM	4. DESIGNING AND CONSTRUCTING	5. COMPLETION AND EVALUATION
Nominate the project sponsor	Develop the strategic brief for the project	Decide contracts	Develop the project brief	Ensure the work is ready for use
Obtain professional advice	Develop the project execution plan	Select the project team	Develop the concept design	Complete the project
Appraise options			Develop the detailed design	Evaluate feedback
Confirm the business case			Start construction	
Develop a strategy for the project			Manage and resolve any problems	
Select client project manager			Review progress and quality	

CLIENT TASKS

Appoint the project sponsor	Confirm the strategic brief	Appoint the project team	Agree the project brief	Take possession of completed work
Appoint the client advisor	Approve the project execution plan		Agree the concept design	Learn from Experience
Confirm the business case			Agree the detailed design	
Appoint the client project manager			Make payments	
			Maintain an Overview	

Figure 1.34: Practice organisation as suggested by the Latham Report.

Of course the involvement of the client in the design process is important, but should this be carried out in direct consultation with the architects rather than through intermediaries?

4.8 Models are useful, but an exciting new development is 'Knowledge Based Engineering' (KBE). This system has been developed in manufacturing industry, both for aeroplanes and cars. It enables product managers and designers to see new ideas either through advanced computer aided design or 'Virtual Reality'. All aspects of the design, manufacture, assembly and use of the product can then be presented in one entity. Research carried out by the University of Reading and the British Airports Authority is showing that it is possible to use KBE in the design of individual construction projects. This development could have a massive effect in placing real choices before clients, and producing better construction performance. If clients can clearly understand the likely outcome of projects at design stage, their wishes can be better met. Some industry experts believe that KBE is the technology of the 21st century, and that the software needed will be too complex and expensive for all but the most prestigious projects commissioned by the wealthiest clients. I suspect that the information technology revolution will produce speedier solutions than that, and will be client driven. Paying a higher fee to the designers for such information will be repaid many times over if it ensures a well planned project which meets the client's aspirations. The establishment of common standards for the exchange of electronic data would be highly desirable and further considerations should be given to this issue. (op. cit.)

The emphasis on the presentation of design alternatives to clients through KBE techniques implies that '*known*' solutions are already prescribed within computing systems, and clients can choose or modify these.

4.10 To achieve co-ordination in the documents available to the constructors on site seems basic common sense. As one client commented 'If Knowledge Based Engineering is tomorrow's technology for construction, CPI ought to be yesterday's. Surely we can harmonise the basic works information?' The CIEC's final report also recommends the use (with some modifications) of CPI in civil engineering. (op. cit.)

Recommendation 7: Co-ordinated Project Information
4.13 CPI is a technique which should have become normal practice years ago. In conjunction with the preparation of a full matrix of documents, its use should be made part of the conditions of engagement of the designers. If, as a result of the client's own instructions or through some problem on the part of the design team, the design drawings and specifications are not fully complete, and provisional sums are used, the consultants must make the client aware of the risks of incomplete design. The consultants should get specific approval through a 'signing off' procedure, whereby the client is aware of the consequences for the construction programme in terms of possible cost and delay. Throughout the process, the emphasis must be on meeting the client's needs and keeping the client fully informed of potential risks. (op. cit.)

Although CPI (co-ordinated project information) is also desirable, we should question whether this is better achieved through management and documentation, or through more intrinsic qualities of digital technologies and representations. Some of the later case studies will reveal the potential of the latter to achieve co-ordination with little if any need for documentation.

6.12 The Interim Report found 'widespread acceptance amongst consultants that a lead manager should always be appointed for the design process, to head an integrated design team'. This in the past was the traditional role of the architect or engineer. Because of the complexity of modern construction techniques, it has become increasingly difficult for designers to be responsible for all aspects of design of a large project, and also act as contract administrators. Clients have looked for a single person/firm to pull the whole process together for them. They have tended to go through a number of stages. The first is to seek one leader of the consultants' team, who may not be the principal designer. The second is to ask the leader to be responsible for advising upon the appointment of the other consultants. The next stage is for the leader to become the channel between the client and the contractor. From there it is only a small step to becoming a single Project Manager who is responsible, as the representative of the client, for dealing with the contractor and the other consultants. Some forms of contract such as the New Engineering Contract and the BPF system recognise the Project Manager (or client's representative) as the specific representative of the employer. (op. cit.)

The emphasis on project managers controlling projects in the Latham Report has encouraged clients to employ them on many contemporary projects, irrespective of the specific contexts of such schemes. This represents a return to the old-fashioned principles of scientific management, specifically of Taylorism, especially by emphasising the separation of planning from design implementation. Placing importance on value engineering leads to inflexibility and prescriptive design solutions. Value analysis (Miles, 1961) can reduce costs and improve functional performance when functions are clearly defined, but can lead to dull and standardised design solutions.

Latham's recommendations in relation to project management suggests that complexity is better dealt with by someone who may know very little about architecture, and does not appreciate why architects have traditionally had this role. The potential disadvantages of appointing project managers are not addressed. Consider one of the many observations made by Bijl on this subject:

In the course of designing, architects have to exercise control over demarcations between overt and intuitive design procedures. Any externally imposed and fixed demarcations will have the effect of reducing the scope of a designer's intuition and, therefore, will reduce design responsibility. In order to practice[,] architects must refer to their intuitive knowledge about other people[,] and this reliance on intuition leads to the conclusion that design procedures must necessarily be idiosyncratic to individual architects. (Bijl, 1989, pp. 63–64).

There are many examples of good architecture that arose out of unmanaged projects, and even out of badly managed projects. Consider Sydney Opera House, for example. Once Utzon had been announced as the winner of the competition in January 1957, the Opera House Committee decided on a three-phased construction programme: Phase 1 – site and platform; Phase 2 – building and roof construction; Phase 3 – finishing work (glass facades, interior, auditoriums, etc.), all of which was expected to be completed by January 1963. The management of the project was effectively in the hands of the government of New South Wales, with both Utzon and the appointed structural engineers, Ove Arup, answerable directly to it (Steiner, Pirker and Ritter, 2001).

Since the focus during phases I and II is on the structural construction, Ove Arup & Partners are given the responsibility of fulfilling the contract and producing the work plans. Only for Phase III – when the focus is 'architectural' – will the structural engineers take on the usual role of consultants to the architect. This approach is completely unknown even in Australia and leads to a poorly defined division of responsibilities, which will later become one of the main causes for the collapse of the collaboration. (op. cit.)

Of the many problems requiring resolution on this project, a major one was to provide a solution to the implementation of Utzon's design for the roof structure. A structural solution for the roof wasn't produced until 1961, after Ove Arup had worked for four years on the structural implementation of what was then a completely new form of roof for the two concert halls. Utzon's proposal was a shell structure, but generated problems because from his sketches it was impossible to calculate a regular geometry for it. Peter Rice of Ove Arup developed computer software to carry out the geometrical calculations, but the resulting solutions, though technically feasible, were not acceptable to Utzon. After all the work carried out by Arup, Utzon himself came up with a design solution in which all surfaces of the roof shell were generated from a single sphere.

> *The spherical vaults were extruded in the manner of a quatered orange, and were geometrically identical, easily calculable and simple to prefabricate.* (op. cit.)

By this time Arups had invested 375,000 man-hours in the development of the solution.

> *. . . the whole problem became a vicious circle; more bending meant thicker concrete shells had to be used, making the shells heavier, meaning that higher bending moments were generated. The final form took years to develop, and the strains produced by this process led to the architect leaving the project before it was completed, and never visiting the finished building.* (Popovic and Tyas, 2003, p. 41).

Utzon's Sydney Opera House design, however, was a counterexample to this, in that the lightweight concrete shell structures that he originally anticipated for this scheme were not structurally feasible without generating enormous bending stresses.

Utzon's vision was to isolate the auditoriums from the external skin for symbolic and acoustic reasons. His intention was to suspend both the opera hall and concert hall from the roof structure, developing a system of large plywood girders forming an optimum acoustic shape. A detailed account of the organisational, political and financial problems of this project is given by Steiner, Pirker and Ritter, and according to them:

> *Utzon's working method was rooted in the European tradition of developing new products and production methods in collaboration with selected firms, instead of embarking on a project with detailed studies, a complete plan and subsequent commissions.* (Steiner, Pirker and Ritter, 2001)

Since this approach didn't correspond to Australian conditions of competition and construction, many conflicts subsequently arose.

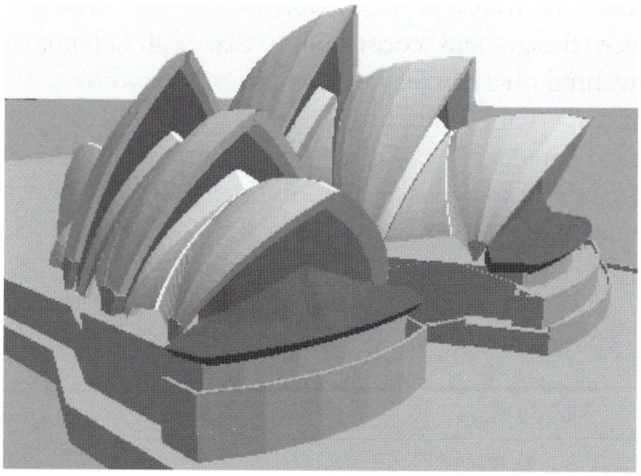

Figure 1.35: Sydney Opera House.

1.6:   Integrating CAD into the Manufacturing Process

Much has been written about the nature of the design process itself, typically starting with specifications arising out of the design brief, which in turn lead on to feasibility studies in which background design information is collected (e.g. typological precedent studies). This part is often referred to as design *synthesis* from which emerge formulations or conceptualisations of early stage design ideas. In order to progress further, models (physical or computational) are constructed that can then be subjected to some form of *analysis*, often corresponding to structural or environmental criteria (e.g. Sebestyen, 2003). It is not too difficult to envisage how computational techniques might be applied to prescribed analytical fields such as lighting, structures, acoustics, energy, etc.. Once key design decisions have been made, however, the application of computing to the *evaluation* of design choices is less clear. It is exactly from this point of the design process that the most dramatic developments in computing applications in architectural practice are currently being made. One computational technique in the evaluation phase that will be referred to in more detail later is that of *rapid prototyping*, in which prototypes of design elements are constructed through machining or stereolithographic processes. The evaluation of prototypes will often lead to redesign and further analysis. Successful re-evaluation then leads on to the preparation of information for the manufacturing processes. If this information can be provided directly to the fabricators in digital form, then further productivity gains can be made.

Just as CAD systems are central to the representation of design schemes in architectural offices, a range of CAM (computer aided manufacturing) software is used in the manufacturing process. CAM software includes computer-aided process planning (CAPP) systems , software for computer numerical control of machine tools in the production phase (CNC), inspection software, and assembly software. In mechanical engineering applications, for example, improvements in the *integration* of CAD and CAM software are viewed as leading to greater productivity and competitiveness. This is also true for the fabrication of architectural components, but the productivity benefits in this case are not necessarily economic ones. They can also increase the expressive potential of design schemes, in that complex CAD-modelled forms may be no more expensive to fabricate than simpler forms, provided the CAD/CAM integration is good.

The essence of integration between the computer-based modelling of design schemes and the fabrication of often complex design elements is the ability to communicate representational information in compatible digital forms between these two stages of architectural or engineering projects. The following case study begins to introduce on a small scale some of the connections between design and construction that will become more significant in the later larger-scale architectural case studies.

1.7:   The Shoal Fly By Project

The Shoal Fly By project is a project that was developed in the context of a practice-based research programme at the Royal Melbourne Institute of Technology (RMIT), Australia, in the Spatial Information Architecture Laboratory (SIAL). The research aimed to develop a design process that transferred scaled freeform curves into digital space, transcribing the curves as tangential arcs for construction through a computer numerical controlled (CNC) tube bending and fabrication operation. Despite the existence of dedicated research and development departments in construction practice, innovation in project-based work is hard to make explicit (Gann and Salter, 2000). The SIAL research programme responded to this with a dual role methodology of design research for both practice and education. Its intention was to offer innovative technical solutions whilst encouraging new kinds of design activity.

3-D curves proliferate in digital space, yet curves in built space are generally planar, separated into tangential arcs during the shop drawing process, and fabricated by welding similar profiles of different lengths and radii. Vehicle exhausts made from the conjunction of a few bends and straight tubes is about as complex as it gets. The ability to build fully 3-D curves on the other hand, requires a radical departure from the conventional *slice and dice* approach based on 2-D profiles extracted from plans, sections and elevations. Powerful representational techniques that can help to achieve this include nonuniform rational b-spline (NURBS) curves and surfaces.

Mathematically, curves can be represented as parametric functions in one variable *(u)* that map a line segment onto a curve. Surfaces are parametric functions in two variables *(u,v)* that map a 2-D region into 3-D space. Surfaces can be composed of multiple surface elements called *patches*. If either *u* or *v* is fixed, and the other parameter varied, then an isoparametric curve (called an *isoparm*) can be created on the surface. i.e. 2-D lines become curves on surfaces in 3-D space (**figure 1.36**). Isoparms are lines *with a fixed number of points* lying on a NURBS surface.

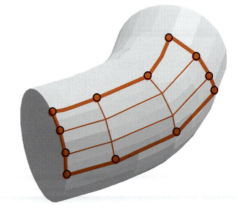

Figure 1.36: NURBS surface with isoparms.

Shoal Fly By is a public artwork comprising a collection of five separate sculptures intended to represent movement through water (**figures 1.37–1.38** opposite). The artists Cat Macleod and Michael Bellemo handcrafted models at a scale of 1:100 composed of freeform curves using wire as a malleable medium. This enabled them to capture small bends and kinks, a seamless but not smooth aesthetic that they wanted to retain in the final work. The sculpture was awarded first prize in a competition for construction on the foreshore of the docklands precinct in Melbourne, Australia, which is currently undergoing massive redevelopment as a place to work and live. The artists had previously built relatively simple curved forms in steel, developing an appreciation of the fabrication processes involved. Through their own research they knew that without establishing tangential relations between the constituent parts of the work, the result would be an exposition of joints, preventing a reading of the whole – in this case a network of freeform stainless steel tubes.

Figure 1.37: The Shoal Fly By sculpture.

Figure 1.38: The Shoal Fly By sculpture.

The research process began by attempting to accurately measure the physical model. Repeatability using a point probe on a three-dimensional digitising arm proved inaccurate. This then led to a non-contact method of 3-D digitisation using a laser scanner and then tracing NURBS curves through sub-millimetre clouds of points. The smoothness of NURBS curves and NURBS surfaces can be controlled with *control points* that do not necessarily lie on the curves and surfaces themselves. An algorithm was developed to approximate the wires to a series of tangential arcs. This involved assimilating the information required by the tube bending machine and the fabrication procedure with a method for fragmenting NURBS curves into arcs. This is mathematically difficult and the result is always an approximation. This is because a curve is continuously changing in curvature whereas an arc is of fixed curvature and so *steps through* curvature change. The process developed through a series of visual iterations, finishing with eight constraints which could be varied for each curve, such as minimum arc length, radius and maximum curvature change. The physical process of tube bending is controlled by CNC processes in which tubes pass either through rollers or around a fixed die. Most bends are planar and of fixed radius, although it is possible to offset a radius to generate helical extrusions.

Figure 1.39: The construction of the Shoal Fly By sculpture.

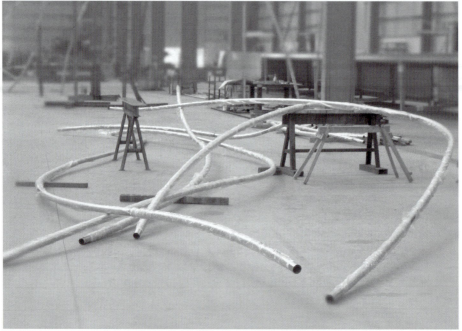

Figure 1.40: The curved steel elements.

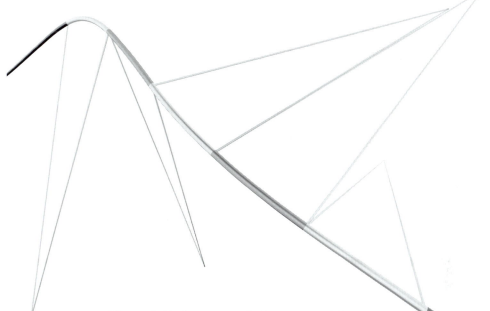

Figure 1.41: A curve made from tangential arcs.

Some tacit knowledge was developed when reconciling the physical design with its expression in arcs. Since the artists did not want a *smoothed* result, a balance was sought between using a greater number of smaller arcs for a very close approximation, and longer arcs with fewer joints to achieve a more economical budget (**figure 1.41**). The collaborative nature of the work, between those not normally collectively associated with the design development of built work – artists, fabricators, students, programmers and surveyors, brought an unanticipated method of representation to the project. The largest sculpture, composing 420 arcs and conveying almost 3800 pieces of information, was fully documented using spreadsheets, together with a digital model for cross-referencing. Although such methods of representation can be found in a research project of this nature, they are radically different from the working practices of many architectural offices. However, some of the later case studies will show the extent to which the profession is changing.

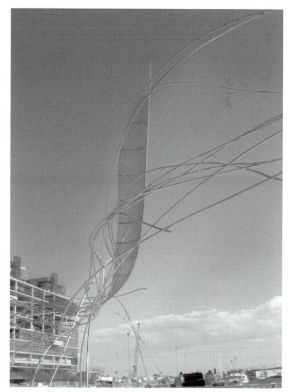

Figure 1.42: The Shoal Fly By sculpture.

Chapter 2: Simple Visualisation of Complex Forms

The following is a case study from the office of Szyskowitz-Kowalski in Graz, Austria. It shows the design development of a complex contemporary building project to be sited in the Ruhr area of Germany, but which was ultimately unbuilt. The design proposal evolved through a series of sketch drawings, in which the 3-D visualisation of form became progressively more complex. The complexity arose from the spiral structural form at the centre of the scheme. In this case, basic CAD modelling techniques, and the ability to visualise proposed design elements, became an extension of conventional sketch design techniques.

2.1 What you see is what you get

The four key areas of sketch design may be viewed as *space, structure, surface,* and *decoration* (Edwards, 1994, p. 174). There is a dependent relationship between space and surface, since space is defined in terms of surface. These four key design areas that relate directly to the visual perception of design schemes need to be integrated, and balanced with the surrounding physical context (**figure 2.1**).

Figure 2.1: The physical context.

In this particular case study, the design focus was primarily upon the structural form. The intention was to create an office space in the form of an independent free-floating body within the space defined by an existing building envelope (**figure 2.2**). This was referred to by the architects as the *house-in-the-house*. Essential parts of the conversion of the interior were to be the demolition of the floor level at 6m, the staircase and parts of the foundations. Initial sketch design ideas attempted to relate the new design proposals for the interior to the existing buildings and site context.

Figure 2.2: The building envelope.

As [inquirers] frame the problem of the situation, they determine the features to which they will attend, the order they will attempt to impose on the situation, the directions in which they will try to change it. In this process, they identify both the ends to be sought and the means to be employed. (Schon, 1983, p. 165)

The end in this case was the resolution of building form with structure, circulation, and environmental aspects. Visualisation through sketching, physical and digital modelling was the means used to achieve this.

According to Clark and Pause, . . . *circulation and use-space represent the significant dynamic and static components in all buildings. . . . Together, the articulation of the conditions of movement and stability form the essence of a building.* (Clark and Pause, 1985, p. 5). Ching states that: *The pattern of circulation and movement within a centralized organization may be radial, loop, or spiral in form. In almost every case, however, the pattern will terminate in or around the central space.* (Ching, 1996, p. 191). The spiral has been a prevalent geometric form in architecture from Tatlin's monument to the 3rd international in 1919, through to Frank Lloyd Wright's Guggenheim Museum in the 1940s, and more recently Daniel Libeskind's proposal for the extension to the Victoria and Albert Museum in London. The mathematics of the spiral will be looked at more closely in relation to the case study presented in the following chapter. In this particular case study, however, the spiral was the dominant organising force regarding *circulation*, thus having a more indirect effect on the building form. The design possibilities of a spiral circulation were something that was explored and analysed over and over again in the early hand-drawn sketches (**figure 2.3**).

Figure 2.3: Preliminary sketch indicating circulation.

The idea was that terraced steps should lead from the ground floor level via a staircase to the first floor level (+3.24m), where a cafe and office entrance were to be located. From here, all offices at the levels +6.48m, +7.02m, +9.90m and +13.14m could be reached, via an atrium, that forms, as a central circulation space, the centre of the building. The atrium also works as communication and recreation space. A second fire-staircase was to be located in the north-western corner of the hall, with direct access to the outside. The exploratory sketches reflect the design issues under investigation, and as these issues become more detailed, computer-generated sketch models may be needed.

2.2 Sketching prior to Digital Modelling

Designers set out the key aspects of design proposals through a fast and spontaneous method of drawing known as sketching. Sketches are characterised by an economy of line and rendering, and provoke further, more detailed, design development.

But why sketch? Why is it necessary to externalize the idea conceived in the brain, and then have the brain examine it? For a composer, the keyboard serves as the sketchpad. In every creative act we observe this bootstrap process in which nascent ideas are externalized and then taken in again by the brain to be reexamined and modified in a creative loop. (Harth, 1993)

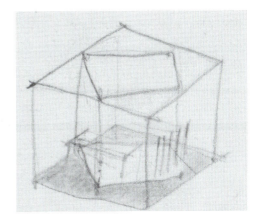

Figure 2.4: Preliminary sketch indicating form.

The idea of *reflection-in-action* was developed by Donald Schon in connection with various forms of professional practice (Schon, 1983), and seems to be applicable to the reflexive process of sketching in architectural design.

The practitioner allows himself to experience surprise, puzzlement, or confusion in a situation which he finds uncertain or unique. He reflects on the phenomenon before him, and on the prior understandings which have been implicit in his behaviour. He carries out an experiment which serves to generate both a new understanding of the phenomenon and a change in the situation. (Schon, 1983, p. 68).

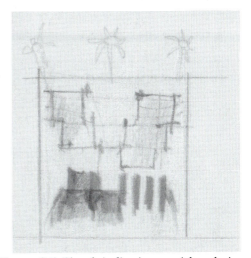

Figure 2.5: Sketch indicating spatial analysis.

Figures 2.4–2.6 show some of Szyskowitz-Kowalski's intial sketch analyses of formal and spatial arrangements for the Ruhr scheme. The simplicity and immediacy of the medium of freehand sketching was conducive to the generation of externalised expressions without fear of interruption by software prompts or other digital distractions. If this fact can be recognised by those involved in the development of digital environments, then digital support for design development from the early stages might be improved. Some potential support mechanisms will be investigated later. Parts of **chapter 8** will look at methods of digitally capturing some of the intentions embodied with the sketching process.

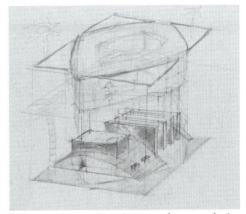

Figure 2.6: Sketch indicating form analysis.

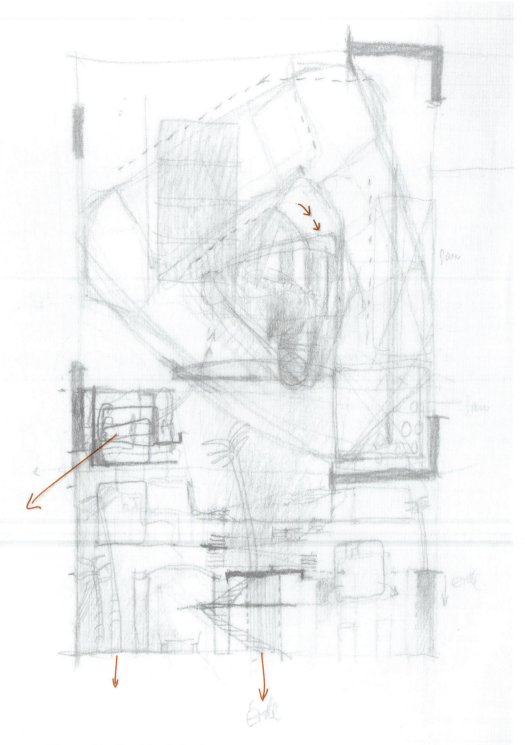

Figure 2.7: Combined plan/elevation sketch exploring circulation issues.

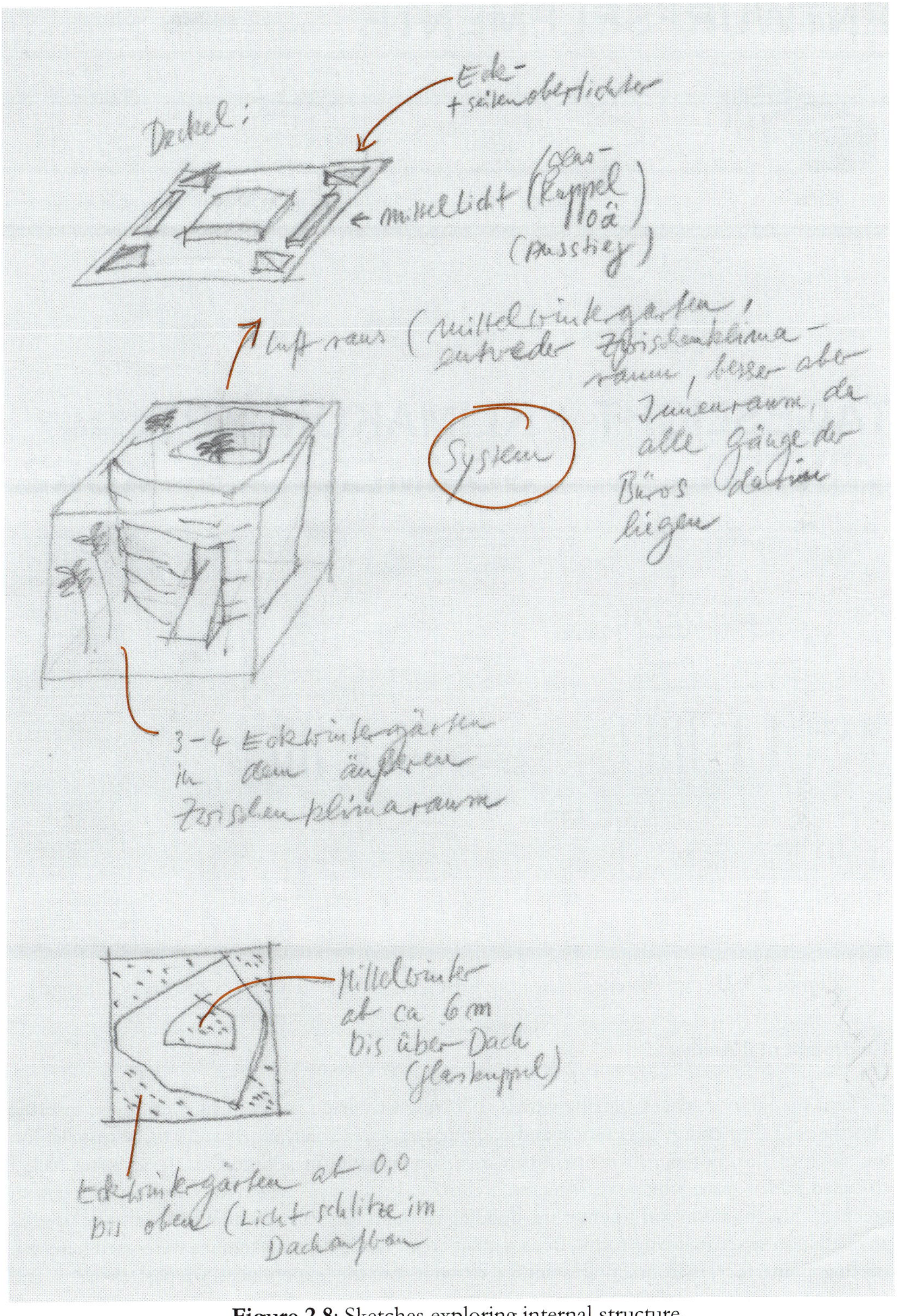

Figure 2.8: Sketches exploring internal structure.

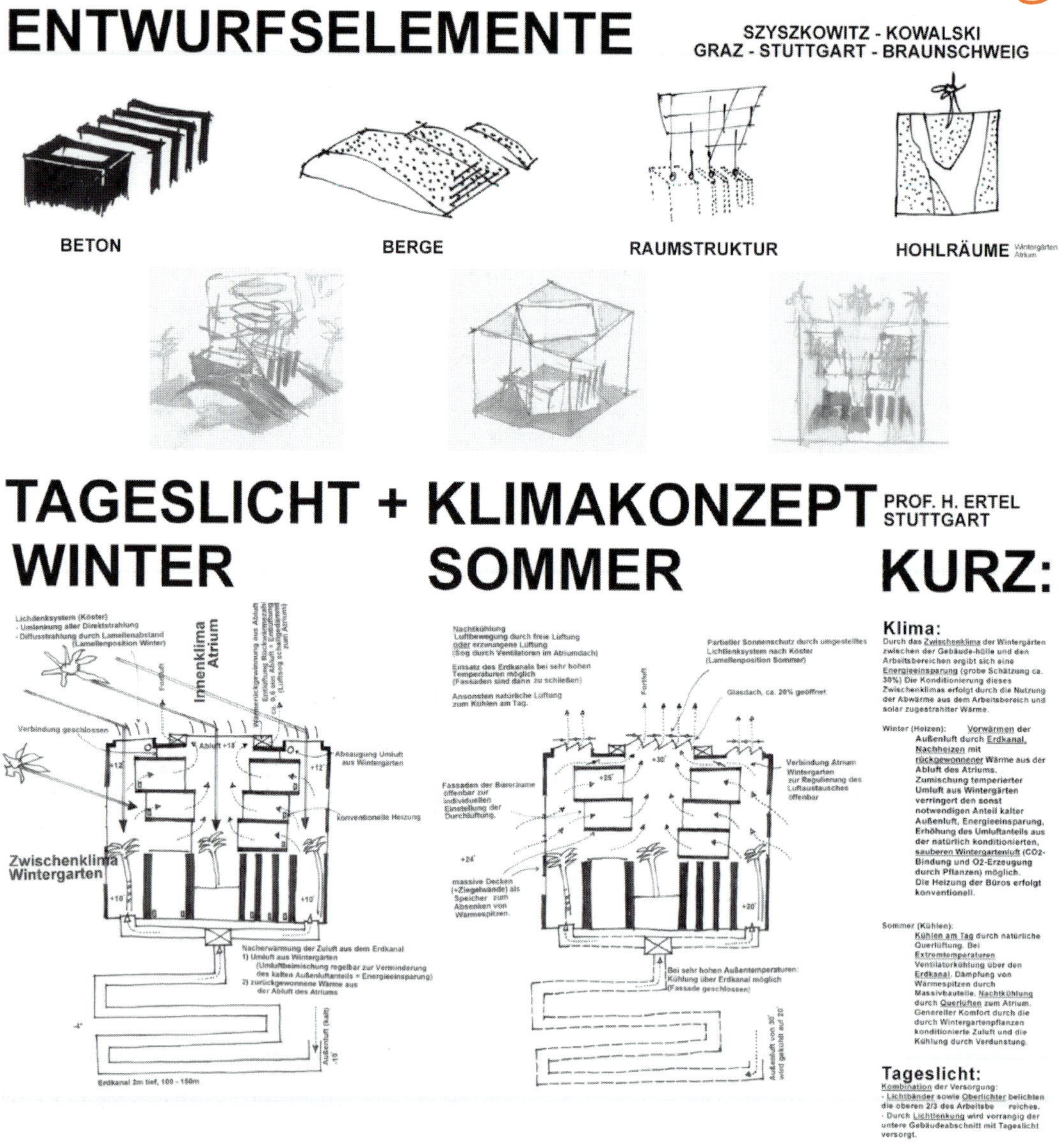
ENTWURFSELEMENTE
SZYSZKOWITZ - KOWALSKI
GRAZ - STUTTGART - BRAUNSCHWEIG
BETON
BERGE
RAUMSTRUKTUR
HOHLRÄUME
TAGESLICHT + KLIMAKONZEPT
PROF. H. ERTEL
STUTTGART
WINTER
SOMMER
KURZ:
Innenklima
Atrium
Zwischenklima
Wintergarten
Klima:
Tageslicht:

Figure 2.9: Design sketches indicating solar gain, natural ventilation and heat exchange.

Environmental Analysis

To light the interior spaces, glazing panels following the shape of the plan, were to be inserted into the roof. For energy generation and cooling, large-area solar panels were to be installed on the slope of the roof-skin. An open-plan form was created in addition to the existing hall, a so-called *interim space*, which was seen as a climatic buffer and which was to be planted with greenery. The intention was to enter the building through this space, which could also be used as an exhibition space, meeting room, or as a quiet area. Again, design sketches were used here as a starting point for environmental analysis, drawing on the experiences of past projects and applying them to the current context.

2.3 Visualisation Supporting Designers' Perceptions

Central to this scheme was the ability to visualise structural clashes between the inner and outer forms in three dimensions.

. . . if we are to perceive the structure of things at all, some correlate of them must be there in the stimuli. This is important in a great number of respects, and especially perhaps in connection with depth perception. (Hamlyn, 1957, p. 86)

3-D freehand sketches such as the one shown in **figure 2.10** may not necessarily reveal all salient details, and this is where digital modelling comes into play.

Gibson . . . points out that objects are on a ground which stretches from us to them and beyond them. The geometrical projection of this ground with the objects upon it corresponds to the structure of the visual field, so that the visual field and the retinal image coincide. (Hamlyn, 1957, p. 87)

A basic property of 3-D digital models is the ability to perceive them through dynamically changing viewpoints.

The three-dimensional, rationalized space of perspectival vision could be rendered on a two-dimensional surface by following all of the transformational rules spelled out in Alberti's De Pittura and later treatises by Viator, Durer, and others. The basic device was the idea of symmetrical visual pyramids or cones with one of their apexes the receding vanishing or centric point in the painting, the other the eye of the painter or the beholder. The transparent window that was the canvas, in Alberti's famous metaphor, could also be understood as a flat mirror reflecting the geometricalized space radiating out from the viewing eye.

Figure 2.10: 3-D visualisation sketch.

Figure 2.11: Sketching directly onto image of 3-D CAD-generated sketch model.

Significantly, that eye was singular, rather than the two eyes of normal binocular vision. It was conceived in the manner of a lone eye looking through a peephole at the scene in front of it. Such an eye was, moreover, understood to be static, unblinking, and fixated, rather than dynamic, moving with what later scientists would call 'saccadic' jumps from one focal point to another. (Jay, 1998, p. 68)

2.4 The Role of Physical Modelling

Physical models are an inherent part of architectural design proposals. They have tactile qualities that can be matched neither by conventional drawings nor by digital models. As a consequence of the increasing trend towards client involvement in design projects, they form an important part of this process.

Typically, models such as those shown in **figures 2.12–2.14** are used for presentation purposes. Such models are relatively time consuming and expensive to construct, and are therefore produced only after completion of at least the concept design stage.

To use Schon's terminology, the process of reflection-in-action is followed by *reflection-on-action*. The act of reflecting-on-action may crystallise some of the ideas that were being explored through sketching in the form of physical models.

Some of the later case studies will also illustrate an increasing trend towards the production of more conceptual and less expensive physical models. The role of such models is as 3-D design sketch models, but also as models that encourage client interaction at earlier stages of the design process.

The use of 3-D digital design data to generate model prototypes using CNC milling machines or stereolithographic techniques is an emerging issue in contemporary architecture that also needs further exploration.

Figure 2.12: Physical models.

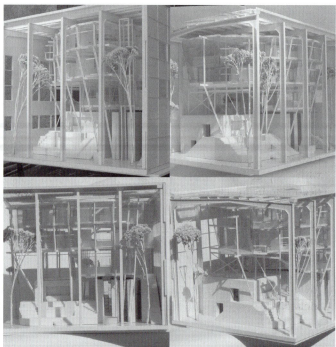

Figure 2.13: Physical models.

Construction Models

One of the aims of the physical models shown in shown in **figures 2.12–2.14** was to indicate the extent to which the internal form was independent from the external form for construction purposes. There was to be no structural connection between the hall facade and the internal office complex. The construction of the steel frame and floor plates for the office levels was to be built on the existing foundations.

Massing Models

In between the massive existing foundations, which were going to be partially demolished, spaces for meeting rooms, archives and plant rooms were to be created.

In the existing hall, office space in the form of a free-standing structure was designed, generating what the architects called their *house-inside-a-house* principle.

Models indicated that for internal reconstruction, the stairwell along with parts of the foundations needed to be dismantled. From the environmental analysis, the roof glazing was to follow the outline profile of the internal installation. In order to support passive solar gains, whilst at the same time allowing cooling when necessary, an inclined roof skin was developed.

Figure 2.14: Physical models.

Figure 2.16: Detailed ground floor plan drawing.

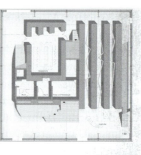

Figure 2.17: Detailed +3m floor plan drawing.

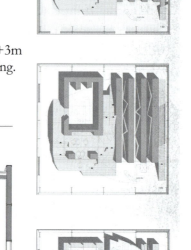

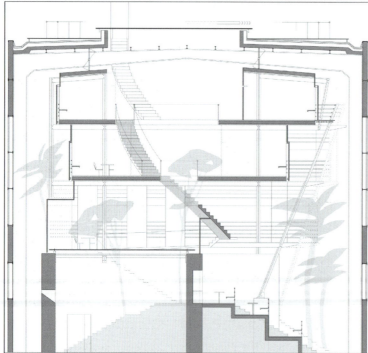

Figure 2.15: Detailed elevation drawing.

Significantly the 2-D plan and section drawings in **figures 2.15–20** were obtained as a by-product of the same 3-D digital model that was central to the generation of visualisations such as that shown in **figure 2.21**.

Figure 2.18: +6.50m plan.

Figure 2.19: +10.4m plan.

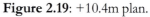

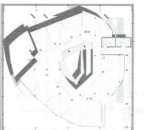

Figure 2.20: +14m plan.

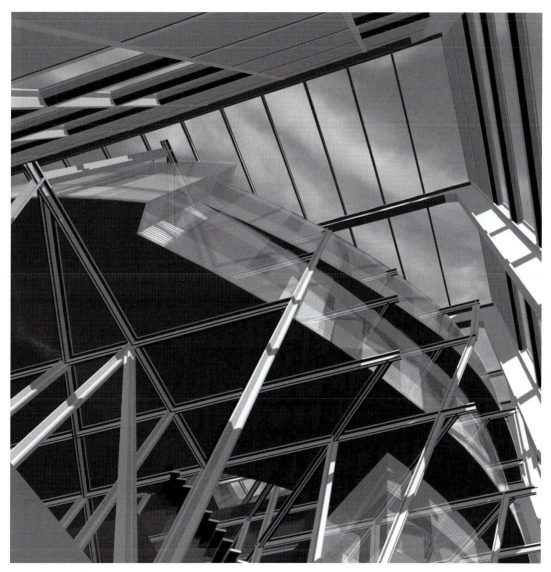

Figure 2.21: The key CAD-generated perspective view resolving sketch design analysis of relationship between interior and exterior structural forms.

The progression from sketching through to physical modelling and then to digital modelling allowed progressively more detailed visualisation of the developing design scheme. Movement in and around digital models revealed structural and constructional issues in relation to building components that would have remained unresolved in physical models. The first and simplest advantage of 3-D digital modelling, therefore, is to be able to quickly visualise the consequences of model changes without the need for complex 2-D redrawing work.

The digital tool is not the instrument of abstraction, of a final transcendence of the design; it simply increases the range of an exploration of dimensional changes as well as perceptual and visual changes. (Migayrou, 2001, p. 9).

Chapter 3: Pure Form: Solidifying Mathematics

Organic architecture is rooted in nature and natural forms, and is based upon the natural world's biological forms and processes, and emphasises harmony through the use of free-flowing curves and expressive forms. It is a move away from the rectilinear, orthogonal mode that came to dominate much of 20th century architecture. (Pearson, 2001)

The previous chapter was concerned with both conventional and digital support for the visualisation of sketch design ideas. This chapter will look at some complex but essentially geometric design ideas, and the capabilities of mathematically-based digital environments to model them. For example, a well-known geometric relationship is the golden section, and a generator of the logarithmic spiral. This is exactly the form that was adopted in one of Peter Hubner's recent projects that we shall look at shortly. By mathematically constraining the ways in which geometric objects can behave when modelled in CAD systems, it becomes possible to *digitally simulate* (however abstract one might consider this to be) natural processes.

Frank Lloyd Wright once defined organic architecture in fifty-one different ways. Jencks reduced these down to the central one of *organic geometry* in which the process of construction was integral to the structure itself (Jencks, 1973). This idea manifests itself in Wright's schemes when buildings rise out of their sites without necessarily looking like natural organic forms. We saw in section **1.4** how it is possible to think of the construction process when modelling structure in CAD systems. Another way of thinking about organic architecture is in its relationship to already known and typically natural, or biological, forms. In Padovan's description of the debate between the two distinct and mutually antagonistic wings of the functionalist movement, he made this observation:

The 'organicists' regarded the artifact as a biological phenomenon, like the nest of a bird, while for the 'positivists' or 'mechanists' it was the product of calculation and geometry, like a machine. (Padovan, 1994, p. 71)

Le Corbusier's approach was to impose simplistic geometric forms from the outside and then to justify them in terms of their aesthetic qualities - designing from the outside in.

It seems clear to us that the two greatest form-makers of twentieth-century architecture - Frank Lloyd Wright and Le Corbusier - were able to innovate largely because of their appreciation and deep understanding of symmetry and pattern-structure. (March and Steadman, 1971, p. 86)

The emphasis of geometry in the work of Wright and Le Corbusier had a huge influence on the development of digital representations such as *shape grammars*, for example (Stiny, 1975; Krishnamurti, 1980). These were based on the assumption that designs could be reduced to abstract geometric structures, but have had limited application in real design generation.

An alternative and less prescriptive approach was adopted by organic expressionist architects such as Eric Mendelsohn, Hans Scharoun and Hugo Haring. They were interested in finding ways of integrating their free-form sketches with clearly defined functional plans – designing from the inside out. The latter approach subsequently had a strong influence on architects such as Louis Kahn and Alvar Aalto, and appears to be reemerging again in contemporary architectural projects (see **chapter 8**, for example).

3.1   Fractal Geometry

The aspiration towards organicism, therefore, inevitably resulted in geometric approximation. One such approximation to the representation of natural form is *fractal geometry*. Van der Laan's qualification is relevant to both the mathematical and computational representation of form:

> *Wherever the human intellect intervenes as the formative principle, there immediately appears a breach with the homogeneous world of natural forms.* (Padovan, 1994, p. 72)

In *Fractals: Form, chance, and dimension* (Mandelbrot, 1977), the central concept was that of *self-similarity* - symmetry across scale. Zooming in or out of fractal forms reveals self-similar, but not necessarily identical detail. Fractal geometry can be used to describe natural shapes such as leaves, tree branches, waveforms, and coastlines. The architectural concepts of rhythm and composition can also be digitally represented in terms of fractal properties, sometimes referred to as *textural progression*. Fractal geometry allows the representation of complex underlying patterns through the repetitive transformation of simple geometric equations, and can be dealt with using high-speed computing resources. Attempts to digitally represent real-world fractal phenomena have focused on certain characteristic features:

> *Real systems signal their presence through three factors:*
> * *They are dynamic, that is, subject to lasting changes.*
> * *They are complex, that is, depend on many parameters.*
> * *They are iterative, that is, the laws that govern their behaviour can be described by feedback.*
> (Becker and Dorfler, 1989, p. 5)

It should be borne in mind that any iterative process can be directly translated into a set of recursive function definitions (Brady, 1977, p. 160). In other words, fractal geometry implies *recursion*, or patterns inside patterns.

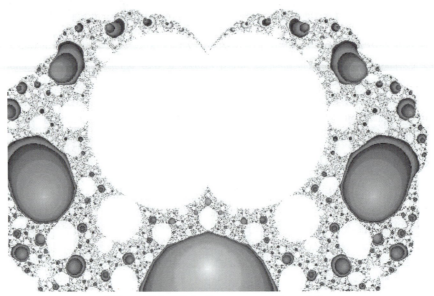

Figure 3.1: Digitally generated fractal form.

3.2   Logarithmic Spirals

Patterns and forms in nature can be viewed as the end-products of internal laws of growth, such as spirals and fractals, *combined with* external forces acting on them, such as sun, wind, and water. A commonly encountered natural law is the Fibonacci series, the infinite number sequence in which each new number is generated by the sum of the two preceding numbers, i.e. 1, 1, 2, 3, 5, 8, 13, 21, 34, 55, 89, etc. It governs *phyllotaxis* (the arrangement of leaves on a stem) to give optimum chlorophyll production. It also describes spiral growth patterns of objects such as sunflowers (**figures 3.2** and **3.3**), pine cones, seeds, and seashells. The number series generates the golden section, the ratio of 1:618, and the golden rectangle, whose sides are in that ratio. Padovan distinguishes natural from artificial forms by emphasising the importance of whole numbers in nature:

> *And nature itself seems to prefer whole numbers. In the example that Hambidge cites – phyllotaxis – it is not the irrational number* ϕ*, approximately 1.618, but the whole number Fibonacci series 1, 1, 2, 3, 5, . . ., that plants actually exhibit.* (Padovan, 1999, p. 47)

> *Nature employs whole numbers because she is counting, not measuring. It is a matter of the number of seeds in a sunflower, or of branches from a stem. One seed is possible, or two, but not an irrational number of seeds.* (Padovan, loc. cit.)

Figure 3.2: Sunflower.

Figure 3.3: Spiral phyllotaxis.

Mathematically, logarithmic spirals can be described in terms of polar coordinates, and can be graphically represented as exponential curves. Stretching a logarithmic spiral is equivalent to rotating it. A logarithmic spiral is a curve whose equation in polar coordinates is given by:

$$r = ae^{\beta\theta} \qquad\qquad (1)$$

where r is the distance from the origin, θ is the angle from the x-axis, and α and β are arbitrary constants. The logarithmic spiral is also known as the growth or equiangular spiral, and spiral. It can be expressed *parametrically* as:

$$x = r\cos\theta = \alpha\cos\theta e^{\beta\theta} \qquad\qquad (2)$$

$$y = r\sin\theta = \alpha\sin\theta e^{\beta\theta} \qquad\qquad (3)$$

3.3   Hubner's Stammheim Church

Peter Hubner of Neckartenzlingen, Germany, is an architect with strong roots in the German tradition of organic architecture. In many of his schemes this is combined with an emphasis on community participation and self-build projects. He sees the role of computing as supporting these aims, particularly with regard to minimising costs. This is achieved by exploiting the relatively quick modification of computer models, and associating alternative arrangements with construction plans and schedules.

Hubner has a reputation for working with communities to develop low-cost self-build architecture, often with the assistance of computational methods not only for mathematical and geometric calculations, but also to assist with construction and the schedule of work. This particular project was a self-build timber construction for a church in Stammheim, Germany. The building form was based on a form resembling an ammonite fossil (**figure 3.4**), which itself has logarithmic properties. The scheme focused on a central point from which 24 timber connecting pieces about 15 metres long radiated outwards.

The entire construction was developed as a CAD sketch model using the Nemetschek AG Allplan software. The digital sketch model then became the basis for structural and constructional analysis, which in turn led to modifications of the structure. The CAD model along with physical models also allowed the contractor to establish a plan of work from the early stages of the project. As the CAD model was updated, so were the planning phases. CAD plan and isometric views are shown in the **figures 3.5–3.7** opposite.

Timber cross-sections were assessed in terms of the economy of their production, as well as ease of on-site handling i.e. without complicated tool-intensive operations. The wood used was douglas fir. The roof timbers were fixed onto a steel thrust ring, with each timber element being different in terms of span, angle, and height. Initial dead weight structural calculations resulted in simplification of timber cross-sections. Connection between wooden elements needed to take into account shrinkage tolerances. The roof performed structurally as a membrane with a clearly defined apex. Membranes can be thought of as thin shell structures such that the significant structural forces are tension forces in the membrane surface. The representation and analysis of a more complex membrane structure will be described in the following chapter.

The roof was clad with laminated wood cut according to CAD-generated drawings. The facade design was developed as a consequence of complex computer animations and light simulations. Hubner made a virtue out of the fact that the cost of the entire building project was 350,000DM. His view is that low-cost self-build projects, assisted with appropriate computer-based technologies focuses minds on the production of deliverable constructions.

Hubner's project was based upon the mathematical idea of the logarithmic spiral. Such a building form requires the digital expression of parametric rules and setting out points for its generation. There does appear to be a trend amongst architects and engineers to try to digitally exploit mathematical systems in the development of new structural forms that diverge from more traditional engineering solutions.

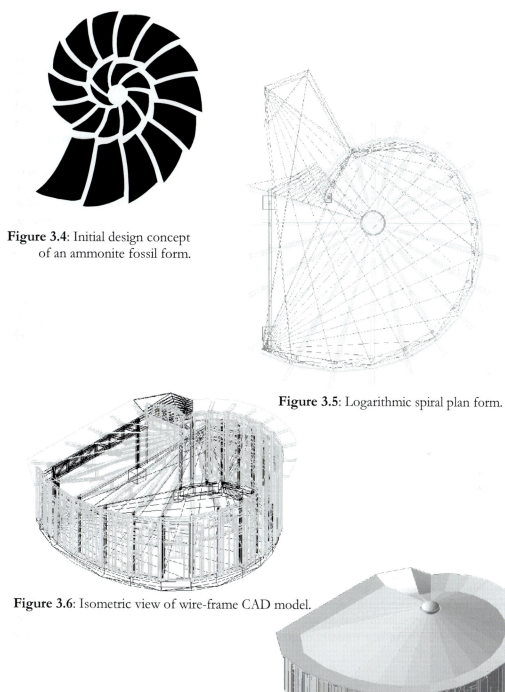

Figure 3.4: Initial design concept of an ammonite fossil form.

Figure 3.5: Logarithmic spiral plan form.

Figure 3.6: Isometric view of wire-frame CAD model.

Figure 3.7: Isometric view of rendered CAD model.

3.4   Dynamic Symmetry

Arcs defined by the radii of squares in golden rectangles of increasing size generate continuous logarithmic spirals. This section gives a simple geometric explanation of the development of architectural compositions with the dynamic symmetry proportional system (Hambidge, 1926). This method can also be used to analyse existing compositions or to proportion given areas. It also has the interesting property of allowing perfect reduction or enlargement of compositions.

Ratio is a quantitative comparison of two things, typically of lengths, areas, or volumes. The constructions in **figures 3.8-3.15** show the continued progression of the development of *root* rectangles. The *root-three* rectangle extension in **figure 3.15** is slightly less than that of the *root-two* rectangle extension in **figure 3.11**. Padovan makes it clear that what is important if such constructions are to be architectonically useful are not individual proportional moves, but the whole series. In other words, a system of proportion only becomes architecturally visible when a series of successive proportional moves have been applied throughout a design scheme.

> *Hambidge's construction can be taken further, however, and must be, if the four ratios are to reveal their full potential, and become systems . . . i.e. interwoven grids. For by themselves, the geometric progressions based on* $\sqrt{2}$, $\sqrt{3}$, $\sqrt{4}$ *and* $\sqrt{5}$ *have negligible additive properties, and are of limited use as systems of proportion. But the systems produced by adding the unit to the square roots of 2, 3, 4 and 5 – that is, 1+* $\sqrt{2}$, *1+* $\sqrt{3}$, *1+* $\sqrt{4}$, *and 1+* $\sqrt{5}$ *– are additive, and their additive potential is further increased when they are interwoven with their parent square root progressions.*
> (Padovan, 1999, p. 49)

The method of adding onto a unit square and successively extending a rectangular shape can be carried out many times. By adding diagonals to each new rectangle, constructing arcs to the base line and then a new right-hand side, new *root* rectangles are formed. The series of constructions up to *root-five* is commonly found in architecture. Other series of a greater number of constructions have also been used. The *root-five* rectangle has similar properties to the golden section and golden rectangle, but the golden rectangle is not part of a geometric progression as are the dynamic symmetry's *root* rectangles. Once the construction of dynamic symmetry *root* rectangles is understood, it is possible to apply this idea to various architectural arrangements of space. The golden section was used widely in classical and renaissance architecture. Padovan (op. cit.) discusses a variety of proportional systems in addition to the golden section that have been used in architectural design. His interest in systems such as the golden section and Van der Laan's plastic number stem from their capacity to generate designs that are both ordered and complex.

> *Broadly speaking, one can say that the potential complexity of a system is directly proportional to its wealth of additive properties, whereas its ordering capacity is inversely proportional to the density of measures. In other words, the more additive permutations a system offers, the greater the potential complexity, while the larger the basic multiplier, the greater the order.* (op.cit., p. 55).

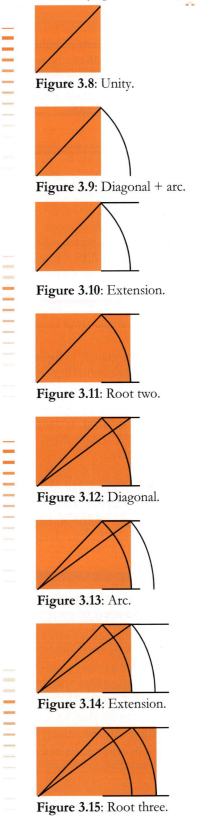

Figure 3.8: Unity.

Figure 3.9: Diagonal + arc.

Figure 3.10: Extension.

Figure 3.11: Root two.

Figure 3.12: Diagonal.

Figure 3.13: Arc.

Figure 3.14: Extension.

Figure 3.15: Root three.

Begin with a square of one unit. Construct a diagonal line from the lower left-hand corner of the square to the upper right-hand corner of the square.

Next, construct the arc of a circle with centre at the lower left-hand corner of the diagonal, starting point at the top right-hand corner of the diagonal, down to the level of the lower base line of the initial square. Then extend the top and bottom lines of the square to encompass the new arc.

By constructing a vertical line from the bottom of the arc to join with the extended upper line, a resultant rectangle is produced, known as a *root-two* rectangle.

Next, to create a *root-three* rectangle, draw a diagonal from the lower left-hand corner of the original square to the upper right-hand corner of the last extension. Again, construct an arc of a circle with centre at the lower left-hand corner of the diagonal, starting from the upper right-hand corner of the new diagonal.

Construct another arc from the top corner down to the bottom of the previous *root-two* rectangle. Now extend the lower and upper lines to the right to encompass the new arc as was done with the *root-two* rectangle. Finally, draw another vertical line from the top to the bottom where the latest arc ends. This now becomes a *root-three* rectangle.

. . . etc.

Hambidge shows how a spiral form such as that shown in **figure 3.16** can be represented in terms of straight lines that can then be used to resolve compositional problems according to rules of proportion (**figure 3.18**).

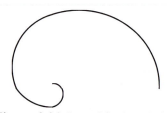

Figure 3.16: Logarithmic spiral.

> . . . *between any three radii vectors of the curve, equal angular distance apart, the middle one is a mean proportional between the other two.* (Hambidge, 1926, pp. 5–6)

The way in which dynamic symmetry can be constructed in a rectangular plan form is as shown in **figure 3.19**. Once the diagonal **AB** has been determined, **CD** then cuts **AB** at right angles. **ACBDE** are points on a logarithmic spiral. This process can be continued by constructing a vertical from **E** and so on.

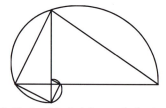

Figure 3.17: Embedded right-angled triangles.

The shaded rectangle in **figure 3.19** defined by extending a horizontal line from **D** is known as the *reciprocal* of the larger initial rectangle. If the reciprocal is half the size of the initial rectangle, then the larger rectangle is a root-two rectangle, 1/3 is root three, 1/4 is root four, 1/5 is root-five.

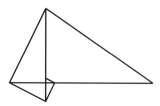

Figure 3.18: Proportional composition.

It should be noted that although Hambidge's method may seem at first sight to be a formulaic geometric approach, he also maintains a broader perspective to design where rational control is balanced by a more intuitive vision.

> *In art the control of reason means the rule of design. Without reason art becomes chaotic. Instinct and feeling must be directed by knowledge and judgment. . . . The present need is for an exposition of the application of dynamic symmetry to the problems of today. The indications are that we stand on the threshold of a design awakening.* (Hambidge, 1926, p. xvii)

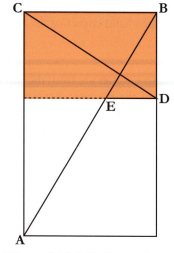

Figure 3.19: 2-D diagonal cuts.

Creation is more than technique. Hambidge's observations are beginning to come to pass with new developments in digital technology.

Figure 3.20: 3-D diagonal cuts.

The progression to 3-D geometric forms is relatively straightforward. Rules of proportion can be expressed initially on the surfaces of modelled 3-D forms as in **figure 3.20** by switching from one *working plane* to another as and when required. Working planes represent 2-D slices through 3-D space to which the usual geometric drawing constraints (angles, lengths, offsets, etc.) can be applied.

The expression of relationships between objects in 3-D space requires another level of representation altogether. *Parametric modelling techniques* allow users to change the dimensions of specific parts of a model and to see the effects of these changes propagate through the rest of the model without needing to redraw or to remodel the other parts. Parametric modelling techniques can be broken down into two components: parametric geometry and variational geometry. *Parametric geometry* refers to one-way relationships; *variational geometry* to bi-directional ones, and is therefore a more general and powerful technique of digital representation.

Computer-modelling technology is increasingly being used to model complex curved forms to which parametric modelling techniques can then be applied. If parametric constraints can be related to physical properties, then greater digital integration can be achieved between building form and building structure. *Structural optimisation* is a numerical technique for the determination of an optimum material distribution in a given space. This technique uses parametric relationships to express constraint conditions that can in turn be used to find optimal solutions. The default methodology is to find the smallest volume of material for a given load, by seeking maximum stiffness for a minimum of stored elastic energy. Such developments could be applied to the problem of engineering a structure of a given shape to optimal dimensions. Mathematical methods of finding an optimal topology with only forces and material characteristics as parameters are now being developed (Golay and Seppecher, 2001).

3.5 Form Constrained by Environment

The recent re-emergence of organic design in projects such as Ted Cullinan's Downland Gridshell completed in 2002, is critically dependent upon the capabilities of CAD systems to model such organic forms. The naturalism embodied within these forms arises as a consequence of the fact that geometric objects are constrained by the mathematical description of key physical properties. In the case of the Downland Gridshell, . . . *the mathematical model had to contain bending stiffness during form finding, otherwise compressive stresses produced wrinkling.* (Williams, 2000, p. 47). A key idea, therefore, is the *strength through shape principle*, in which curved forms such as arches, vaults, domes, and spheres have the added benefit of providing structurally efficient building structures (see **Chapter 7**). Optimally structurally efficient curved forms in turn stem from studies of natural forms which are then abstracted and applied to the design of built form.

A recent example of the simulative power of CAD modelling relates to Gaudi's *equilibrated structures* i.e. those composed of catenary, hyperbolic, parabolic arches and vaults, and inclined columns and helicoidal piers. Gaudi predicted complex structural forces via string models hung with weights, known as *anti-funicular models*. *Funicular models* are those in which all structural members are in compression, whereas anti-funicular models consist of tensioned members. Such structural models can now be simulated directly within digital environments (Andreu, 2003). The primary modelling objects within such systems are flexible elastic cables, which when suspended from both ends form parabolic or catenary curves. Parabolic curves arise when there is an equal loading of force per unit horizontal distance (the r.h.s. of **figure 3.21**). Catenary curves are natural curves for cables in which the load at each point is related to the slope of the cable and to its curvature (the l.h.s. of **figure 3.21**). In mathematical terms, for catenary curves the load at each point is related to the second derivative of the curve.

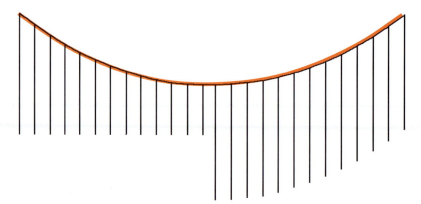

Figure 3.21: Forces determine catenary or parabolic curvature.

The equilibrium equations of forces for catenary (hyperbolic cosine) curves are well known, and hence they can be digitally modelled according to these equations. Systems of catenary curves such as those in funicular models can be represented computationally as sets of non-linear equations which are *approximately* solvable using numerical analysis methods. Researchers at UPC in Barcelona (op. cit.) have developed a more intuitive mathematical method of representing the relationships between structural forces in shell structures by digitally modelling these structures as nets of elastic cables, in which the cables represent lines of compression along the edges of arches.

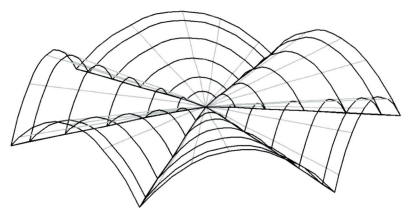

Figure 3.22: Wire-frame CAD model of shell structure derived from funicular geometry.

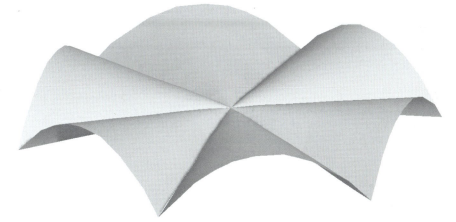

Figure 3.23: Rendered CAD model of shell structure derived from funicular geometry.

Digital representations of this sort have implicitly embedded within them sets of, rather than unique, design solutions. According to Lynn:

> . . . *the forms of a dynamically conceived architecture may be shaped in association with virtual motion and force, but again, this does not mandate that the architecture change its shape. Actual movement often involves a mechanical paradigm of multiple discrete positions, whereas virtual movement allows form to occupy a multiplicity of possible positions continuously with the same form.* (Lynn, 1999, p. 10).

The case study in the following chapter will describe an application of parametric modelling technology to the generation of a complex curved roof structure in which multiple configurations needed to be explored through a virtual and digital design process.

Chapter 4: Parametric Form: Variations on a Theme

This case study is concerned with the use of parametric equations to effect changes in architectural form. Parameterisation is concerned with the manipulation of variables within mathematical functions. The manipulation of such variables leads to the generation of a range of formal possibilities, and is particularly useful in the systematic control of complex curved surfaces. There will be indications in later chapters such as **chapter 8** as to how such control is increasingly being exploited in other design disciplines such as ship and aircraft design, for example. For such mathematical techniques to be useful in the early design stages in architectural and structural engineering disciplines, their outcomes need to be presented in visual form. There are existing architectural engineering projects in which it was essential to be able to control curved forms in very direct ways in order to be able to *propagate* small changes to other related forms. A good example of this was the design of the Waterloo train terminal in London. The mathematical representation of the arched form shown in **figure 4.1** was modified in order to propagate a series of 36 arches along the length of the train shed. The direct user-control of the arch's parameters meant that subsequent curves could be generated exactly according to the design constraints (e.g. path in plan, width of span, height of arch). In this way relationships can be defined between parts of structures and other associated parts. In this example, the form of the train shed emerged from the application of parametric expressions to regular geometry. There is also a connection between the use of parametric modelling techniques and compositional design, in which whole design schemes are broken down into component parts, which can then be distributed amongst various manufacturers. This approach is well established in industrial and mechanical design and manufacture design disciplines.

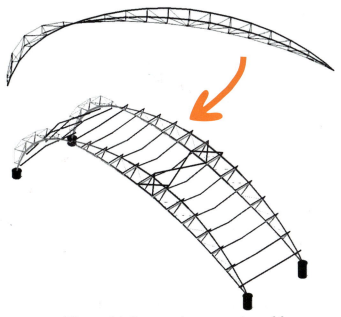

Figure 4.1: Parametric propagation of form.

4.1 The Design of the British Museum Great Court Roof

Following an international design competition with architects Fosters and Partners, Buro Happold were appointed as engineers for the design of the roof on the Great Court of the British Museum. Fosters' proposal began with the demolition of four book-stack buildings that filled the Great Court, creating an open volume of space and thus reflecting the original design in 1850 by Sir Robert Smirke (Anderson, 2000). The solution focused on forming a large internal public square with the restored Reading Room as a centrepiece, all sited under a steel and glass roof covering the whole courtyard, and so maximising the sun-filled space. The roof was to be as lightweight a structure as possible, in order to preserve the splendour of the Reading Room and the existing classical Georgian facades of the museum that surround the court. The unusual support conditions in the Great Court had a major influence on the structural behaviour of the roof. The existing buildings could not resist horizontal thrusts from the arch action of any new roof. This meant that besides axial forces, significant bending moments and shear forces develop within a grid structure. The *toroidal* form of the roof evolved as a consequence of having to provide a transition from the circular form of the reading room to the quadrangle of the surrounding museum buildings. A rigorous non-linear computer analysis of the structural form under the differing load patterns was undertaken to tune the design and determine the roof's stiffness and deformed shape. With the help of parametric digital modelling techniques, combined with a very high level of engineering, complex roof forms such as this can be designed, analysed and constructed.

Initial Form Finding

Initial form-finding studies focused on the computer generation of stress-controlled surfaces. This technique is more commonly applied to the design of membrane structures in which loads can be effectively resisted by doubly curved surfaces, and in which tensional forces play the most important role (**figure 4.2**).

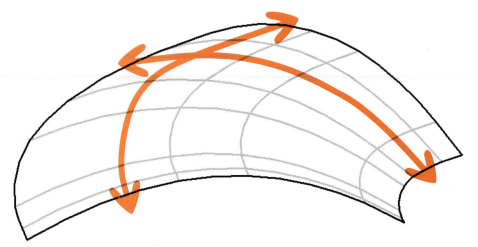

Figure 4.2: Doubly curved membrane form.

Every curved surface has an optimum curvature that will carry loads such that the least strain is in the plane of the surface. By exploiting the *opposing curvatures* of a doubly curved surface, it is possible to *parametrically* control the loads with a membrane surface. The role of parametric form-finding algorithms in the initial design of the Great Court roof was to optimise (through the method of *relaxation*) curvatures of opposing sign. The initial stress-controlled surface approach generated forms analogous to those a soap film bubble might produce if it were stretched and gently inflated between the perimeter of the courtyard and the inner circle of the Reading Room. Coincidentally, when several bubbles come together, they share a flat wall that meets at 120° angles, since this arrangement requires the least amount of bubble film to enclose the air inside (**figure 4.2**). This is relevant to the geodesic dome structures that will be investigated in **chapter 7**. The German architect Frei Otto famously experimented with bubbles and soap film to figure out how to enclose the greatest possible volume with the least material (Otto, 1973). These studies enabled him to design giant temporary exhibition pavilions, and to move onto more precise mathematical studies. His scheme with Gunter Behnisch for the design of the roofs of the main sports arena in the Olympiapark, Munich, initiated the use of computer-based procedures for determining the forms of tensile structures.

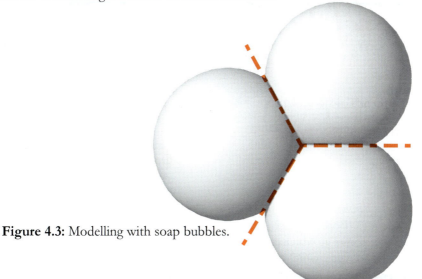

Figure 4.3: Modelling with soap bubbles.

Although the stress-controlled surface approach to modelling was instructive, it tended to create a form that was too bulbous in the corners and too constrained in the narrow areas. In order to *take control* of the form, the ultimate model was geometrically defined using parametric equations representing something between a soap film shape and a free-form inflated skin. The shape of the roof was undoubtedly the most important factor in terms of its load-bearing properties. In the original scheme, the roof surface was defined as a single *spherical* form with straight plan cuts defined by the courtyard perimeter. A two-way structural grid was then superimposed onto this surface running at 45 degrees to the north-south axis. Because of the relative flatness of this initial roof form, it acted as a bending plate, with no circumferential constraints or shell action. To reduce self-weight for this flatter roof, and to allow double glazing to be used in place of the proposed EFTE cushions, the structural efficiency of the roof was improved by increasing the curvature and turning the two-way grid into a *three-way grid* to generate in-plane stiffness.

4.2   The Optimisation of Shape and Topology

Shape optimisation keeps the topology constant while modifying the shape. Topology optimisation involves the addition and removal of elements such as nodes and members in a truss structure. In both approaches, key design variables computationally define form. There were already several initial topological constraints: a fixed rectangular form with a circular hole, the need for a roof surface with opposing (concave and convex) curvatures across its surface, so that loads (e.g. $W_1 - W_4$ in **figure 4.4**) could be transferred as tensile forces into the plane of the roof.

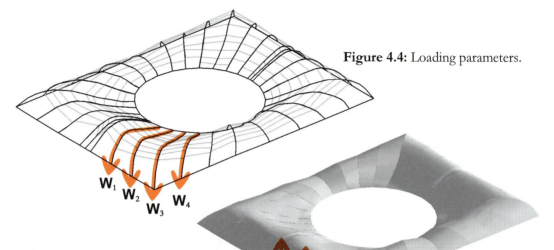

Figure 4.4: Loading parameters.

Figure 4.5: Stress parameters.

If the co-ordinates of nodes on the inner (circular) and outer (rectangular) boundaries could be established as being fixed points, all intermediate points could be considered as being *design variables*, and therefore subject to *parameterisation* of their individual co-ordinates. Both internal and boundary nodes are points at which loads could be applied, and with which stress parameters could be associated (e.g. $\phi_1 - \phi_4$ in **figure 4.5**). The stress values at particular points were initially derived from the stress function approach to form finding (**figure 4.6**). The problem with the stress-function approach was that although it embodied a direct relationship between load and form, its parametric equations did not express other constraints, e.g. height restrictions due to planning regulations, for example.

Figure 4.6: Stress function.

The parametric design process, therefore, begins with establishing control points on the boundary geometry of the structure, and by modelling the structure as a mesh (**figure 4.7**).

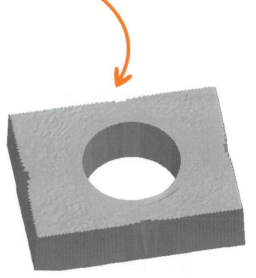

Figure 4.7: Mesh form in elevation.

The graphical elements from which this mesh is composed can then have specific (physical) properties associated with them. For example, nodal points, and both linear and curved segments of different types can be associated with loading characteristics. A visual representation of uniform loading across the space of the Great Court is shown in **figure 4.8**.

Figure 4.8: Loading characteristics.

Good practice in the use of form-finding software is first to estimate maximum displacements, and then to rerun the software with the nodes in the displaced position. This will determine whether the predetermined form can support the maximum shape deformation, or whether local high stress points exist, perhaps leading to a collapse of the structure. Ideally, parametric form-finding software should allow users to define form, apply loads, measure dynamic responses, check maximum displacements and check the form against that maximum displacement.

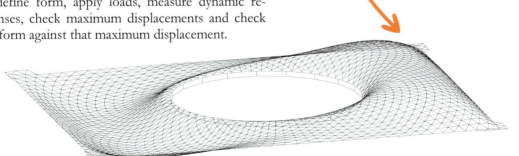

Figure 4.9: Possible collapse.

4.3 Shape Optimisation through Parametric Geometry

To meet the planning requirements, therefore, the parametric representation of the roof developed from a stress-defined form to one defined *geometrically*. This parametric model was then used to determine the actual structural member grid. This was a essentially a shape optimisation procedure in which the values of the optimal roof shape were determined. The advantage of this procedure was that sizing optimisation becomes a by-product of shape optimisation. The layout of the mesh was generated by a series of radial members starting from equally spaced points on the inner circle. These radials were each divided into an equal number of segments. The intermediate members were then defined as connectors between consecutive points on the radials. This process generated the spirals that are a feature of the roof, and ensured that the roof grid ended in nodes along the whole of the perimeter. The final form included a degree of shuffling of members across the surface in order to control glass panel sizes, but the principle for initial generation was the same. The result was a smooth flowing roof that kept to height restrictions, whilst curving over the existing stone porticos in the centre of each of the quadrangle's facades.

The basic form of the roof surface was defined analytically in terms of the equations defined in (**1**), (**2**) and (**3**).

$$z/h = \left(1 - x/b\right)\left(1 + x/b\right)\left(1 - y/c\right)\left(1 + y/d\right) / \left(1 - ax/rb\right)\left(1 + ax/rb\right)\left(1 - ay/rc\right)\left(1 + ay/rd\right)$$

$$\text{where} \quad r = \sqrt{x^2 + y^2} \qquad (1)$$

$$z/H = \left(1 - x/b\right)\left(1 + x/b\right)\left(1 - y/c\right)\left(1 + y/d\right)\left(\sqrt{x^2 + y^2}/a - 1\right) \qquad (2)$$

$$z/\lambda = \left(\sqrt{x^2+y^2}/a - 1\right) \Big/ \begin{bmatrix} \sqrt{(b-x)^2 + (c-y)^2}/(b-x)(c-y) & + \\[2mm] \sqrt{(b+x)^2 + (c-y)^2}/(b+x)(c-y) & + \\[2mm] \sqrt{(b-x)^2 + (d+y)^2}/(b-x)(d+y) & + \\[2mm] \sqrt{(b+x)^2 + (d+y)^2}/(b+x)(d+y) & \end{bmatrix} \qquad (3)$$

The parameterised co-ordinates defined by these second order equations were constrained to satisfy architectural, planning, structural, and clearance requirements (Williams, 2000, p. 47).

Because of the three-way grid system that was adopted, the roof became a shell structure, and thus allowed the member sizes to be reduced dramatically. The geometry inevitably became more complex but the roof became more elegant and transparent as a result. Generally, the larger the change from a flat plane, the more efficient the surface will be. The calculations proceeded from a mathematical grid which through the method of relaxation developed into a final precise form, and this mathematical grid was in turn associated with three member grids **(figures 4.10–4.12**), which when combined as in **figure 4.13** could generate the intended roof structure. The detailed initial and final mathematical and member grids are shown in **figures 4.14–4.17** respectively.

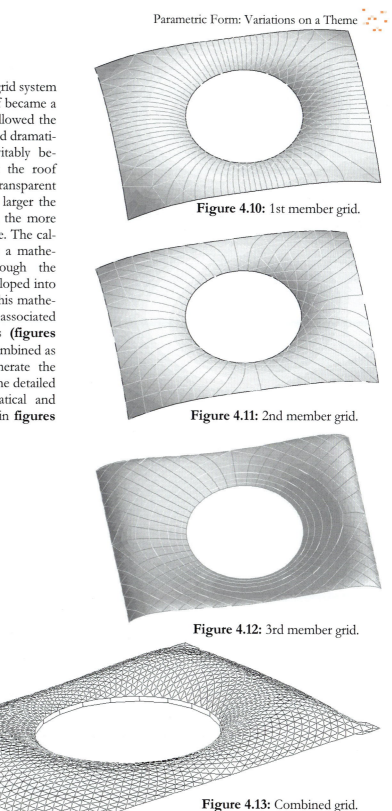

Figure 4.10: 1st member grid.

Figure 4.11: 2nd member grid.

Figure 4.12: 3rd member grid.

Figure 4.13: Combined grid.

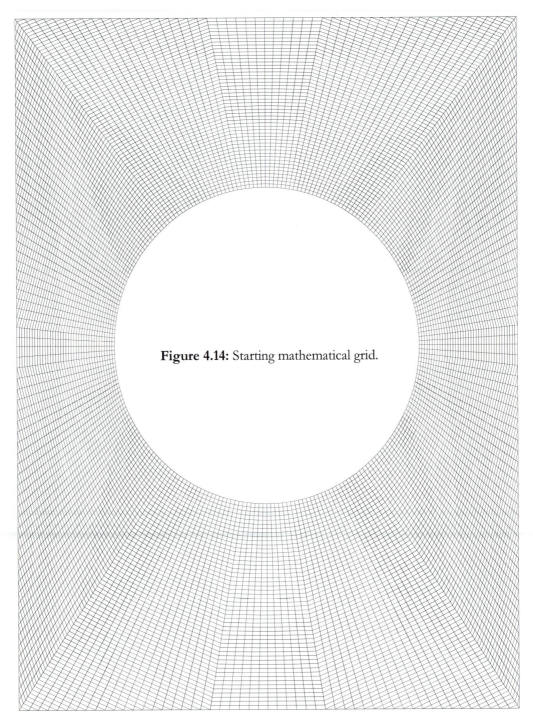

Figure 4.14: Starting mathematical grid.

An iterative numerical analysis procedure known as *relaxation* (a kind of optimisation technique) was applied to the initial grid of surface co-ordinates shown in **figure 4.14**. Interior 3-D surface co-ordinates were then calculated, starting from points on the fixed boundary, in terms of the weighted average of the four points surrounding the current nodal point.

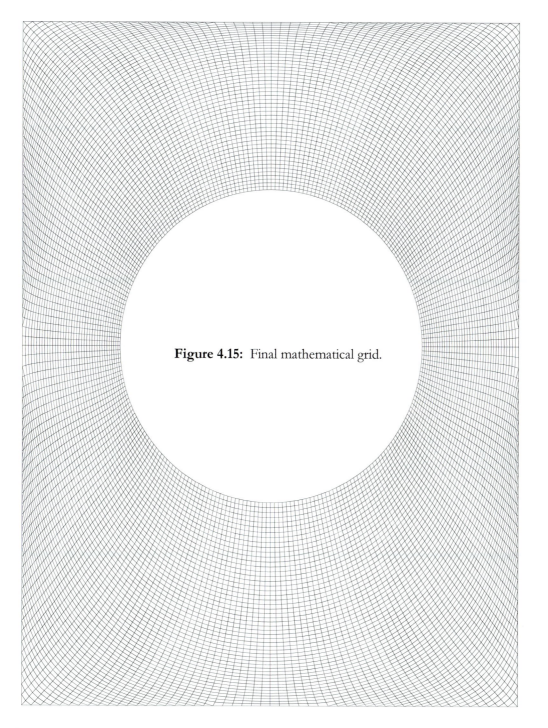

Figure 4.15: Final mathematical grid.

The current nodal point is then changed by moving to the next point. Each nodal point is recalculated a number of times (an *iterative* process) to a level that is acceptable. The relaxation procedure was then repeated thousands of times for the whole structure until the final grid in **figure 4.15** was determined.

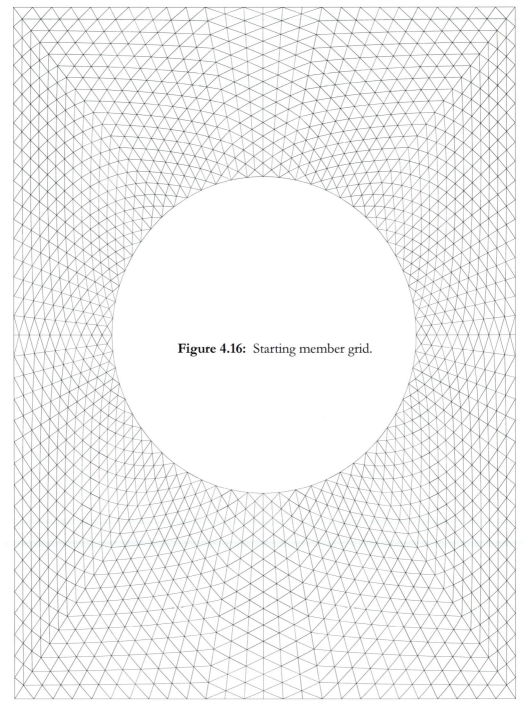

Figure 4.16: Starting member grid.

It was important to find a structural grid, which would ensure that the three-way lattice resolved at node points coinciding with the perimeter boundary line. To achieve this, the layout of the mesh was generated by a series of radial members starting from equal-spaced points on the inner circle. These radials were each divided into equal numbers of segments.

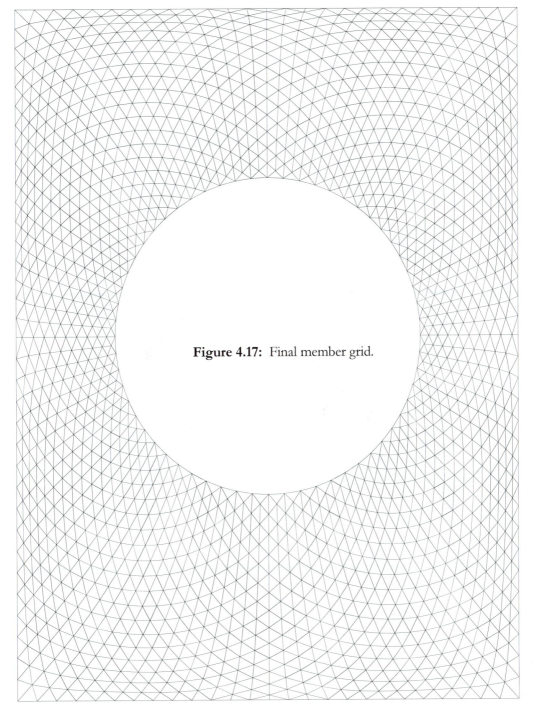

Figure 4.17: Final member grid.

The intermediate members were then defined as connectors between consecutive points on the radials. This generated the *spirals* that are a feature of the roof and ensured that the roof grid *noded-out* along all the perimeter. In the final form there was a degree of shuffling of members across the surface to help control glass panel sizes but the principle for the initial generation was not changed.

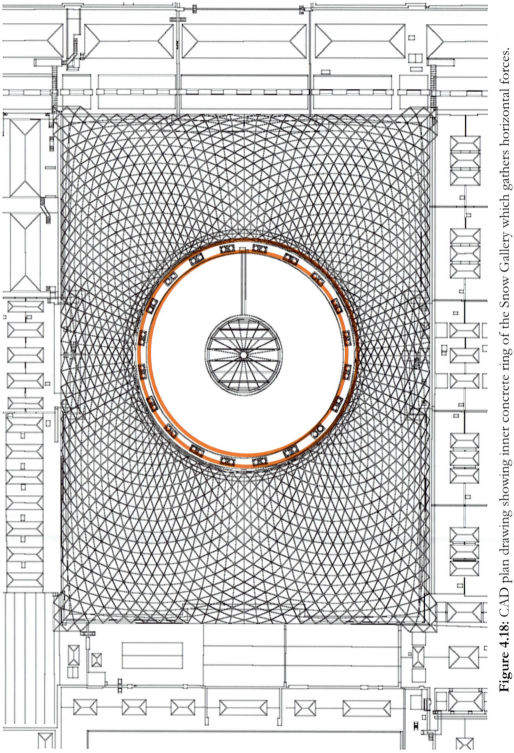

Figure 4.18: CAD plan drawing showing inner concrete ring of the Snow Gallery which gathers horizontal forces.

4.4   Structural Materials

In all wide span structures, the structural elements need to be efficient, reducing residual dead load as much as possible. A wide range of materials was considered for the construction of the roof structure before steel was considered to be the most appropriate (Brown, 2000, p. 285). Steel is commonly selected for wide span structures, because it provides high strength and stiffness at low cost, is easily connected by bolting or welding, and has good weathering characteristics with additional surface coating.

Structural analysis techniques were used to ascertain the most suitable form of *sectional profiles* for the steel roof elements. As the roof developed into a net structure, tubular sections were investigated. The research began by examining hot rolled *circular sections*, but as the roof form, together with the support conditions, demanded that the members were particularly efficient in bending, design thinking progressed to *square hollow sections*. In order to further reduce the residual dead load, *tapering fabricated box sections* were developed, allowing the steel to be placed in the most efficient configuration to meet the stress requirements in different sections of the roof. A final structural analysis procedure was to optimise the section sizes. Steel sections had a standard width of 80mm to support the glass. However, their depth varied from 80mm near the Reading Room to 200mm at the   perimeter. Similarly, according to the structural requirements, the flange plates of the boxes also varied in thickness from 10mm up to 40mm and the web or side plates varied from 5mm to 10mm.

Figure 4.19: Steel roof members.

The manufactured box sections had the additional advantage of being able to taper the sections, allowing the sections to gradually increase in depth as they move away from the Reading Room. This ensured that the lines of thrust remained constant, eliminating the potential of awkward secondary moments being developed in the joints should the members have stepped up in size. (Brown and Cook, 2001).

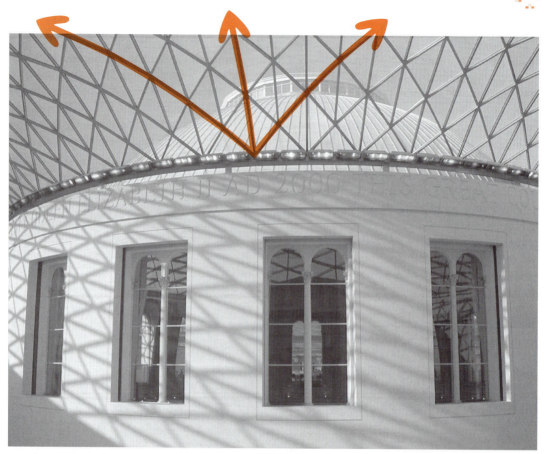

Figure 4.20: Three-way roof lattice.

The parametric modelling approach generated a lattice shell structure spanning in three directions. The three-way lattice of steel members provided in-plane stiffness, creating a very efficient form. The roof shape itself was curved to a tight radius of approximately 50m, which meant that it behaved like a dome, but still imposed minimal loads onto the surrounding structures. Each of the 3312 triangular glass panels is different in size and shape. The steel members in the roof consist of smaller members towards the centre, and larger ones towards the perimeter, the largest at the corners.

The curvature of the roof allowed Buro Happold to develop a lightweight construction relying on *arch compressions*. The curvatures of a perfect toroid are usually steep so that it acts in an arching fashion, converting vertical loads into compression in radial members. The Great Court roof was restricted in height and the outer perimeter unrestrained laterally. The roof's structural grid followed that of the glazing, supporting each panel along its edges and minimising the complexity of the glass fixing. The maximum size of glass available determined the final structural grid size.

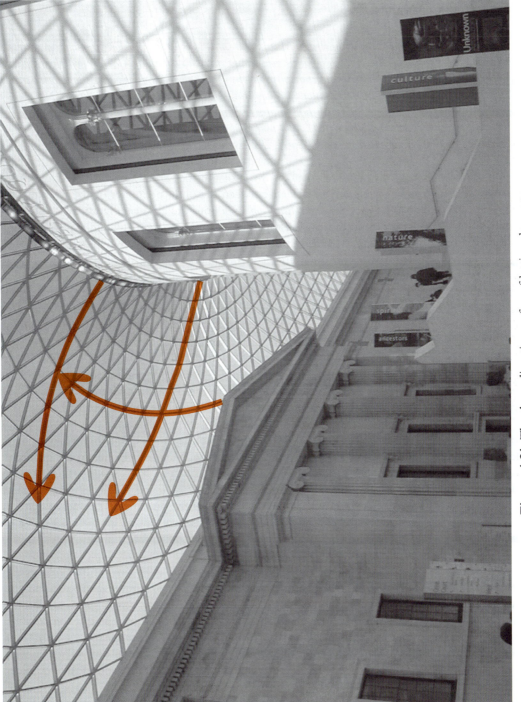

Figure 4.21: The three directions of roof lattice elements.

4.5   Design Constraints

. . . the new roof to the Great Court at the British Museum (architect Norman Foster) faced a major constraint in the geometry of the surrounding buildings that the roof had to match - a central circle and an outer rectangle. A second consideration was to make the structure invisible - using as little material as possible so that the sky would be more visible that the roof. A third consideration was to keep the height down to satisfy the planning constraints imposed on the design. A fourth was to ensure that it could be built whilst the museum was working. A fifth was to ensure a pattern of roof elements that would support the glass skin and flow naturally between the circle and the rectangle like a single 'web'. (Cook, 2004, p. 47)

An important planning constraint was that the *height* of the roof should be restricted. A related constraint was the *visual and structural relationship* between the outer perimeter of the roof and the quadrangle. There was to be *no visual or structural intrusion* onto the classical Georgian facades that faced into the Great Court, even though the roof needed to be restrained laterally. The solution was to insert cross bracing between vertical posts in the centre of each side where the horizontal spreading movement of the roof was one-dimensional. The bracing was hidden from view behind four existing stone porticos in the courtyard internal facades. The high points of the roof, particularly at the northern and southern ends, were not located in the centre of the spans as they would be for normal arch action, but were moved out more towards the perimeter. This not only assisted in resolving the *physical constraints* of lifting the roof over the porticos, but also resolved the roof's support conditions. Moving the high points out had two positive effects on the structural performance of the roof. First, the relatively gradual slopes down towards the Reading Room ensured that the lateral forces exerted on the Snow Gallery from opposing sides of the roof were generally balanced. Second, the steeper slopes down onto the museum buildings minimised the lateral thrust at the perimeter and therefore the spreading effect of the roof under load.

No significant additional horizontal load could be applied to the museum quadrangle, nor could additional loads be applied to the Reading Room. To avoid applying lateral loads to the quadrangle buildings around the outer perimeter, the roof was separated from the existing original buildings using a series of sliding bearings. These bearings allowed the roof to spread laterally under load, normal to the relevant facade, and independent of the buildings. This meant that for the roof to hold its form, the outer radial members near the perimeter quadrangle *need to work in bending and compression*. These effects then pass through the joints in all directions.

At its perimeter, the roof is supported on short vertical posts placed at 6m centres around the parapet, separated from a continuous concrete ring beam also at parapet level. Around the Reading Room, the roof is supported on twenty columns. At the Reading Room's roof level, these columns are rigidly fixed to a new 2m wide horizontal concrete ring known as the *Snow Gallery*. This ring forms an important part of the roof (**figure 4.18**). By *acting in compression*, it distributes the horizontal thrusts from opposing sides of the roof around the Reading Room. The concrete ring itself is supported on sliding bearings. A continuous movement joint around the perimeter of the Reading Room's dome separates it from the Reading Room.

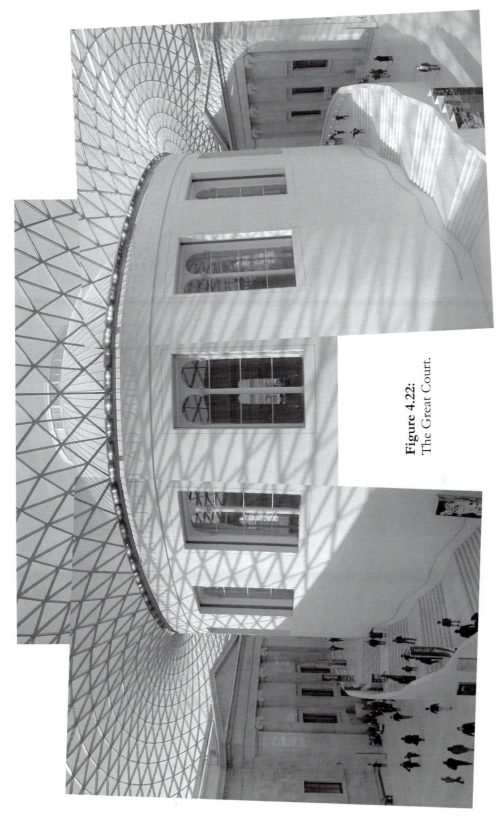

Figure 4.22:
The Great Court.

Figure 4.23: The Great Court.

The complexities of the design together with construction on a confined site surrounded by a live building was made possible by the close collaborative working of the project team. This began with the building of a close relationship between client (Great Court client committee), architect (Spencer de Grey and Giles Robinson of Foster & Partners) and engineers (Buro Happold). It should be noted at this point that at the first meeting of the client committee in September 1996 it appointed a client project manager responsible for the programme and budget. Having expressed some reservations in section **1.5** about the interventionist role of project managers on smaller-scale projects, it is essential to have reliable management on projects of this scale and complexity. The issue of project management will be revisited in **Chapter 6**.

During the design process, this team was joined by the construction manager and specialist trade contractors who brought their fabrication and installation knowledge into the design process (e.g. Waagner Biro). The digital representation of the roof structure also contributed greatly towards the process of information transfer, allowing the roof form and structural design to be developed initially between the designers, and then to be shared with the specialist roof materials contractors to be used as input data into the robotic manufacturing process.

Work on the construction of the roof began in September 1999 and was completed with a formal de-propping ceremony in April 2000. The project was completed and opened to the public in December 2000.

Figure 4.24: The Great Court.

Figure 4.25: The Great Court.

4.6   Detailing

The roof covered the whole area of the Great Court, 95m long and 74m wide. The Reading Room is not exactly in the centre of the Great Court, but is located 5m towards the North, which means that as far as the glazed roof goes, there is only one line of symmetry. This in turn meant that the geometry of all of the nodes and members within the net are individually different. The span of the roof in the north end of the Court is 23.8m with an arch height of 6.4m, in the east and west it has a span of 14.4m and in the south it has a span of 28.8m with an arch height of 5.48m.

The roof's structural grid followed that of the glazing, supporting each panel along its edges and minimising the complexity of the glass fixing. Apart from the cost considerations, structurally this allowed the thickness and dead weight of the glazing to be minimised. The 6100 square metres of glazing was made up of 3312 separate triangular panels of an average area of 1.85m². The grid itself was formed by distorted radial elements spanning between the Reading Room and the quadrangle buildings, interconnected by two opposing spirals that form a shell with six-way connections at each node.

The glazing panels are supported on a fine lattice made up of 5162 purpose-made steel box beams that intersect at 1826 structural six-way nodes, each totally unique in its x, y and z co-ordinates and rotation angles. (de Grey, 2000, p. 281)

To achieve the environmental and safety requirements of the roof, each panel was a double glazed unit with the bottom pane being a laminated safety glass and the upper pane treated to control the solar gains within the occupied space below. This was achieved by tinting each glass pane with an ultraviolet filter and shading out 65% of the light with a white ceramic frit that was baked on to the outer surface. This latter process controlled the maximum size of the individual panels, as the maximum width available was 2.05m. The maximum size of glass determined the final structural grid size. All connections are fixed joints, transferring the forces and moments between all the structural elements.

Wind tunnel testing was carried out by Bristol University, which provided information on external and internal pressures under varying wind conditions. The results demonstrated that the wind flow separates at the outer perimeter of the museum buildings and does not reattach over the new steel and glass roof. This means that the wind pressures on the roof are small, and consistently negative (uplift). On this basis the net once-in-50-years uplift force is well below the total dead load, or weight of the double glazing units.

It was necessary to allow for a given pre-tension in the erected structure as a value during the initial form finding. This pre-tension, sometimes as high as 1–1.5 tons per lineal metre of membrane, usually measured at the perimeter, was required to provide the out-of-plane stiffness to prevent buckling or wrinkling and was an intrinsic part of the actual membrane design.

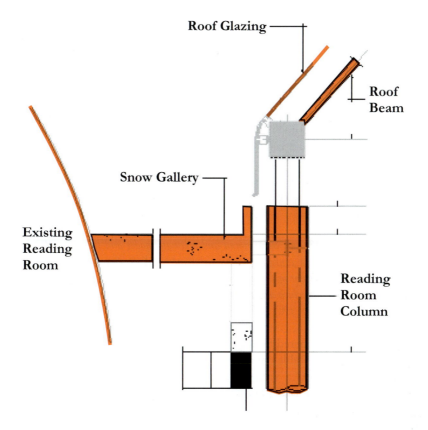

Figure 4.26: Snow Gallery construction detail.

The new columns surrounding the Reading Room carried the weight of the roof directly down on to the foundations (**figure 4.26**), ensuring that no additional load was applied to the iron frame of the Reading Room. The columns were of a structural steel/concrete composite construction that achieved the required fire rating and stiffness to span 20m unrestrained from floor level to the Snow Gallery, while remaining slender enough to be hidden behind the new stone cladding of the Reading Room. The columns were designed in accordance with *Eurocode 4*, and were fabricated using hot rolled tubular steel with an outer 457mm diameter circular section, reinforced with an inner 250mm square section, both filled with concrete.

4.7   The Physical Node

One of the main challenges, after understanding the geometrical and structural implications, was to develop a node detail which allows the connection of all members and transforms forces, and especially bending moments through the node. (Sischka, 2000, p. 201)

The nodes of the mathematical grid had to be developed into physical structural nodes connecting the roof members. Each node allowed the connection of six members, and a distribution of structural forces and bending moments between them. The angle of the incoming members varied between a minimum of 26 degrees and a maximum of 110 degrees. The members themselves were tapered, so that all the members connecting into a single node were of the same depth (**figures 4.27–28**). This allowed an increase in size of the members as they spanned away from the Reading Room, and eliminated the complexities of secondary moments being induced at the nodes should members increase in size.

The first proposals for the node design, using round and prismatic nodes and starting with triangular frames for each glass pane which had to be connected on site using intermediate elements, were not successful, neither in terms of the visual appearance nor of the economical aspect. After rejecting versions 1 to 7, including some sub-versions and a lot of sketches which were never tabled, the final idea was suddenly born. It was version 8 - the one to be built. (Sischka, op. cit.)

Different proposals were considered for the node in search of a solution that would allow a simple, aesthetic and precise, but repeatable connection of all the members. Starting with a circular node, options quickly developed into a variety of different, star-like forms. At this point specialist steelwork contractors Waagner Biro joined the project team. Using their skills and knowledge in working with steel, a final node solution was developed in which the triangulated ends on the members were plugged in between the arms of a star. The triangulation of the member ends not only allowed precise installation, but also simplified the on-site welded connection of the members to the nodes (Brown and Cook, 2001). The top and bottom plates of the members were butt welded to the nodes. Triangulation increased the length of weld, and therefore reduced the required depth. This reduced the risk of deformation of the lattice through thermal shrinkage and also reduced the risk of high thermal stresses that can develop in deep welds if the temperature is not strictly controlled. The flanges or side plates of the members were fillet welded to the ends on the arms of the node to transfer the shear and small torsional moments.

Figure 4.27: Tapered steel members joining star-shaped node.

Figure 4.28: Computer rendering of evenly distributed node with welds.

4.8   Robotic Manufacture

An essential factor to determine the net geometry was the maximum possible size for the glass panes from the fabrication point of view considering the required glass performance. The final net is comprised of 4878 members and 1566 nodes within the net, all of them different from each other. (Sischka, 2000, p. 199).

From the computer analysis, the roof members were robotically manufactured and erected to very tight tolerances. Because of the number of different pieces, members and nodes, it was essential to fully define all the steps of the manufacturing process, and to automate the fabrication as much as possible. To do this, it was important to precisely define the geometry and structural coherence of the roof, in order to understand exactly how the lattice would deform under load. As the roof had to be constructed on temporary props, to achieve the final required geometry, the deflection due to the roof's dead load or self-weight was added in the opposite direction as compensation. This became the *zero geometry*, and was the geometry to which the individual components were manufactured and assembled.

Each roof member component was positioned in a precise orientation, so that the minor principal axis of each member bisects the angle between adjacent supported glass panes. This ensured that each triangular pane of glass was adequately supported on all sides, avoiding pressure points and effecting a proper weather seal. To achieve this, the triangular-shaped ends on the members were individually cut at an angle so that when they were slotted into the nodes, the member was orientated to exactly the right angle to receive the glass. An added benefit of this approach was that only the right member could fit between two adjacent nodes, minimising the risk of installation errors on site. The roof was assembled on site to very tight tolerances of +/-3mm. This ensured that the glass panels fitted on to the steel and that the construction team understood how the roof performed structurally during the de-propping process.

To achieve this precise construction requirement, it was necessary to develop a robotic manufacturing process that could automatically ensure the tight geometrical requirements of position and orientation of each of the structural components every time. The node fabrication method was to flame-cut parts out of thick steel plates, using computer-controlled cutters to achieve the required tolerances. The positioning of the nodes within the steel plate was also automated, and took into account the different configurations and production sequence. During the cutting process, the node centre was marked and each node had its number defining its final position and orientation etched into the top surface.

Member fabrication also needed to be automated as much as possible, although this was more difficult due to the complex end geometry. (Sischka, 2000, p. 202)

The members were assembled by first tack welding the pieces together. The longitudinal welds were done using submerged arc welding with a double head. At this stage, the centre line and member number were robotically etched into the top surface. Finally, to meet the overall allowed tolerances, the triangulated ends of the members were precisely cut using a welding robot. This was a complex procedure as the gas pressure required to cut the ends depended on the plate thickness. As the flange and web plates were of different thickness, the gas pressure had to be varied automatically within the process.

4.9   Computing the Construction Process

Since the construction site was surrounded by a working museum, the roof elements could not be stored on site. This, together with the dimensional advantages of prefabricating large pieces of the roof on specially designed jigs under workshop conditions, suggested off-site construction options. The roof was divided into sections or *ladders*, defined by the largest sized elements that could fit onto an articulated lorry. 152 *ladders* were prefabricated and transported to site on a *just-in-time* basis. Using this method, many of the steel roof members, and all of the nodes were formed into the ladders, which were then stitched together with the remaining loose members on site.

Once on site, the roof was only stable once the entire steel lattice was complete. The roof was installed on a forest of 600 strategically placed temporary props. To allow work to continue on the redevelopment of the rest of the Great Court underneath, the props themselves stood on a watertight temporary deck. The temporary deck covered the entire court, and was supported on scaffold towers 20m high rising from the reinforced concrete courtyard below. As the roof was constructed, increasing the load on the temporary deck, the props were continually adjusted to allow for any resulting deformations, ensuring that the roof remained in its predetermined position prior to de-propping. The roof erection process started in the north of the Great Court, moving out in both clockwise and anti-clockwise directions around the Reading Room simultaneously. The erection of the temporary deck progressed just ahead of the steel work, with the installation of the glass following on behind. The computer generated 3-D design model of the roof was referred to by an independent surveyor during the installation process. From his measurements, the height of the temporary props was adjusted. The two opposing halves of the roof met in the south six months later with a final tolerance of 2mm.

The de-propping process was begun only when all the glass had been installed. Because of the complex geometry and structural form, the relaxation of the roof under its own weight was not uniform. A detailed de-propping procedure was developed to lower the roof in a controlled fashion to avoid overstressing any part of the structure. After a further in-depth computer analysis of the de-propping options, and the consequential behaviour of the roof, a process of 48 individual steps was developed that gradually released the roof to its final form. The maximum theoretical deflection was 142mm. During the process, which was carefully monitored throughout, the roof settled approximately 125mm and spread by some 70mm.

The project team, including the client architect, engineers and trade contractors, aided by computer technology, showed that it was now possible to develop and construct complex projects such as the Great Court roof within acceptable cost parameters. The construction of the roof over the Great Court demonstrated that remarkable solutions are now achievable for costs which are not too far removed from comparable costs for more standard solutions. Although parametric software was an important aid to the design process, an in-depth understanding of the engineering principles was also needed to make this work successfully. A continuous *digital information chain* throughout this project, beginning with design, demolition of the existing structure, construction of the foundations and roof, and concluding with the fabrication and installation, was essential for its success. The digital propagation of design information across all design stages reflects an emerging trend in contemporary design practice.

4.10   Stress, Strain, and Tensors

The modelling and analysis of the initial roof form was dependent upon the concepts of stress and strain in elastic solids. What is of interest from the perspective of computational representation is the need to make connections between *geometric* and *physical* properties of design elements. According to Synge and Schild:

> *The theory of strain belongs to geometry; it consists of a systematic mathematical description of the deformations that can occur in a continuous medium. The theory of stress involves a study of the internal reactions that can occur in a continuous medium.* (Synge and Schild, 1949, pp.202–203)

In rigid bodies, the distance between any two particles remains unchanged by a displacement. In elastic bodies, the analysis of *strain* begins with measuring the changes in length of lines between particles. *Stress*, on the other hand, is a generalisation of the concept of pressure, and is concerned with the actions of forces. The theory of elasticity brings these two concepts together so that stress becomes a linear homogeneous function of strain (op. cit.). The multi-dimensional mathematical notation that brings together both physical forces and geometry is the *tensor*.

The initial form-finding notation for the stress function associated with the roof membrane involved the use of tensors, and, despite the fact that this was eventually abandoned in favour of a more geometry-based approach, this idea has interesting implications for the representation of architectural form . Simplistically, a tensor can be viewed as a generalisation of a vector. In **figure 4.29**, a rod of elastic material fixed at **B** is twisted, bent and stretched by forces $\mathbf{F_1}$, $\mathbf{F_2}$, and $\mathbf{F_3}$ applied respectively at **A**. Within the rod, the stresses at any point **P** vary with direction. The face of any small element of the rod at **P**, oriented in any direction (given by three co-ordinates), is in equilibrium under forces in three directions. The stress at **P** is therefore given uniquely by nine components (Glenn and Littler, 1984, p. 207). These form a tensor of order two, and can be represented by a 3x3 matrix. A vector with three components can be thought of as a tensor of the first order. The laws governing the distribution of stresses through the rod are independent of the co-ordinate system being used, and so the elements of the tensor can transform from one co-ordinate system to another. A tensor can be thought of as a system that allows this kind of invariant transformation.

The stress equation used in the initial analysis by Williams (Williams, 2004, p. 84) has similarities to the following equation given by Green and Zerna in which the evaluations of stresses of membrane theory can be reduced to the solution of one second order linear differential equation:

$$\varepsilon^{\alpha\gamma}\,\varepsilon^{\beta\rho}\,Z_{|\alpha\beta}\,\phi_{|\gamma\rho}\ =\ q$$

where $\phi_{\gamma\rho}$ represents the stress function, and $Z_{|\alpha\beta}$ the displacement.

$\varepsilon^{\alpha\gamma}$ and $\varepsilon^{\beta\rho}$ are skew-symmetric tensors that represent the double curvature of the surface, and **q** contains the loads acting on the shell (Green and Zerna, 1968, p. 390).

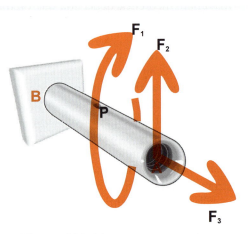

Figure 4.29: Tensor representation.

4.11   Hyperspaces and Hypersurfaces

Tensors are derived from the concept of multi-dimensional space. A point in **n**-dimensional space has **n** co-ordinates e.g. x^1, x^2, ... , x^n. A space of **n**-dimensions is known as *hyperspace*. One can imagine mapping an **n**-dimensional hyperspace onto the ordinary Euclidean space of three dimensions. For purposes of illustration, consider mapping three-dimensional Euclidean space onto two-dimensional Cartesian space. This actually corresponds to the age-old interface problem in CAD of identifying parts of 3-D objects on flat 2-D computer screens. In **figure 4.30**, for example, one can imagine co-ordinates ξ^1 and ξ^2 in Euclidean space mapping onto co-ordinates in Cartesian space at some particular moment in time t_1. Under any kind of viewing transformation of the Euclidean space, the co-ordinates ξ^1 and ξ^2 appear to shift in Cartesian space at a different time t_2 (**figure 4.31**).

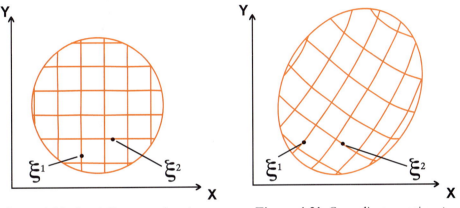

Figure 4.30: Co-ordinates at time t_1.   **Figure 4.31:** Co-ordinates at time t_2.

Cartesian (two-dimensional) space is known as a *subspace* of Euclidean (three-dimensional) space, and corresponds to a surface in it, since it subdivides neighbouring portions of Euclidean space into two parts. Similarly, any hyperspace V_{n-1} is a subspace of the hyperspace V_n. V_{n-1} is commonly referred to as a *hypersurface* in V_n, since it divides V_n into two parts. These two parts are usually defined in terms of functions which turn out to be positive on one side of the hypersurface, negative on the other side, and zero on the hypersurface itself. Green and Zerna (op. cit.) extended their analysis of membrane shell structures in terms of the tensor representation of differential equations, and derived the following conclusions:

 •   If the middle surface of the shell has positive Gaussian curvature everywhere, the differential equation is elliptic.

 •   If the middle surface of the shell has negative Gaussian curvature everywhere, the differential equation is hyperbolic.

 •   If the Gaussian curvature is zero everywhere, which means that the surface is *developable*, the equation is parabolic.

The concept of *developability* and its importance for the construction of complex forms will be expanded in **chapter 8**. The idea of representing hypersurfaces through architectural form arises in the following chapter.

Chapter 5: Express Vision: The Changing Face of Architecture

Despite its complex double-curved geometry, its extensive use of acrylic materials, the lean structural efficiency of its triangulated steel shell and the quiet sophistication of its low-energy environmental control systems, the kunsthaus is not about high-tech expressionism. For this we had neither the budget nor the inclination. The technological mutation of which this building is a symptom is a deeper one, which lies is the radical change of the design process itself and its new connection with automated manufacturing processes. A non-Euclidean object such as this cannot be designed and represented by means of conventional plans, sections and elevations; it's only meaningful manifestation is as a set of 3D data in a computer software package, later to be directly linked, at the production stage, to cad-cam manufacturing tools. It is in this fundamental shift towards 3D modelling, not as a representational tool but as the only legitimate conceptual milieu for contemporary design, that the true technological revolution lies, leaving us, at times, feeling like dinosaurs on the eve of a major climatic change. This is just the beginning of the surprises that await us in the 21st century: architecture will never be the same again and this building is at the transition point. (Colin Fournier, in Cook and Fournier, 2004)

The Kunsthaus Graz was designed by Peter Cook and Colin Fournier along with other architects, and is characterised *geometrically* by its *blob-like form*. In the 1960s, Peter Cook was part of the influential Archigram group of architects, and many architects refer to the Kunsthaus as the first Archigram building that has actually been built. Once Graz was named as the European Cultural Capital for 2003, Volker Gienke's competition jury strongly supported Cook and Fournier's blob proposal, known as *the friendly alien*. The aspiration to design *a non-Euclidean architectural form*, however, was driven as much by the need to develop synthetic spaces appropriate for a 21st century art house as it was by pure geometry of building form.

> *Here the viewer is no longer consumer in a mausoleum of objects but traveller and discoverer in a latent space of sensual information, whose aesthetics are embodied both in the coordinates of its immaterial form and in the scenarios of its interactively manifest form.* (Shaw, 1997, p. 154)

Just as non-Euclidean geometry has influenced modern art (Henderson, 1983), the concept of *the architectural blob* is a reflection of the technological developments of the 1990s. *Blobitecture*, as it is sometimes referred to (Waters, 2003), is not a radical re-interpretation of Euclidean geometry and rationalist perspective space (in 1854 Riemann described more general non-Euclidean geometries than those of Bolyai and Lobachevsky in 1829), but more akin to Greg Lynn's idea of *the evolution of a form and its shaping forces* (op. cit.). The significant shaping forces in this case are the building's functionality together with the process of digital production. The 3-D curvilinear nature of the blob form is an expression of the totality of these digital design processes.

Digital blob modelling techniques are based on *B-spline surface modelling* technology, which allows complex curved forms to be precisely modelled. The particularly powerful form of B-splines that is now common in mainstream CAD software is referred to as *NURBS* (non-uniform rational B-splines), and will resurface again in **chapter 8**. The power of NURBS surfaces derives from the fact that a NURBS surface equation is a unified internal representation of several commonly encountered surfaces, such as spheres, cones, cylinders, parabolic and hyperbolic surfaces. *Parametric* NURBS surfaces are also user-definable within CAD systems by virtue of the fact that their boundary curves are NURBS curves defined by control points. Parametric equations of surfaces allow the interactive display and manipulation of these surfaces at fine levels of detail (Lee, 1999, p. 190). These technical factors have made it possible for architectural offices to explicitly model free-forms such that they can subsequently be detailed and hence constructed.

Greg Lynn's initial encounters with blobs were as follows:

When I first used the term it was completely technical. The term Blob modelling was a module in Wavefront software at the time, and it was an acronym for Binary Large Object – spheres that could be collected to form larger composite forms. At the level of geometry and mathematics, I was excited by the tool as it was great for making large-scale single surfaces out of many small components as well as adding detailed elements to larger areas. At a conceptual and technical level, I loved it and I do not expect this kind of nerdy involvement with the details of my profession to be shared or understood. (Rappolt, 2003)

It is clear, however, that the development of the Kunsthaus form did not arise out of the definition of algorithms and computational methods that automate the generation of architectural form. The automated generative approach is the direction towards which Lynn's work has increasingly been moving. Sometimes referred to as *algorithmic design*, it involves the use of programming or scripting languages that are available as components of 3-D CAD modelling software, such as the Maya Embedded Language (MEL), for example. Cook and Fournier's competition entry on the other hand, consisted of a basic form made from plasticine, from which a model was then cast in acrylic glass. Subsequent hand-drawn sketches and physical models were represented as Microstation computer models.

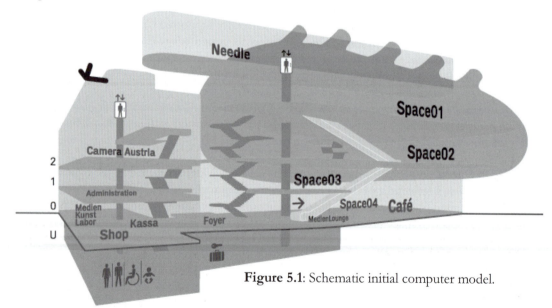

Figure 5.1: Schematic initial computer model.

Perhaps surprisingly, given the current blobby zeitgeist, we did not consciously set out to give the Kunsthaus the biomorphic appearance it now has. This was not so much a stylistic decision as the unplanned outcome of a number of accidental circumstances: partly the fact that the site given to us had a complex geometry from which the curvaceous outline of the building's footprint emerged; partly the fact that we had originally proposed, for the previous Kunsthaus competition (at a time when it was to be developed as a cavity within the Schlossberg) a double-curved inner lining that we had grown fond of and were keen to recycle; partly the fact that since we wanted to establish the 'alien' nature of the new object, a sleek continuous surface was the best way to smooth out the conventional differentiation between elements such as roof, walls and floors; and partly, quite simply, because we wanted it to look cuddly and friendly. To us, the form of the building has more to do with the 'strength of the inevitable', to borrow one of Bernard Tschumi's favourite formulas, than with aesthetic rhetoric. (Colin Fournier, in Cook and Fournier, 2004).

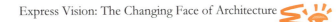

The structural engineers Bollinger & Grohmann had previous experience of the structural analysis of blob forms, although at smaller scales. The Graz blob was 60m x 40m rather than a 24m x 16m one they developed for BMW, and consequently had greater wind and snow loading. The structural digital model began as a *sphere* which was then distorted by pulling on *parametric control points* in Rhino 3-D. The structural modelling process cycled through fifteen variations of load-bearing structure. The end result was determined by optimising in relation to manufacturing criteria such as rod lengths, distances and structural conditions.

Figure 5.2: Daytime rendered CAD model.

Figure 5.3: Night-time rendered CAD model.

In the final scheme, skylight nozzles emerged out of the skin of the building (**figure 5.4**), with one of these pointing to the clock tower on the Schlossberg hill on the opposite side of the river. Another important feature at this top level was the *needle*, a cantilevered glass-enclosed structure that was to be an exhibition space with views over the city. Three links connected the ground and first two floors to an important historic building adjoining it known as the Eisernes Haus, a prefabricated cast iron flat-roofed building made in Sheffield in 1848, which itself was a radical building for its time (Lyall, 2004). The Eisernes Haus formed the main entrance, gallery and museum administration for the Kunsthaus.

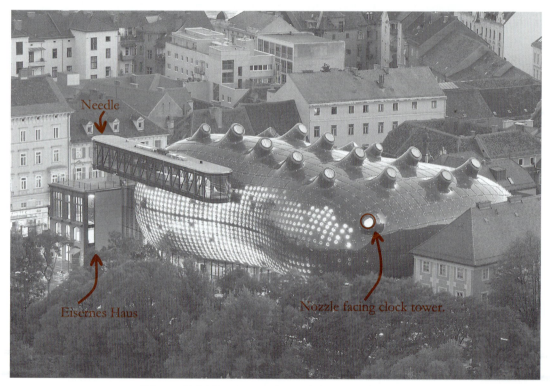

Figure 5.4: The site context of the Kunsthaus, Graz.

The intention for the exhibition spaces inside was not to have permanent exhibitions, nor to have storage or research facilities. The building was meant to serve the presentation and mediation of a wide range of contemporary artistic productions, and as a place for multidisciplinary exhibitions and activities, offering a highly differentiated programme of spaces and functions. While the interior works as *a black box of hidden tricks* (Cook and Fournier, 2004), its outer skin is a media facade which can be changed electronically (see section **5.3**). The Kunsthaus satisfies modern functional and technological standards for international art exhibitions. It has innovative, cost-saving climate-control systems which meet the requirements set by important lenders. For the professional realisation of exhibition projects, the building provides spacious receiving and handling areas, storage space and workshop areas, as well as modern lighting and security systems.

5.1   Modelling the Kunsthaus, Graz

The primary way of thinking about the Kunsthaus during the design phase was to generate 3-D models with separate models for different aspects e.g. structure, cladding system, ventilation , etc. This process began with an early stage CAD model for the skin as shown in **figure 5.5** through to more detailed models such as that shown in **figure 5.6** indicating the cladding system. The figures on the following pages illustrate the range of 3-D models created.

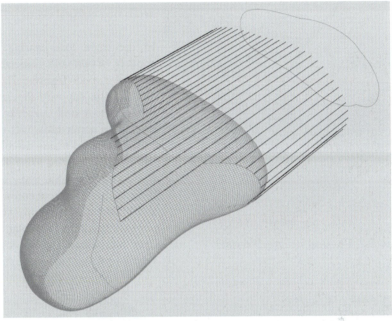

Figure 5.5: Early CAD sketch model of skin form.

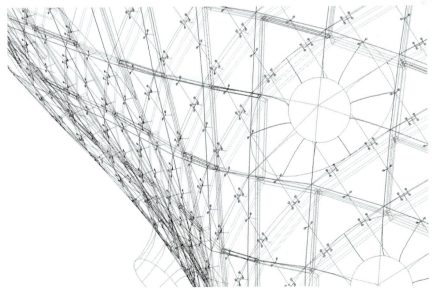

Figure 5.6: Detailed CAD model of cladding system.

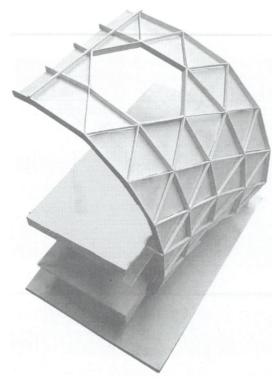

Figure 5.7: Physical structural model.

An important area of structural investigation focused on minimising the supporting elements (pins). Another important factor was the development of the material, the shape and the structure for the shell (skin) of the blob in order to create a translucent free-form body that could withstand the weather and, at the same time, satisfy the needs of a cultural centre.

In the main load-bearing structure, the concept of two tables, one above the other, was developed (**figure 5.7**). The lower table was to support the blob, span the ground floor and serve as an exhibition level. The upper table was to be a second exhibition level inside the blob. The lower table was developed as a solid steel framework needing only five supports. Two bean-shaped concrete cores with space for access and infrastructure were to serve as reinforcement. A 40m long, inclined travelator was selected as the means of linear access from below.

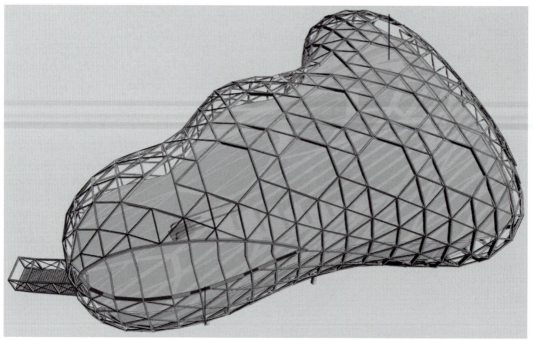

Figure 5.8: CAD model showing primary and secondary structural elements.

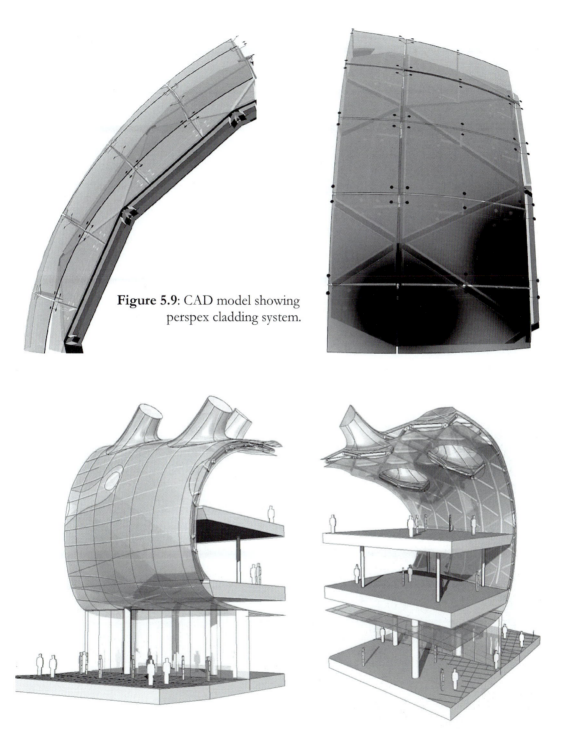

Figure 5.9: CAD model showing perspex cladding system.

Figure 5.10: CAD model with sectional cuts indicating scale of spaces.

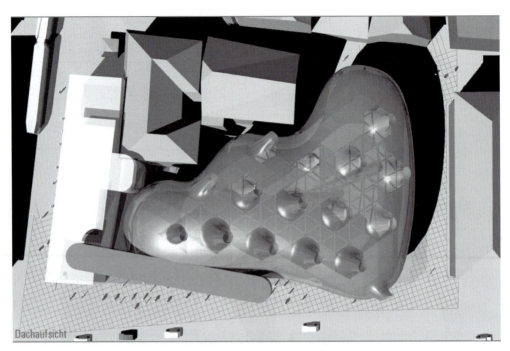

Figure 5.11: Bird's-eye view of rendered CAD model with transparency.

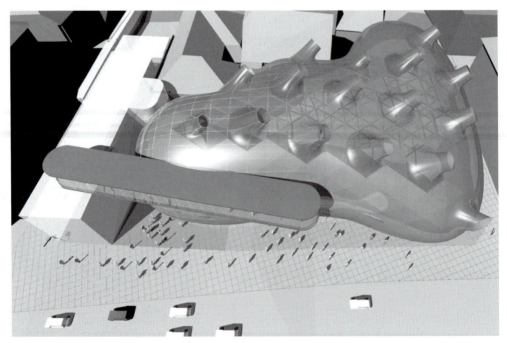

Figure 5.12: Aerial view of rendered CAD model with transparency.

. . . digital workflow also changes the clear division between the roles of architects and civil engineers, and that the performance profiles, which are defined separately in the HOAI (German honorary fee structure for both architects and engineers), begin to merge. This is true of the design phase in which engineers, too, develop solutions on 3-D models. In doing so, they must consider not only material properties, but also from the very beginning the structural design of an entire 'layer', as well as the production processes. Even in the preparation of the necessary planning documents for execution, the tasks are less clearly divided. In digital planning, architects no longer draft working drawings, and engineers draft formboard-layouts and reinforcement plans. Instead, a joint '3-D model' is created, complete with all the pieces of information and implementation necessary for the execution. This 3-D model is the basis for the workshop-planning of each firm. 'Conventional' 2-D planning is used only for the master details. It is interesting to observe how many firms still approach their actual work-shop-planning via the 'detour' of two-dimensional preparation, for building is traditionally a 'two-dimensional' trade; in other words, it isn't quite ready for digital production techniques. Hence, the executing firms must be in constant communication and consultation from the outset to jointly develop solutions that can be realized and financed. (Kloft, 2000)

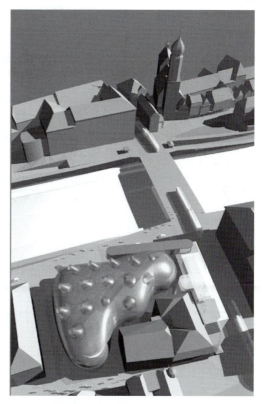

Figure 5.13: Aerial CAD view of model and site.

The development of an enclosure without recognisable roofs, walls and floors depended upon the manipulation of digital 3-D surfaces such that topological relationships could be preserved. The 3-D aerial views shown in **figures 5.11–5.14** were especially useful in the visualisation of the relationship between the doubly curved form and the the irregular geometry of the site boundary. The information needed for fabrication of the curved elements was obtained by further detailing the topological 3-D model.

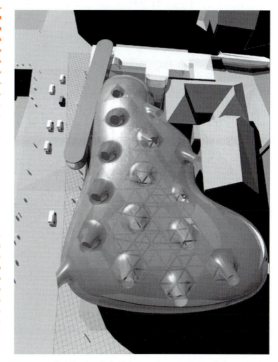

Figure 5.14: Aerial CAD view of model and site.

Figure 5.15: Structural CAD model with bridge element between Kunsthaus and Eiserne Haus.

Figure 5.16: Structural CAD model.

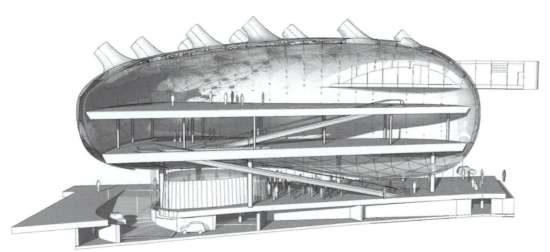

Figure 5.17: Sectional model of Kunsthaus.

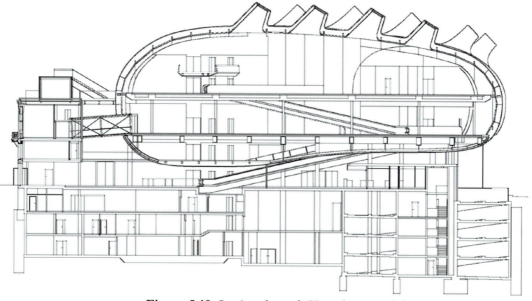

Figure 5.18: Section through Kunsthaus model.

Spanning up to 60 metres in width, the biomorphic construction enveloped two large exhibition decks. From the surface of the acrylic glass outer *skin*, *nozzles* project outwards to admit daylight, and are inclined to the north to provide optimum natural lighting. The glass-walled ground floor contains a bar, an event space and various communications amenities as well as the foyer, from which the *pin*, a travelator, leads to the upper exhibition rooms.

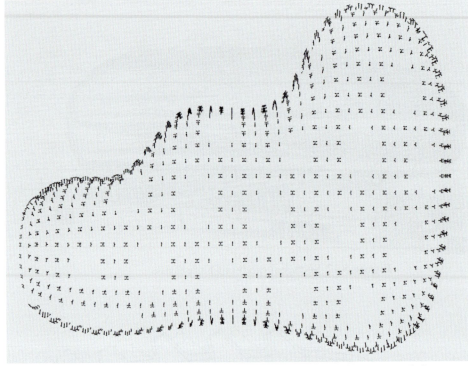

Figure 5.19: CAD model with 3-D co-ordinate information of clamps.

Figure 5.20: 3-D contour model of Kunsthaus form
with clamp geometry.

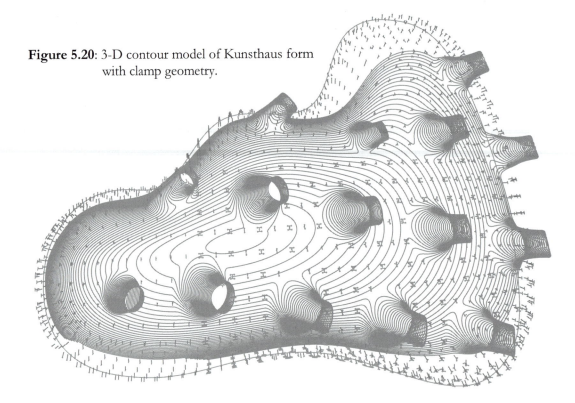

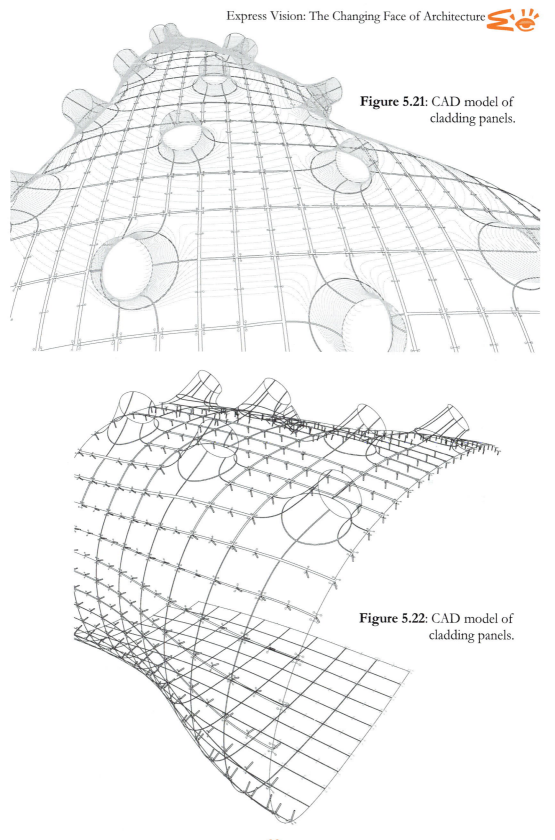

Figure 5.21: CAD model of cladding panels.

Figure 5.22: CAD model of cladding panels.

5.2 Planning in 3-D

To fully exhaust the range of new digital options in working with free form, and of translating free-form structures into reality, all those involved in the planning process must develop new working methods. . . . It is important to note that for these projects all planning parties must collaborate from the very beginning, and do so with much greater intensity than in 'conventional' projects. Forging new paths always means that there are few models to rely on and that new solutions must be developed from scratch. (Kloft, 2000)

The design and construction of the Kunsthaus was predominantly an *outside-in* process. Initial project planning centred on the master geometry of the structural 3-D model developed by the engineers. Once a structural form had been established in consultation with the architects, architectural planning could then proceed in more detail. This process was also a three-dimensional one. 2-D plan drawings were derived from 3-D models by slicing through the blob form as and when required. **Figures 5.23–5.28** show some of these plans.

The Kunsthaus consists of 11100m² of usable space, with a delivery area, various depots, workshops, and an underground car park with space for 146 vehicles.

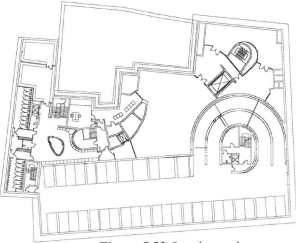

Figure 5.23: Level one plan.

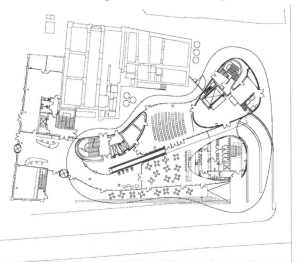

Figure 5.24: Level two plan.

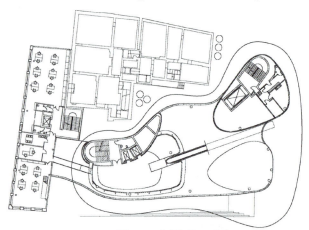

Figure 5.25: Level three plan.

The glazed ground floor is a meeting place with two main entrances. This floor was designed to be a versatile space with information, communication and entertainment facilities. These include the Media-Art-Laboratory as well as a reading and media lounge, an art bookstore/museum shop, and a 24-hour cafeteria. A large multipurpose event space at the rear of the building can be linked to the cafe, expanding it into one vast public area.

On a 30-metre-long travelator known as the *pin*, visitors ascend into the blob. This passes through an area designated for children and young people, and ends at the level of the first exhibition space.

A second travelator takes visitors to the upper exhibition deck, which is enclosed within the structural shell. The ceiling height here is 8 metres at its highest point. The exhibition area is equipped with adjustable daylight and artificial light sources, provided by the cones of the nozzles, which have the added effect of giving a distinctive structure to the inner surface of the building's skin.

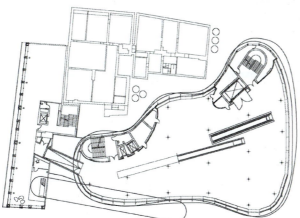

Figure 5.26: Level four plan.

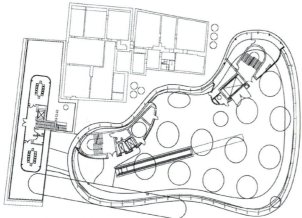

Figure 5.27: Level five plan.

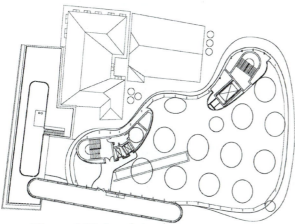

Figure 5.28: Level six plan.

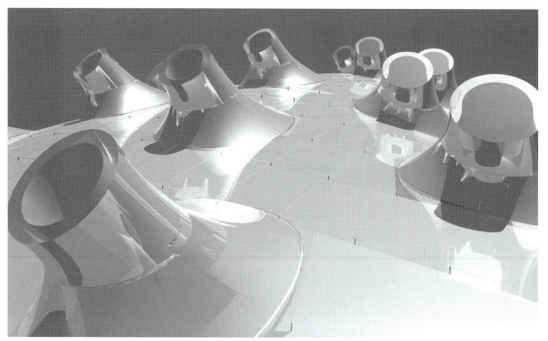

Figure 5.29: CAD model of roof nozzles.

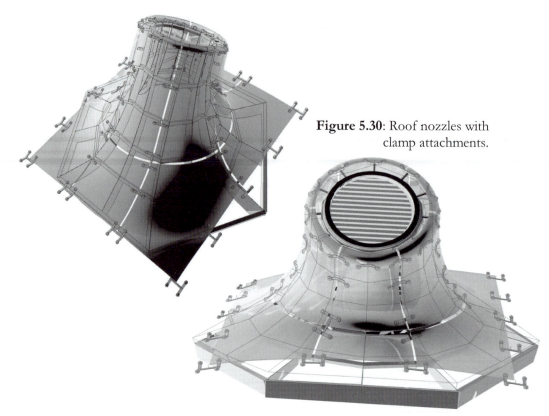

Figure 5.30: Roof nozzles with clamp attachments.

5.3   Media Facade

The total thickness of the roof construction was around 90cm. The primary structure consisted of polygonal, rectangular, steel box girders, arranged parallel to each other. Between them, standard square tubes were structured in a triangular formation, transforming the load-bearing layer into a shell (Schmal, 2004). On the inside, the steel girders were covered with a fire-resistant coating, and the shell was closed off from the outside with steel sandwich panels and then insulated and sealed. This follows the usual fire-protection and insulation procedures for industrial roofs. Although the connecting details appear as normal, they are geometrically different at each point on the skin and were therefore time-consuming and expensive to make. All acrylic glass elements of the doubly curved smooth skin were individually heat-shaped. The nozzles were also made of individual acrylic elements and dyed a blue-green colour. The big advantage of acrylic is that it can be shaped by heat at relatively low temperatures. The disadvantage is that it is inflammable. Because of this, sprinklers were fitted in the outer 70cm air gap.

The BIX (*big pixel*) media facade was developed by *realities:united*, a Berlin-based office famous for its facade treatment of Renzo Piano's KPN headquarters building in Rotterdam.. The BIX facade began as a much more ambitious concept that was to incorporate photovoltaics and sensors into the skin of the building. The actual pixel-based system that was developed consisted of circular neon tube light sources uniformly positioned under the acrylic skin. A total of 925 conventional, circular 40 watt fluorescent tubes were integrated into the acrylic glass facade. These lights turn the facade into a 45m-wide and 20m-high low-resolution grey scale display on the complex double-curved facade. The innovative aspect of this concept was the computer control system, by means of which light intensity values could be adjusted between 0% and 100%. This method of controlling the neon lights allowed the projection of signs, graphics and simple animations onto the skin.

This media facade is a unique feature of the Kunsthaus that integrates architecture with media technology. The giant low-resolution screen surface can display simple image sequences and varying text streams. Each ring of light functions as a pixel which can be centrally controlled, thus making the skin of the Kunsthaus an innovative medium for digitally presenting art and other information. The skin is used by the museum to communicate with the outside world, and also as a medium for artists to work in. The designers of the facade refer to it as a *lo-tech matrix for productions of media artists who engage themselves with work in the public realm*. The media facade also reflects one of the major themes of the institution, which has no permanent collection, but aims to foster work in digital media through hi-tech facilities, a *media laboratory*, and an artist-in-residence programme, along with more conventional exhibition space.

The media facade is seen by some as an *urban screen*: a new instrument and platform for artistic production. The Kunsthaus uses the media facade to present itself to the outside world. The media facade functions as a membrane between interior exhibitions and events, and the exterior public realm.

Figure 5.31: The BIX media facade.

With a digital control system, abstract animations, graphics and textual messages can be displayed at speeds of up to 20 frames a second. The low-resolution (925 pixels) and monochromatic images have the effect of generating abstract rather than realistic images and animations, which seems appropriate for an urban screen display. Psychophysical and perceptual evidence supports this fact:

Human viewers tend to position themselves relative to a scene such that the smallest detail of interest in the scene subtends an angle of about one minute of arc (1/60°), which is approximately the limit of angular discrimination for normal vision. (Poynton, 1994, p. 387)

In order to achieve a viewing situation where a pixel subtends 1/60°, viewing distance expressed in units of picture height should be about 3400 divided by the number of picture lines. Computer users tend to position themselves closer than this – about 60 to 75 percent of this distance – but at this closer distance individual pixels are discernible. (loc. cit.)

The formula given is : distance$_{PH}$=3400/lines, where distance$_{PH}$ is distance expressed in *picture height* units.

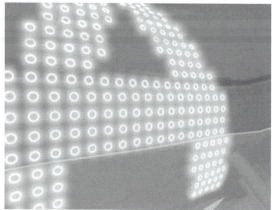

Figure 5.32: A BIX character display.

A display such as that in **figure 5.32** indicates approximately 20 picture lines spaced approximately at 1m intervals, giving an ideal viewing distance of 2-3km. Since in reality it would only be viewed at a distance of a few hundred metres or less, the image will always be pixelated and abstract.

Figure 5.33: BIX facade: exterior view.

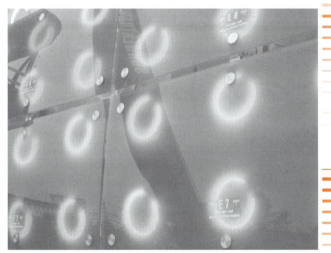

Figure 5.34: BIX facade: zooming in.

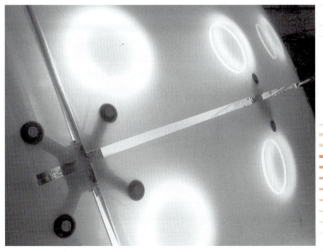

Figure 5.35: BIX facade: close up.

Ambitions for the facade go beyond visual imagery to include the additional communication channel of sound to complement the textual and graphical displays. Psychological research indicates that human communication is most effective when all perceptual modes work together.

At the building's inauguration in September 2003, a foretaste of the exhibitions to come was provided by *Eintönen* (*tuning in*): a series of sound installations which preceded the opening exhibition. The opening focused on the theme of perception with an exhibition called *Einbildung*. The exhibition specifically examined art from the perspective of being a creative science of processes within people's minds, and of the ways in which minds create images and ideas.

Discoveries in cognitive psychology and neurophysiology indicate that cognitive processes and neural networks determine our visual and aural perceptions in very specific ways.

Audio is an important communication channel and, in some cases (e.g. involving human emotions), the most appropriate and efficient. We all know the richness of the subtle cues transmitted by inflection in the voice. Audio provides three-dimensional cues (e.g. in the back of the head) that are not available to other human sensory systems. (Strawn, 1994, p. 67)

In the main exhibition, visitors were immersed in installations, and viewed photographs, paintings and sculptures all focusing on the idea of perception. Visual and acoustic impressions combined with other sensory perceptions to provide a comprehensive set of multimedia stimuli.

5.4   Interactive Surfaces

A new aesthetics comes to the fore. The art-work is more and more embodied in the interface, in the articulation of a space of meeting between the art-work and the viewer, and even in the articulation of a space where the art-work as an artifact seems to disappear altogether and only communication between the viewers remains.

While the success of an interface is constituted simply by its efficacy as a mechanism of conjunction, the artistic quality of an interface is the extent to which this conjunction embodies new cultural values. The interest now focusing on the raw creative modalities of interactivity, virtual reality, hypermedia, telepresence and networking comes from a recognition of the implicit shift in cultural paradigms these techniques embody. But the liability is of course an enthusiasm that merely articulates the metaphoric and anecdotal values of these techniques. In this situation, the poetic and conceptual rigour of traditional art practice may remain exemplary for all our efforts in the digital domain. (Shaw, 1997, p. 157)

Jeffrey Shaw's involvement from the 1960s onwards in the development of soft and transformable architecture through projects involving inflatable structures, combined with the projection of images onto their surfaces, demonstrated his pragmatic approach to art and architecture. More recently, projects such as Marcus Novak's *paracube* (Novak, 2001, p. 316), in which parametric relationships between surfaces in 4-D space were used to define a 3-D spaceframe structure, also illustrate how concepts such as multidimensional or *trans-Euclidean* space can be explored and investigated with digital technology.

Similarly, the Kunsthaus project explores not only dynamic responses to the surrounding environment, but also its interaction with it. This is a step beyond the environmental responses of intelligent buildings in terms of lighting, heating, ventilation and shading. The low-resolution computer-controlled facade display is capable of projecting abstract animations of perfomances inside the building out into the city (**figure 5.36**). Microphones placed around nozzles pick up ambient urban sounds, which are then mixed and projected back into the city from speakers that sit on top of the needle, creating a low-frequency *sound cloud* (Lyall, 2004). The BIX media facade constitutes an architectural language which is far removed from the sensually numbing applications of electronic billboards as found in some major western cities, in which commercial products are advertised consecutively to the point of banality. Instead, it is concerned with communication outwards with, and identification through, media.

The digital BIX media facade is also a part of the structure of the building, and therefore an architectural element as much as other parts. The light rings are integrated into the complex form of the architecture in such a way that only activated pixels become visible during the external broadcasting of internal art events. The interactivity of the surface of the media facade with interior events creates the impression that the architecture itself is the generator of images and pictures. The media facade becomes a *communication membrane* for the dissemination of artistic information to the general public.

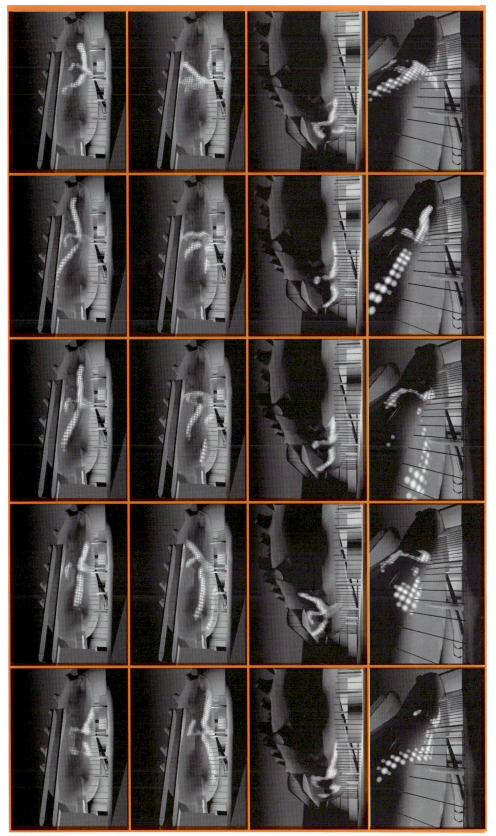

Figure 5.36: Keyframes from a BIX animation.

5.5   Toplogical Relationships

Architectural topology means the dynamic variation of form facilitated by computer-based technologies, computer-assisted design and animation software. The topologising of architectural form according to dynamic and complex configurations leads architectural design to a renewed and often spectacular plasticity, in the wake of the baroque and of organic expressionism. (Di Cristina, 2001)

The Kunsthaus was designed through a process of deformation of a digital model of a sphere. This process was in turn dependent upon the preservation of connectivity relationships during the course of a series of deformations. The digital model in this case had an elastic quality that meant that it could be continuously contorted and deformed. The realisation of a detailed building model that could ultimately be constructed was dependent upon this digital representation technology.

The geometries represented by digital topological models are not static, and can be continually transformed. Topology is concerned with those elements that remain constant as the entire system undergoes change, or those relations that remain constant under transformations and deformations. Through the use of what is referred to as *anexact geometry*, computers are able to represent forms previously prohibited in traditional architectural practice. *Anexact geometry* involves non-developable forms, or forms that cannot be flattened. As a result, and in contrast to Euclidean geometric forms, it is impossible to describe such forms as an algebraic equation. Lynn describes abstract geometries as those that *can be determined with precision yet cannot be reduced to average points or dimensions.*

As information and communication technologies become more prevalent in design practice, the impact of digital modelling techniques on architectural form is also having an effect. CAD systems have taken on a role beyond the mere generation of production drawings; they now fundamentally affect the forms and environments that architects create. The ability to represent topological relationships in digital environments has a direct influence on the ways in which architects can now think of buildings:

Topological structure corresponds to quantitative difference and, hence, to service; topological form corresponds to qualitative difference, and, hence, to surface. (Novak, 1998, p. 27)

There have been many recent examples of the application of surface modelling techniques to the generation of new building forms. The Kunsthaus itself fits into this category. It is more difficult, however, to separate ideas of topological structure from the fundamental nature of design. The currently popular Deleuzian view that there is no distinction between process and product (Krauss, 1993) is having a major influence on those wanting to create new forms of architecture. Novak warns of the dangers of omitting technological considerations from such views:

How can the response to a technological, informational, computational virtuality just be that we make stranger forms in conventional space, and arm these forms with more contorted rhetoric? (Novak, 1998, p. 21)

If we are to escape from superficial form combined with talking architecture, then just as in other architectural movements, contemporary digital design practice needs to connect the real to the virtual, the content to the style, the function to the expression.

5.6   Perella's Hypersurfaces

[Hypersurface] is the receipt and re-deployment of the architectural telegrams sent in the 60's by the group Archigram. . . . Hypersurface architecture is a way of thinking about architecture that does not assume real/irreal, material/immaterial dichotomies. (Perella, 1995)

A technique often associated with Stephen Perrella is the *texture mapping* of images onto the surfaces of 3-D digital models. The combination of imagery with surface form often results in the production of very abstract patterned objects. This has led Perrella to formulate his architectural *hypersurface* theories, which are not to be confused with the mathematical definitions of hypersurfaces given in the previous chapter. The *architectural hypersurface* is an attempt to fuse the material surface of structures with virtual imagery, and to use the resultant representations to signify change and technological development in contemporary society.

The material aspect concerns the ways in which digital representations allow a multitude of forms to be conceived and realised. Digital modelling combined with topological deformation techniques are currently resulting in the production of curvilinear architectural forms. By feeding other factors into the modelling process e.g. notions of time and place, it may even be possible to interpret form in a Deleuzian manner. For the result to be regarded as innovative architecture, however, Novak's observations need to be taken seriously, and the form also needs to become a technological event. One can see this phenomenon emerging in the relationship between the Kunsthaus and its media facade - the building is more than a mere location for urban activities.

Perella's virtual aspect of architecture is the medium of information in which contemporary society is immersed at ever greater depths. The topological surfaces of contemporary architecture can potentially be used to communicate and reflect the activities of their surroundings, and perhaps make urban environments more suggestive of peoples' events and experiences.

Perella's concept of hypersurface, therefore, is an attempt to link *hyper*media with topological *surface*. Complex geometries are simultaneously interactive and communicative media. Ideas such as this can potentially lead to more fluid and responsive architecture. At this point I will leave these philosophical deliberations for others to pursue. The major preoccupation of most architectural offices is with the reality of responding to clients' needs by building buildings. Let's get on with that.

PART II

The first part of the book indicated several kinds of digital techniques available to architects, together with illustrations of the types of architecture that these techniques have been applied to. In the second part of the book, although the focus is still on the digital design process, the context of the architectural practices within which digital techniques are being applied takes on a more important role. The three in-depth case studies that follow intend to show that the manner of use of CAD and other digital techniques can be adapted to various styles of office organisation without undermining the integrity of the offices in question. Whether architectural offices have a more corporate nature or are more singularly design-driven, the process of moving from design idea to design sketch to model, and even through to construction, is increasingly being supported through digital representation. It should become apparent from the following three case studies, however, that the extent to which the digital design process supports or replaces more conventional processes is determined by the vision embodied within individual architectural design offices. What emerges, therefore, is contrary to the conventional notion of the word *tool*, in which common implements have known and prescribed functions. Digital tools are whatever design practitioners decide them to be.

Chapter 6: The Well-Tempered Vision: Client as Patron, Quality on Demand

The case study that is the focus of this chapter is a scheme developed by FaulknerBrowns Architects for an IT centre (InfoLab 21) at the University of Lancaster, England. There are several important issues that emerge from the case study presented. These include:

- The role of CAD-generated models and drawings in the design and briefing process.
- The role of drawing types in different design stages (particularly RIBA design stages).
- The production of digital presentational material for the client partners.
- The visualisation and analysis of key design ideas and design alternatives.

Although the primary focus is on the role of CAD and other computing software throughout the design process, this needs to be looked at in the context of other non-CAD generated information (e.g. sketches and conventional models) that are used on schemes such as this. A central theme of this book has been to emphasise the role that computing technologies play in allowing designers to express ideas, whether these are sketch ideas or more detailed ones. One of the features of such investigations is the relationship between *exploratory* and *developmental* expression (McKim, 1980, p. 134). In the *exploratory mode*, designers use both conventional drawing and computer modelling techniques to record the conception of new ideas. In the *developmental* mode, designers gradually evolve an embryonic concept into a mature form. An added dimension to the expression of design ideas is the concept of *fluent and flexible ideation* (Guilford, 1967). According to McKim:

> *Fluent ideation is demonstrated by a thinker who generates many ideas; the yardstick of fluency is quantity – not quality or originality. Flexible ideation is demonstrated by a thinker who expresses diverse ideas; the measure of flexibility is variety.* (McKim, 1980, p. 136)

This chapter will begin to explore some of the wider issues relating to computer-based technologies in architectural practice by looking at the nature of interdisciplinary working, both within and between practices and client partners. The organisational context within which architectural offices in the UK currently operate has been affected by a number of recent government sponsored reports on the construction industry. These include the Latham and Egan Reports, as well as other proposals for the urban environment.

The Latham Report *Constructing the Team* (Latham, 1994), was a review of the procurement and contractual arrangements in the United Kingdom construction industry. The report was critical of the state of the construction industry and made a series of recommendations to address this. A key element in the report was that it identified the *client* as being the core of the construction process, and many of its recommendations were aimed at government departments becoming *best practice clients*. For this to happen, it was recommended that clients should develop detailed project strategies, and obtain advice in the form of feasibility studies (Smith, 2001). The role of the client and the constraints of external bodies provides a context within which both digital and non-digital processes can be described. The significance of this in design practice is that it places importance on enabling clients to visualise design concepts through 3-D digital visualisation techniques. Before looking at the InfoLab IT centre scheme in detail, the images overleaf illustrate a more recent exploratory proposal by FaulknerBrowns for a ski centre, with the now customary curvilinear geometry. Will the client go with further development of this proposal by the architect, or will a project manager succeed in transforming it back into a less-expensive box?

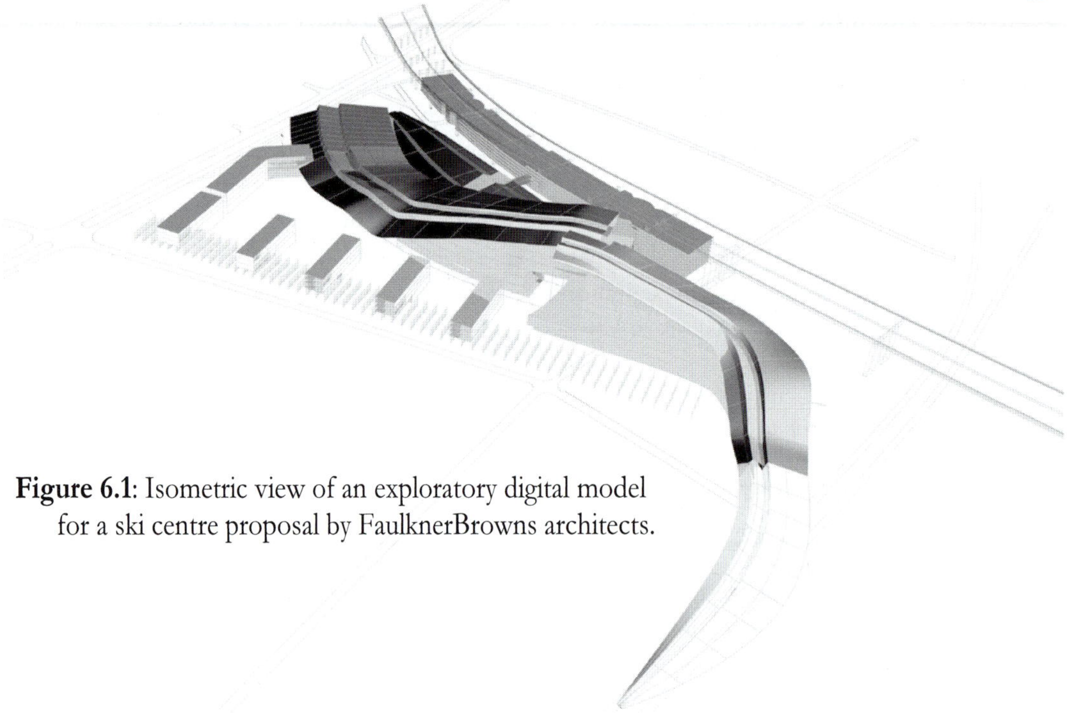

Figure 6.1: Isometric view of an exploratory digital model
for a ski centre proposal by FaulknerBrowns architects.

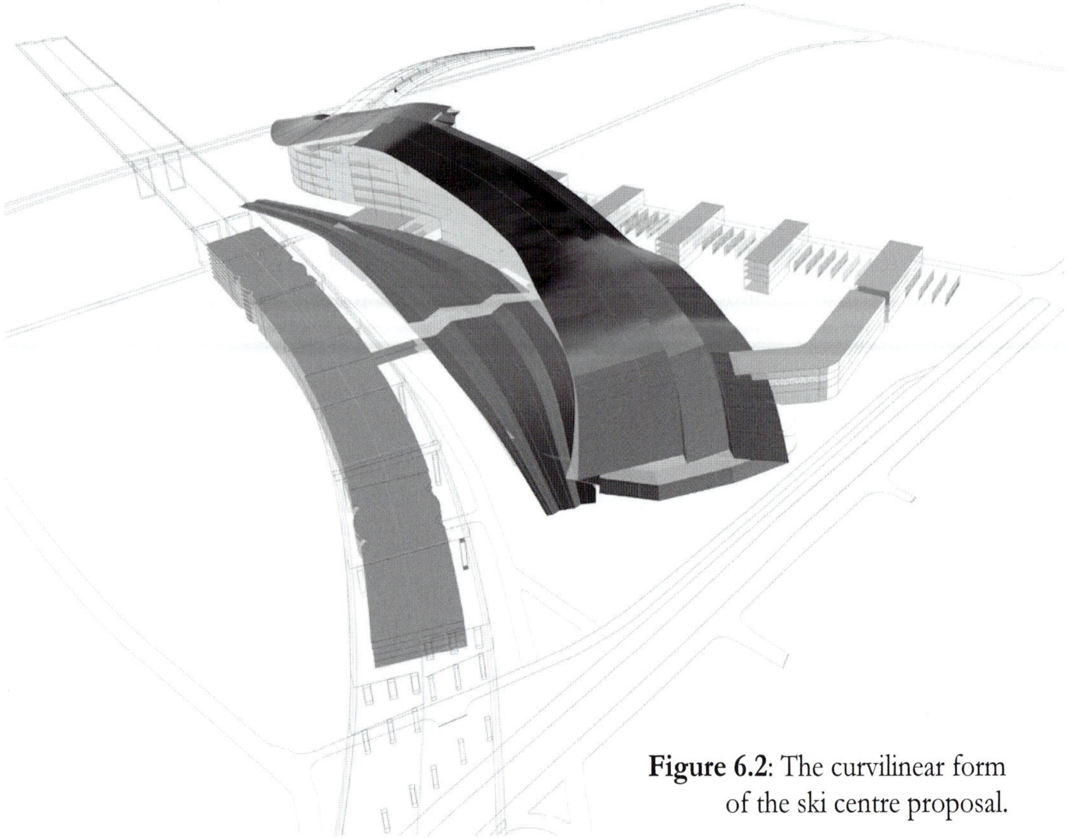

Figure 6.2: The curvilinear form
of the ski centre proposal.

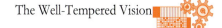
The sculptural curvilinear digital model illustrated in **figures 6.1** and **6.2** opposite was created by lofting a section suggesting glacial topography along 3-D paths set by the geometry of a ski slope along with supporting accommodation. The intent was to create an ambitious external form that conveyed the dynamism of movement on a scale legible from an adjacent motorway, whilst achieving a sympathetic appearance and approach when viewed and accessed from surrounding areas. Such proposals are intended to stimulate excitement and debate about the potential of a site amongst various interested parties *at very early stages of a project*, thus raising the commercial profile, rather than describing a fully developed design. With the popularity of curvilinear geometry in contemporary architecture, digital presentations of early stage design schemes such as this exposes spatial and structural opportunities to potential client partners.

Whatever the answer to the earlier question about the future progress of such a model might be, the point to be made here is that the context in which such models are developed is as much a part of the briefing process as it is of the design process, both of which proceed in a cyclical fashion (**figure 6.3**). To ensure that the views of project partners are balanced and focused in the briefing process, a clear communication structure between them is needed. The demands of each partner can then be assessed within the context of a finite budget

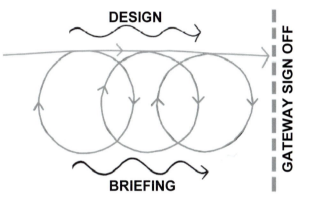

Figure 6.3: The cyclical design and briefing processes.

In the project that will be described in detail in the remainder of this chapter, the intention is to give the reader an impression of the design and briefing effort involved. The design team project leader regularly convened and chaired user group meetings, and a steering group provided an important filtering process for the many demands, ensuring that a single clear point of contact with the design team was provided. This process of testing and refining the brief is frequently iterative in nature, often examining initial concepts in parallel with the exploration of the requirements of the brief. The real opportunities to add value in a design exist at the early stages of a project, since the cost consequences would be far greater later (**figure 6.4**).

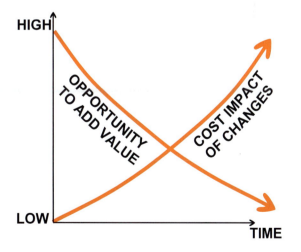

Figure 6.4: Added value in early design stages.

In order to understand the building type that was the focus of this project, it is necessary to look at some recent UK government initiatives in more detail. In *'Our Competitive Future: Building the Knowledge Driven Economy'* (DTI, 1998), the economic benefits of supporting and exploiting new knowledge was identified. This was followed by a further white paper, *'Excellence and Opportunity: a science and innovation policy for the 21st century'* (DTI, 2000), which set out the government's role in creating and maintaining the right supportive climate for innovation and enterprise to thrive. Funding to develop this new knowledge economy was channelled into three principal areas – scientific research studies, university infrastructure, and regional infrastructure.

This increasing influence of external funding on research activity has led to Research Assessment Exercise (RAE) ratings being directly linked to funding formulas. Five-star rated departments (*outstanding research of international standing*) currently receive more than nine times the funding of those rated at zero (*no evidence of research*). A natural consequence of this is the increasing pre-eminence of high-performing research staff creating a 'premier league' of academics. The attraction and retention of these academics and their research teams has become a major consideration for universities if they are to continue to maintain their standing and funding. Consequently, a raised expectation has been created among the academic elite, who now expect facilities comparable to those of the commercial R&D community. The increasing significance of knowledge generation and academic research staff in higher education institutes has brought with it a new set of demands for twenty-first century research buildings.

Over the course of a number of projects, a pattern of nine critical success factors has emerged (Kane, 2003). These are central to the success of any research department, irrespective of the academic discipline, and can be traced back to several factors. First, the drive towards increased research activity has widened the focus of attention beyond laboratories to academic staff areas, in particular the office, interaction and social facilities for academic staff and researchers. Many academics believe laboratories are not the primary space in which new knowledge is created, but instead the location in which it is tested. The combination of an academic's private workspace and the local interaction spaces that provides the mix of quiet contemplative thought and immediate discussion of new ideas is the true medium for the germination of knowledge. Second, there is a constancy of staffing structures across all academic research fields and research programmes. Typically, for every member of academic staff leading research projects there will be about four researchers employed for a specific research project. Third, most academics have to balance research work with a number of other activities, such as administration, interaction with external funding bodies or industry partners, and undergraduate teaching. This interaction with the external community brings with it a common set of concerns about the control of privacy, together with the confidentiality of intellectual property.

As a consequence of this context of research funding, the overall objectives of the InfoLab 21 project were summarised as follows:

- high quality accommodation for academic and research staff
- a building reflecting the research quality and promoting the research output
- business incubation support facilities to encourage technology transfer
- an overall master plan supporting phased growth.

The Latham and Egan Reports, along with the Urban White Paper that followed (DETR, 2000), were all concerned with encouraging improvements in the construction industry. Through the implementation of real projects, these were meant to demonstrate the benefits of:

- more client focused, innovative procurement methods
- streamlined building processes and better measurement of performance
- a team approach to design and construction
- making the most of standardised components and off-site construction.

This series of reports on the whole reflect the widespread perception that there is a need for more multidisciplinary working and for changes in education and training to support this.

Two key professional figures that emerged from the findings of these reports are first the *project manager*, to engage with the more integrated overall project process; and the *urban designer*, to integrate architectural, planning and landscape architecture aspects of planning and design. Since this case study was predominantly an architectural rather than an urban intervention, it is the former figure that came to play a dominant role in this case. The role of the project manager within the project steering group for InfoLab 21 is illustrated in **figure 6.5**. Traditionally architects have always been project managers as well as designers. The modern trend is for the project manager to represent the client whilst the architect manages and leads the design process.

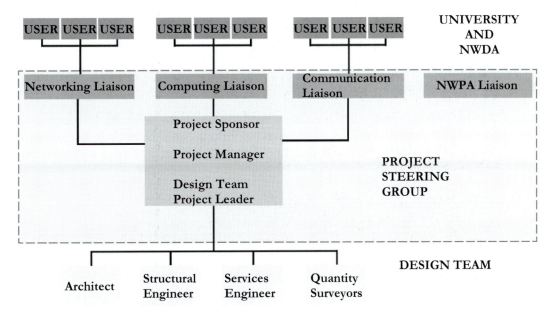

Figure 6.5: The organisation of the InfoLab 21 project.

6.1 Rethinking Construction

The 1998 report *Rethinking Construction* (Egan, 1998), was a review of the scope for improving the quality and efficiency of delivery of UK construction, and compared the construction industry with other industries, with which it tended to compare unfavourably (Smith, 2001). The task force made recommendations drawing on the experience of other industries, from which it identified a series of factors it considered fundamental to achieving an efficient process resulting in good quality. The area of recommendations most relevant to interdisciplinary working was that relating to the integration of the design and construction processes. The report called for an integrated project process that utilises the full construction team, bringing the skills of all the participants to deliver value to the client:

The key premise behind the integrated project process is that teams of designers, constructors and suppliers work together through a series of projects, continuously developing the product and the supply chain, eliminating waste in the delivery process, innovating and learning from experience. (Egan, 1998)

The report rejected the fragmentation in the conventional construction process, as well as the assumption that clients benefit from choosing a new team of designers, constructors and suppliers competitively for every project they do. The report subdivides this integrated project process into four *complementary and interlocked elements*, to each of which can be associated some consequences in terms of interdisciplinary working and skills. The four elements were: product development, project implementation, partnering the supply chain, and the production of components. To improve productivity in the construction industry, the following issues needed to be resolved:

- committed people at top management level
- training in integrating projects at the project manager level
- training at the site supervisor level
- a greater understanding of the needs of clients among designers.

Teamwork was a central concept in this report, involving not only the design professions, but all those that have an input to the construction process, in order to achieve *design that is properly integrated with construction and performance in use*. The practical consequences of this for multidisciplinary working were that:

- suppliers and subcontractors fully involved in the design team
- the experience of completed projects should be fed into the next one
- quality must be fundamental to the design process – *right first time*
- designers should collaborate with the others in the project process
- design needs to encompass whole life costs
- clients also have to accept their responsibilities for effective design.

For the InfoLab 21 project, a team was put together from amongst FaulknerBrowns staff with skills and experience in the design of higher education research facilities, experience of projects of a similar size, cost and complexity, and skills in two-stage procurement. One of the opportunities of the InfoLab 21 facility lay in the potential synergies between the three departments of Computing, Networking and Communications. Key design milestones, both those internal to FaulknerBrowns and those that were needed to satisfy the key RIBA design stages, were defined in value management trees and Gantt charts used for planning and scheduling information. Once preliminary issues have been resolved, and a project is under way, the key issue of the project as far as the client is concerned is the management of the project itself, and a competent practice is well capable of assuring the client that this is taking place. In response to the aforementioned government initiatives, involving the client in the process of design development was a key aspect of this particular case study, and the effective communication of design alternatives and solutions was central to this. The role of CAD models and drawings played an important part alongside more conventional drawing and model presentations, as will be seen in the visual material in the following pages.

The Latham Report placed particular emphasis on the use of co-ordinated project information (CPI), both in architectural practice, and in architectural education. At present, architectural education does not appear to be adopting CPI techniques, partly because of the separation of management from communication skills, and probably because of the lack of IT resources needed for such procedures. Latham goes on to place considerable emphasis on the issue of project management, and suggests that clients should arrange for this either in-house or externally. This particular issue has been a large bone of contention in many architectural offices over recent years, and many architects have felt undermined by appearing to be the clients of project managers.

In relation to partnering, the Latham Report discussed the relationships between clients and contractors, rather than the interrelationships between the professions involved, and noted the advantages in building up expert teams and keeping them together. In relation to teamwork on site, the report discussed the relationships between clients, consultants, contractors and specialist/trade contractors, and it referred to a survey that recommended that subcontractors should be involved earlier, and that their skill and knowledge should be better utilised. The Latham Report itself, however, did not make any detailed recommendations on multidisciplinary working over and beyond mainly contractual matters. Even before Latham, FaulknerBrowns recognised the benefits to clients of offering both specialists in design together with specialists in project administration who can work closely with contracting organisations and manage the design process.

NWDA (North West Regional Development Agency) funding was identified to support the development of research facilities linked to technology transfer facilities in the form of a new KBC (Knowledge Business Centre). The new combined facility was called InfoLab 21 providing the opportunity to establish a national research centre comprising three key components:

- the Informatics Institute
- the Networking Centre
- the KBC.

6.2   Design Stages

Typically, the range of activities in any architect's office are many and varied. These include responding to the brief, addressing cost and timescale considerations, selection and specification of materials and building elements, and construction and contract documentation. Responding to the brief alone involves planning, testing, designing, refining, amending, writing, drawing, sketching, and calculating. Professional bodies such as the RIBA in the UK have provided guidelines for architectural offices to generate more formalised descriptions of their key activities to give greater overall clarity to the design process. The overall project process is defined in terms of RIBA design stages. The updated version of these stages, produced by the RIBA in 1999, was as follows:

Stage A: Appraisal and **Stage B**: Strategic Briefing
In these first two stages, the size, accommodation, performance, durability, costs and costs-in-use criteria are identified and assessed.

Stage C: Outline Proposals and **Stage D**: Detailed Proposals
Overall form, appearance, techniques and materials.

Stage E: Final Proposals
Significant elements examined and determined in detail.

Stage F: Production Information 1 and 2
Specification and detailing decisions become finalised.

Stage G: Tender Documentation
Specification and bills of quantities, documentation standards defined, components listed and quantified.

Stage H: Tender Action and Stage J: Mobilisation
Selected contractors submit price and timescale bids and are appointed.

Stage K: Construction and Implementation On-site
Key objectives include programme, cost, and avoidance of conflicts.

Stage L: Post Completion and Maintenance
After-sales servicing – hopefully promoting long-term customer satisfaction.

The significance of the Latham Report in relation to the above stages and the role of CAD is that it becomes a responsibility of the architects to involve clients much more in the whole design process. CAD models and computer-generated presentations should enable clients to understand and visualise design concepts through 3-D visualisation. CAD visualisations in turn can be used to test design concepts in relation to the brief with the client. Alternative design configurations can be tested and initial concepts can be explored. The design brief can be developed with the involvement of the client.

The design stages that will be used to present this case study vary somewhat from the RIBA stages opposite. First, the role of digital production drawings is well known and corresponds to the common perception of CAD use in architectural practice. What is of interest here, however, is the extent to which CAD modelling is applied in earlier design stages. In many contemporary architectural offices, digital tools are being applied at increasingly earlier stages in the design process. Furthermore, with the introduction of new competitive practices, an additional tendering stage is invariably required, in which architectural offices are required to present their case to potential clients prior to their appointment and full design development. These factors lead to the adoption of the following sequence of design stages:

Feasibility — Stage A — **Tender** — **Briefing** — Stage B — **Concept** — Stage C — **Scheme** — Stage D

Feasibility

This is usually a small commission to investigate whether the site can accommodate the functionality demanded of it. The output is usually a report showing the ways in which the goals might be met, or modified by the constraints uncovered. If the feasibility study shows that the project is viable, the customer can then proceed with the project.

Tender

The European Union (EU) aimed to create incentives for public purchasers by opening up public procurement to competition. The public procurement rules were intended to ensure open competition by and between EU member states for contracts of goods, services and construction projects. These rules affect tenders not only for central governments and local authorities, but also for public utilities, quasi-public bodies, and transportation and telecommunications industries.

Briefing

The brief for an architectural project functions as a message between clients and designers, and should be meaningful to both parties. Briefing plays an important role in focusing effort towards solutions that are relevant to the client's requirements. A written brief typically focuses on specific functional requirements in any project, and ensures that the design team focuses on essential points. In terms of digital data, volumetric analysis and massing studies often feature at this stage.

Concept

Concept design is the creative process of making or taking the client's brief and devising an appropriate design response. Alternative design proposals are analysed before a final concept is put forward. A concept design indicates the general arrangement of a scheme, its likely appearance, its area and broad budget costs, based on an initial specification. A concept design is usually insufficiently detailed to make a detailed planning application, but allows the client to sign off that the approach is the one required.

Scheme

In scheme design, the agreed concept design is developed to include all the major decisions on layout, engineering techniques and materials. The function, form and economics of a scheme are defined prior to final detailing. The material produced at this stage is suitable for a full planning application, though it is standard practice to apply part way through a scheme design to reduce uncertainty.

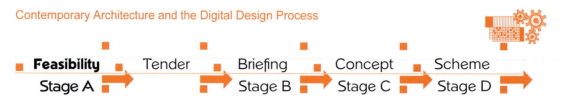

6.3   Feasibility

6.3.1   Feasibility Study for InfoLab 21

The computing department at Lancaster University reached a point where it could no longer support its own research requirements. FaulknerBrowns were commissioned to carry out a feasibility study to develop a new computing centre. A wider opportunity was identified to create a national research centre with opportunities for technology transfer into the local economy. The study investigated the advantages of bringing several research departments into one combined centre along with business support facilities. The existing computer department consisted of predominantly cellular office space, typical of older university facilities, in which the layout and interconnectivity constrained research productivity. The following deficiencies were identified:

- staff offices were cramped and below space standards
- featureless corridors with solid doors did not encourage interaction or mixing of staff
- no defined mix area was available for research staff interaction
- researchers have to share small 12–15m² offices between three to four persons
- dedicated research laboratory space was very limited
- cabling infrastructure was retrofitted to suit research programmes rather than built in
- technology transfer was limited because of the location of the department on campus.

The new proposal aimed to incorporate accommodation for the existing departments of Communications Systems and Information Systems Services (ISS), and in the longer term, the Management School, so that the potential synergies between these three departments could be exploited. The new combined facility was referred to as **InfoLab 21**, consisting of three (renamed) key components: the Lancaster Informatics Institute, the Lancaster Networking Centre, and the Lancaster Knowledge Business Centre (KBC). The objectives of InfoLab 21 could be summarised as follows:

- provision of new high quality accommodation to support and promote research work
- business incubation support facilities to encourage technology transfer (BIC)
- an overall master plan to permit the phased growth of InfoLab 21.

Each of the three components of InfoLab 21 were to have their own well-defined roles and activities. Bringing these components onto one site offered an opportunity to maximise the synergy between them. This synergy and integration was to provide a number of benefits:

- flexibility of space
- long-term technology transfer
- enhanced interaction and shared facilities
- attractive working environment
- cross-fertilisation of ideas from research to business and vice versa.

Feasibility | Tender | Briefing | Concept | Scheme
Stage A | | Stage B | Stage C | Stage D

6.3.2   Feasibility Analysis Sketches

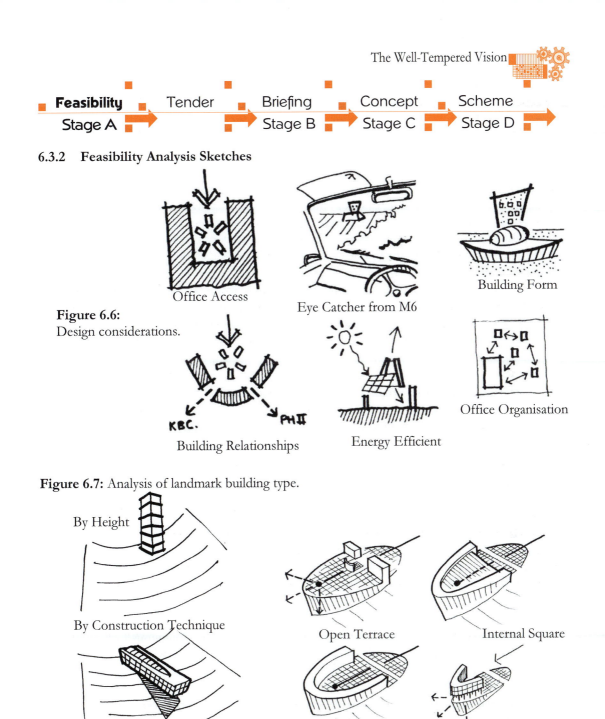

Figure 6.6: Design considerations.

Office Access

Eye Catcher from M6

Building Form

Building Relationships

Energy Efficient

Office Organisation

Figure 6.7: Analysis of landmark building type.

By Height

By Construction Technique

By Form

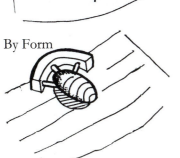

Open Terrace

Internal Square

Visual Stop
From Distance

Allow Views
Through

Figure 6.8:
Analysis of end campus pedestrian spine.

Feasibility	Tender	Briefing	Concept	Scheme
Stage A		Stage B	Stage C	Stage D

6.3.3   Key Relationships

Fundamental relationships arose from an understanding of innovation, and especially that ideas arise as much out of casual conversations as they do out of formal work and meetings. The key to the facility design was to create casual encounters and to encourage social interaction in central hubs, whilst allowing private space for quiet thought. The relationships and aspirations for such a resource were condensed into the following set of objectives:

- To centrally locate academic staff offices to encourage mixing between staff and to dispense with the tradition of corridors and enclosed cellular rooms.
- To foster creativity and serendipity by having an active and impressive public heart with private space accessed off. This space must have the ability to function dually for meeting areas, social occasions and exhibition space.
- To provide visitor demonstration areas located near the entrance/reception to promote examples of completed projects with possibly a video wall.
- To locate Networking alongside Informatics, accessible off a shared entrance and hub space, with easy access to remainder of campus which it supports (**figure 6.10**).
- To create varied workplaces in the categories of hive, cell, club and den, to encourage varied approaches to research (Duffy, 1997).
- An open-plan (hive) approach would greatly assist with staff interaction and, therefore, support research activity for the researchers. These spaces should:
    - (a)   be located adjacent to the academic staff whom they assist
    - (b)   provide quiet spaces for contemplative working and writing
    - (c)   provide flexible shared laboratory spaces.
- Varied private and open meeting areas around the building to encourage interaction.
- A cafe as a social and public meeting point to encourage people into the centre.
- To centrally locate administration and support areas, encouraging movement and interaction.
- Functions such as reception foyers and shared spaces to be different in character from one another and offer functional flexibility serving periodically as Ubiquitous Communication (UbiCom) spaces, showcase laboratories and exhibition spaces. The UbiCom lab should not be separate from the social spaces but integrated to explore people's interaction with new technology in a more naturalistic fashion.
- To fully integrate the KBC into the development allowing direct connection and knowledge transfer yet maintaining a hierarchy of use from teaching to research to business (**figure 6.10**)

A series of preliminary diagrams exploring a range of options for the relationship between the offices, mix space and laboratories was prepared for the Informatics facility (**figures 6.11** and **6.13**).

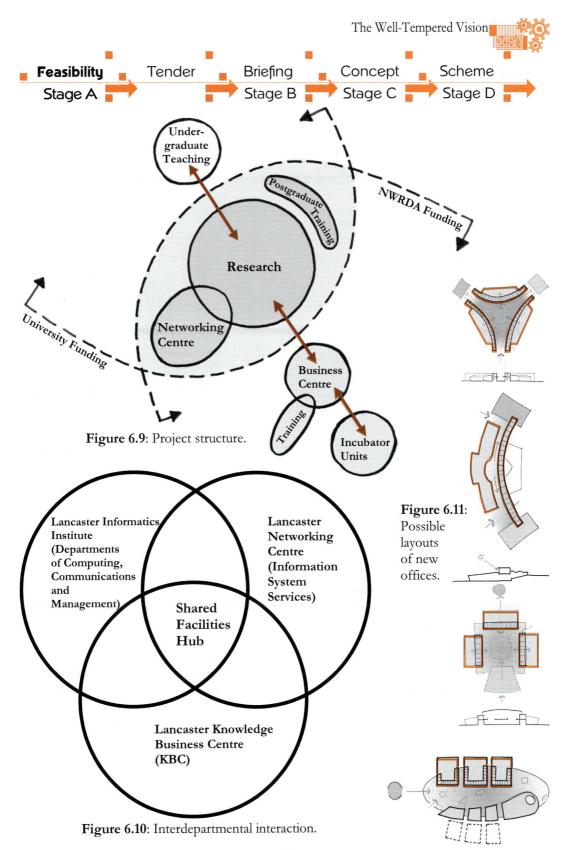

Feasibility	Tender	Briefing	Concept	Scheme
Stage A		Stage B	Stage C	Stage D

Figure 6.9: Project structure.

Figure 6.11: Possible layouts of new offices.

Figure 6.10: Interdepartmental interaction.

Feasibility Tender Briefing Concept Scheme
Stage A Stage B Stage C Stage D

Since research activity was the essence of InfoLab 21, it was vital that the relationships between the internal spaces supported this activity. Studies of workplace activity patterns have shown that four general categories can be identified. These have been summarised as hive, den, cell or club patterns, depending on the level of autonomy and interaction which typically occurs (Duffy, 1997).

Hive: Individual routine process work with low interaction and low autonomy

Cell: Individual concentrated work with little interaction

Den: Group work typically highly interactive with low autonomy

Club: Knowledge work that is highly autonomous and highly interactive

Figure 6.12: Workplace activity patterns.

Research spaces appear to benefit from a *club* type of working. A number of approaches were analysed for the *club* working space layout, beginning with a **cellular** approach. This conventional solution provides individual academics offices and cellular rooms for between two and five researchers, but suffers from the isolation of academics' offices. To encourage a greater level of interaction, a range of more flexible spatial layouts were investigated.

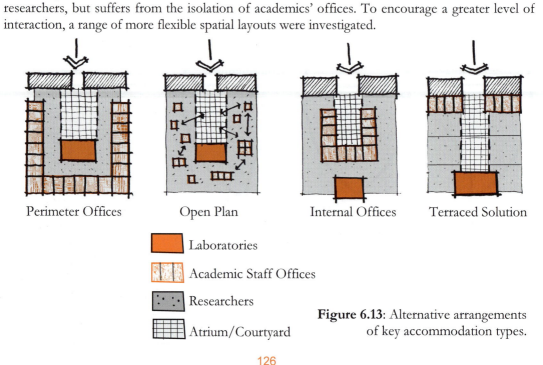

Perimeter Offices   Open Plan   Internal Offices   Terraced Solution

Laboratories
Academic Staff Offices
Researchers
Atrium/Courtyard

Figure 6.13: Alternative arrangements of key accommodation types.

From the sketch ideas developed in **figure 6.13**, a more detailed analysis investigated the properties of each configuration, from which a new candidate began to emerge out of the terraced solution.

Open Plan: Gives optimal informal interaction by means of open plan layout for academics and researchers. It is both efficient in space usage and also highly flexible, but does not support individual working for academics as well as the cellular option, and may lead to disturbance from visiting undergraduates unless dedicated tutorial rooms are provided.

Internal Offices: Facing academics' workspaces onto both a central public space and onto the researchers' work areas gives an excellent balance of interdepartmental (or inter-*club*) mixing in the public realm with secondary *club* mixing adjacent to the researchers. Glazed frontages in each direction can reinforce this benefit. Separate access to the academics for undergraduates via the public space keeps disturbance of research activity to a minimum.

Perimeter Offices: Placing academics offices on the perimeter ensures that they benefit from natural light and ventilation. Researchers are located alongside a central void or lightwell. This arrangement gives good environmental conditions for academics, but does not support informal mixing. Researchers have no external views and may be disturbed by visiting undergraduates.

Modified Combi: A focused *club* meeting space sandwiched between academics' workspaces located on the perimeter with good views, natural light and ventilation. Researchers can be located alongside in flexible space permitting a mix of either open plan or cellular accommodation. Visiting undergraduates do not disturb researchers' work. From this initial analysis, the *modified combi* appeared to provide good relationships, mixing, environmental conditions and flexibility.

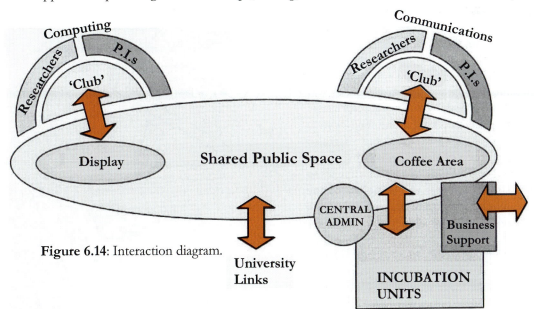

Figure 6.14: Interaction diagram.

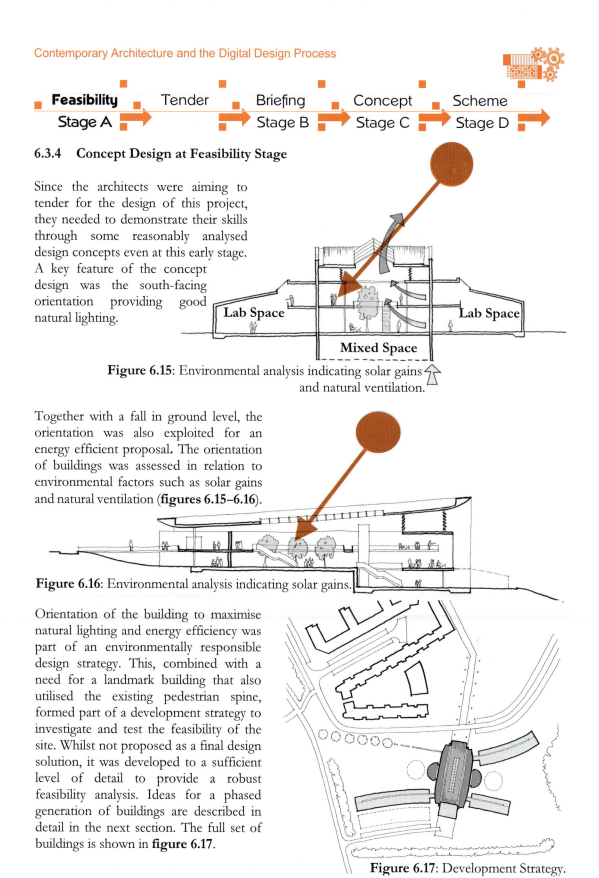

Feasibility · Tender · Briefing · Concept · Scheme
Stage A · Stage B · Stage C · Stage D

6.3.4 Concept Design at Feasibility Stage

Since the architects were aiming to tender for the design of this project, they needed to demonstrate their skills through some reasonably analysed design concepts even at this early stage. A key feature of the concept design was the south-facing orientation providing good natural lighting.

Lab Space · Lab Space

Mixed Space

Figure 6.15: Environmental analysis indicating solar gains and natural ventilation.

Together with a fall in ground level, the orientation was also exploited for an energy efficient proposal. The orientation of buildings was assessed in relation to environmental factors such as solar gains and natural ventilation (**figures 6.15–6.16**).

Figure 6.16: Environmental analysis indicating solar gains.

Orientation of the building to maximise natural lighting and energy efficiency was part of an environmentally responsible design strategy. This, combined with a need for a landmark building that also utilised the existing pedestrian spine, formed part of a development strategy to investigate and test the feasibility of the site. Whilst not proposed as a final design solution, it was developed to a sufficient level of detail to provide a robust feasibility analysis. Ideas for a phased generation of buildings are described in detail in the next section. The full set of buildings is shown in **figure 6.17**.

Figure 6.17: Development Strategy.

Feasibility	Tender	Briefing	Concept	Scheme
Stage A		**Stage B**	**Stage C**	**Stage D**

6.3.5 Programme and Phasing

A phased development strategy was required for InfoLab 21 in order to respond to the requirements of
both the funding streams and site constraints. A development strategy supporting a phased approach consisted of three components:

Phase 1 : Lancaster Informatics Institute
A 3072m² phase providing high quality research facilities for the Department of Computing, and incorporating 220m² of accommodation for the Department of
Communications.

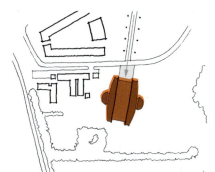

Figure 6.18: Phase 1a: Informatics.

Phase 2 : Knowledge Business Centre
A 1389m² phase providing both business support facilities and incubator business units.

Phase 3 : Lancaster Networking Centre
A 1669m² phase providing high quality research facilities for the Department of Communications and Information Systems Services. Outline programmes were
prepared to indicate the timescales required for the first
phase of the InfoLab 21 based on the following procurement strategies:

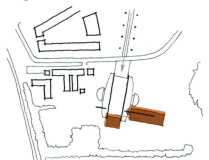

Figure 6.19: Phase 1b: KBC Phase 1.

- Traditional Procurement: preparation of full information by a consultant design team. Selection
  of a contractor on a competitive basis and appointment of a fixed lump sum basis.

- Two-Stage Procurement: preparation of design
  proposals by a consultant design team up to
  mid-RIBA Stage E. First stage competitive selection of a contractor on the basis of management
  approach, preliminaries, overheads and profit.
  Preparation of construction information by consultant team with buildability and cost advice
  from contractor. Appointment of contractor on
  a fixed price lump sum and novation of consultant design team. The two-stage approach provides a number of benefits:

Figure 6.20: Phase 2: KBC Phase 2.

(a) comparable overall programme duration to tra-
    ditional procurement, may be slightly shorter
(b) improved buildability
(c) cost certainty
(d) balanced distribution of risk.

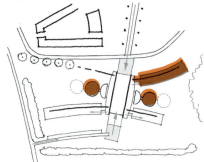

Figure 6.21: Phase 3: Lancaster Networking Centre.

Feasibility ■ **Tender** ■ Briefing ■ Concept ■ Scheme

Stage A ■ Stage B ■ Stage C ■ Stage D ■

6.4 Tender

6.4.1 Value Management

The architects recognised the importance of understanding not only the clients' functional requirements, i.e. numbers of rooms, areas etc., but also their wider objectives. The architects, therefore, placed a great deal of emphasis on the benefits of *value management* as a structured way of testing the objectives of a project. Their view of the design process was one in which a series of value management workshops would play a prominent role, particularly during the briefing process (VM1 and VM2), and subsequently for the evaluation of concept design proposals (VM3) (**figure 6.22**).

The way in which value management was to be applied to the InfoLab 21 project was for a facilitator from the architectural office to host a series of workshops with all of the project stakeholders: users, steering group, NWDA representatives. The end result of the workshops would be a structured set of objectives. Some of the issues that were to be considered in this process included academic objectives, university-wide objectives, capital vs through-life cost balance, sustainability targets, flexibility and security. By scoring nine principal objectives, the architects could then establish a framework of priorities, called a *value tree*, that would become an invaluable tool to assist decision making at later stages.

Digital support for this process would consist of sets of spreadsheets associated with design proposals in which the project objectives were represented in terms of weighted criteria (see section **6.5.2**).

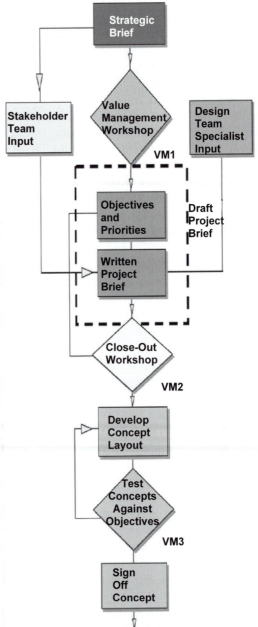

Figure 6.22: The role of value management in the design process.

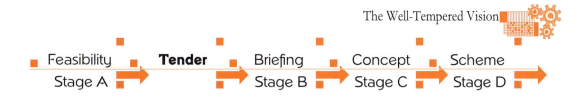

Feasibility	**Tender**	Briefing	Concept	Scheme
Stage A		Stage B	Stage C	Stage D

6.4.2 Design Team Management

At the tender stage, the architectural office proposed a team for the project consisting of specialists in design together with specialists in project administration (**figure 6.23**). This team was to work closely with contracting organisations and manage the design process. The team members brought with them experience of working on other research facilities of similar size and complexity.

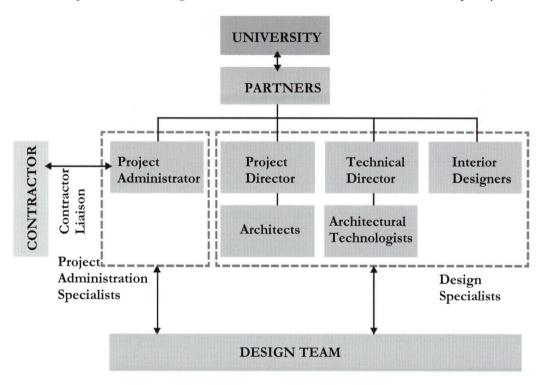

Figure 6.23: Project partners

A further important consideration was the establishment of a clear communication structure between this team and the main university departments involved in the project: Computing, Networking and Communications. The architects proposed a project steering group as already shown in **figure 6.5** to provide a forum for strategic review of the needs of each department as well as the NWDA. Assessment of the demands of each department was carried out by the steering group which included the project sponsor and project manager.

6.4.3   CAD Massing Models

As part of the feasibility exercise, FaulknerBrowns prepared a preliminary concept to test both the site and strategic relationships. Some invaluable feedback was provided by the academic staff and researchers on this design. This particular concept required further development in response to to this feedback. However, for the purposes of this tender response, FaulknerBrowns opted to develop some alternative designs to help demonstrate the approach they might take if successful in being awarded the commission. Digital models were produced at this stage to indicate notional spatial relationships. Two possible approaches were investigated, both of which were based around the *modified combi* form of research area layout.

Approach Number 1

- the pedestrian spine is extended and reinforced by way of paving and canopies across the perimeter road alongside InfoLab 21
- research facilities orientated east/west with a central public entrance adjacent to the perimeter road and extended spine
- the Business Incubation Centre (BIC) is located to the south of the research facilities. A south facing terrace above creates a new landscaped public space on campus
- access to the business support services of the BIC to be situated off the spine, alongside the new public hub of the research facility
- university expansion supported westwards onto the Biological Field Station site at a later date, and the BIC expands southwards onto the lower portion of the site
- public-private balance is achieved between the open public hubspace and the more private *club* spaces within the research areas
- views, natural light and ventilation are provided for all PIs and researchers
- flexibility is provided to reorganise the research area ratio of cellular to open plan space.

Approach Number 2

- the pedestrian spine is similarly extended and reinforced
- research facilities are arranged within two wings linked by a public hub space
- university entrance located within public hub space, adjacent to the perimeter road and spine
- the Business Incubation Centre is located close to the research facilities lying north-south alongside the central hub
- business support areas of BIC to be situated at the south of the hub with a public front door
- expansion for academic and business incubation facilities is flexible both west and south
- internally this option provides all the same benefits as approach number one albeit with a horizontal rather than vertical orientation to the central public hub space.

The following two images are CAD massing models which were part of the tender submission.

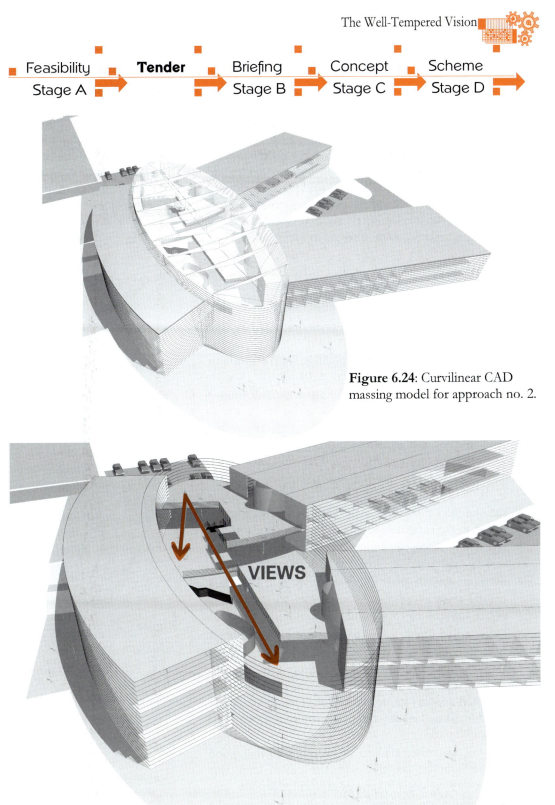

Figure 6.24: Curvilinear CAD massing model for approach no. 2.

VIEWS

Figure 6.25: Curvilinear CAD massing model with view analysis for approach no. 2.

6.4.4 Site Analysis

Lancaster University identified an area to the southern edge of the campus outside the perimeter road, as the preferred site of InfoLab 21. Through its topography and position, the site is an important area on campus, and was identified as an appropriate site for the landmark building InfoLab 21. A number of issues relating to the site had to be ensured:

- the area requirements are sufficient for InfoLab 21 as well as for future expansion
- good links to existing social facilities can be set up
- the site could enliven and regenerate the southern edge of the campus
- the site could provide a focal building for the southern edge of the university
- the site maintains good links with main campus routes.

Figure 6.26: Masterplan.

An analysis of the chosen site was prepared, highlighting key issues, and enabling opportunities for fully exploiting the site. The following issues were identified and are illustrated in the site analysis diagrams (**figures 6.26–6.28**):

- the site sloped down at a gradient of 1:5, with steep slopes to the eastern edge preventing development
- an existing Biology Field Station needed to be retained initially, with possible future expansion into this area
- the campus pedestrian spine was to be extended to a natural ending, offering opportunities to create new public space and a focal point at the end of the route
- the site had direct access to the university perimeter road and parking
- the site allowed opportunities for direct vehicular and pedestrian access from outside the University boundary. A KBC facility located to the lower southern part of the site would create a separate business area with dedicated parking
- the site was orientated to the south, allowing good natural lighting. Together with the fall in level, this factor was exploited for energy efficient solutions
- the elevated natural orientation of the site allowed the outstanding southern views to be utilised through and from the development.

Figure 6.27: Pedestrian spine.

Figure 6.28: Site analysis.

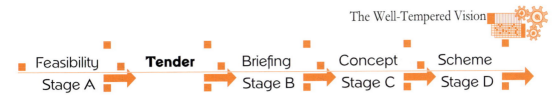

6.4.5 View Analysis

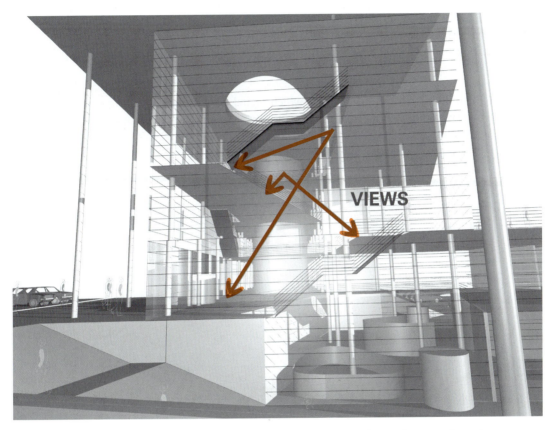

Figure 6.29: CAD building model with view analysis of approach no.1.

Figure 6.29 shows a CAD-generated image produced at tender stage to show the client the importance given by the design team to analysing views in and around design proposals. The activity of analysis is typically carried out in relation to specific criteria. The methodology of analysis, and therefore methods of digital presentation, vary according to different criteria. A primary and important group of criteria include: structure, zonal planning, circulation, servicing, and environmental control. Each of the criteria in this primary group can be assessed against predetermined aspects of a brief or programme. In the case of zonal planning, for example, given pre-established relationship preferences and a set of proposals in a given structured format, performance gradings can be allocated to each. **Figures 6.30–6.31** on the following pages illustrate the importance placed upon the analysis of circulation. A secondary set of criteria may include: volumetric massing, symmetry, cultural implications, proportions and conceptual intention.

Feasibility **Tender** Briefing Concept Scheme
Stage A Stage B Stage C Stage D

6.4.6 Analysis of Circulation

Fundamentally, circulation and use-space represent the significant dynamic and static components in all buildings. Use-space is the primary focus of architectural decision making relative to function, and circulation is the means by which that design effort is engaged. Together, the articulation of the conditions of movement and stability form the essence of a building. (Clark and Pause, 1985, p. 5)

Figures 6.30 and **6.31** illustrate the way in which digital models were used to generate exploded views showing circulation and internal relationships between spaces. These models were part of the tender submission.

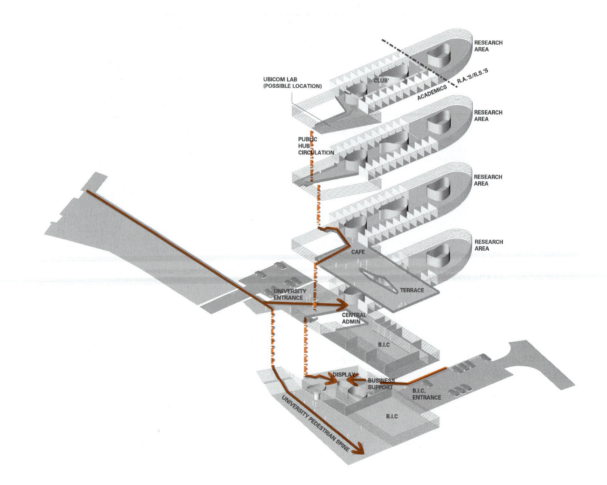

Figure 6.30: Exploded CAD model showing circulation in approach no.1.

Feasibility **Tender** Briefing Concept Scheme
Stage A Stage B Stage C Stage D

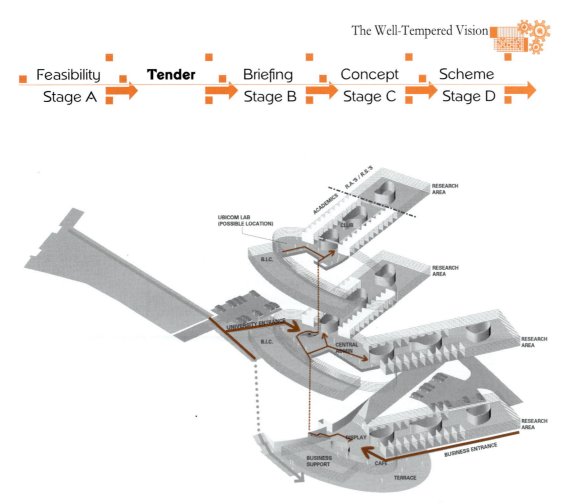

Figure 6.31: Exploded CAD model showing vertical and horizontal circulation.

A surprising aspect of the digital models illustrated in **figures 6.30–31** is that such a detailed analysis of spatial relationships was carried out even before the architects were appointed to this particular project. Tendering for an architectural contract, therefore, is design competition work, and as such involves a great deal of time and energy on the part of the office in question.

During the tender stage alone, the architects carried out substantial analyses of several pertinent design factors which included massing (**figures 6.24–6.25**), the site (**figures 6.26–28**), views (**figure 6.29**) and circulation (**figures 6.30–6.31**). Digital modelling techniques played an important part in this process. The analysis of vertical circulation, for example, can be supported with the layering mechanisms that are common to most CAD systems. These can be used to create exploded isometric views such as those shown in **figures 6.30** and **6.31**, by exaggerating the separations between layers. Such views also maintain connections between the 2-D parti diagrams essential to design development, and the 3-D views that are more more useful as presentations to the client.

Feasibility | Tender | **Briefing** | Concept | Scheme
Stage A | | Stage B | Stage C | Stage D

6.5   Briefing

6.5.1   The Briefing Process

The steering group was responsible for the rationalisation of the extensive information gathered during the briefing stage. This involved the filtering of user requests in order to meet the principal objectives of the project:

- provision of an environment that supports and encourages world class research
- a flagship building which acts as a showpiece for both the university and the region
- world class infrastructure and communication links
- a fine building within budget
- integration of computing and communications to support formal and informal interaction
- provision of business incubation and mature R&D facilities to support regional business, engage with the wider community, generate knowledge and transfer skills
- reinforce links with the wider university
- facilitate expansion within the context of the masterplan
- deliver the building on time.

A detailed schedule of accommodation indicated that 250 university academics and researchers were to be accommodated in 4150m² of space, and that the Knowledge Business Centre would provide incubation, R&D and business support facilities within 1500m² of space.

The architects suggested the following structure for the brief:

- Overall objectives and mission statement
- Site, location, ownership, access, boundaries and parking
- Budget
- Schedule of accommodation
- Objectives hierarchy (from VM1 in section **6.4.1**)
- Programme requirements and critical dates
- Relation/adjacency diagrams for the spaces
- Occupancy numbers
- Process flow chart
- Design life
- Environment and sustainability requirements
- Workspace and environment requirements
- Expansion forecast
- Laboratory requirements
- Specialised equipment details.

6.5.2 Managing Value

The process of value management was important in ensuring that all project stakeholders (users, steering group, NWDA representatives) were aware of and contributed to the assessment of design proposals.

At the briefing stage, the value management process consisted of a lengthy exercise involving visits to several existing buildings of a similar type and then assessing each of these in terms of a set of agreed criteria. The same criteria were subsequently adopted for value management at the next stage of the design process, namely the concept design stage, in order to assess the various design proposals that were under development. Worksheets such as the one shown in **figure 6.32** were filled out by each stakeholder. The quantifiable views of all stakeholders were then combined into an overall spreadsheet that associated agreed weightings with each criterion. This in turn was used as a basis for the further development of the selected proposal.

InfoLab21			Value Management Workshop						
Name									
	Objective 1	Objective 2	Objective 3	Objective 4	Objective 5	Objective 6	Objective 7	Objective 8	Objective 9
	Best Research Environment	Capital cost	Integration of 3 depts.	Showpiece Building	Facilitate Expansion	Infrastructure and Communication	Earliest completion date	Best incubator facilities	Links to main campus
Option A									
Option B									
Option C									
Option D									

Figure 6.32: Value management worksheet.

139

Feasibility   Tender   Briefing   **Concept**   Scheme

Stage A   Stage B   Stage C   Stage D

6.6 Concept Design

6.6.1 Early Concept Design

At the concept design stage, alternative design proposals were still very much under analysis and review before a final concept was taken to the next stage. The process of evaluation of alternatives led to the establishment of an agreed proposal. A concept design proposal such as the one shown in **figure 6.33** indicates the general arrangement of a particular scheme and its likely appearance. Additional information would indicate areas and broad budget costs.

Figure 6.33: Physical model of one of the design options prior to the Stage C report.

The stage C report for InfoLab 21 recorded the development of the project up to the completion of RIBA Stage C. It identified the strategies for architectural, structural and environmental design, and was presented for client signoff prior to commencement of RIBA Stage D design. The brief was developed during C Stage through dialogue and consultation with the user groups and Steering Committee, under the overall control of the Project Executive. This was circulated as a separate document. Value Management workshops established a clear and coherent brief as a robust basis for the development of the design. Inevitably, this structuring process filtered out some user requests, but this in turn ensured that the principal objectives of the InfoLab 21 project were met.

Feasibility — Stage A → Tender → Briefing — Stage B → **Concept** — **Stage C** → Scheme — Stage D

6.6.2 Testing Ideas

Several concept design proposals were analysed and tested alongside further development of the brief. Parts of this process reverted back to hand-drawn presentations such as those shown in **figures 6.34–6.36. Figures 6.37–6.39** were produced on a conventional drawing board.

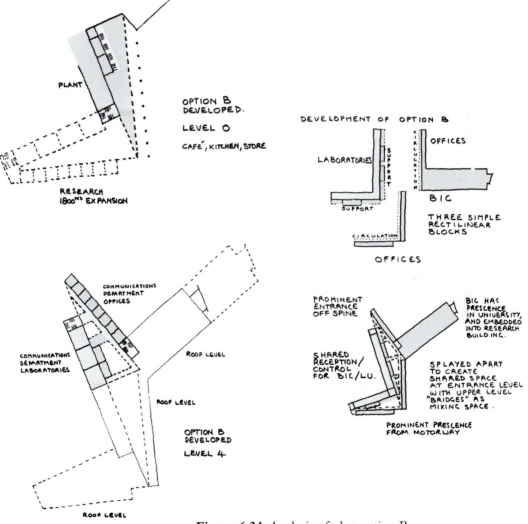

Figure 6.34: Analysis of plan option B.

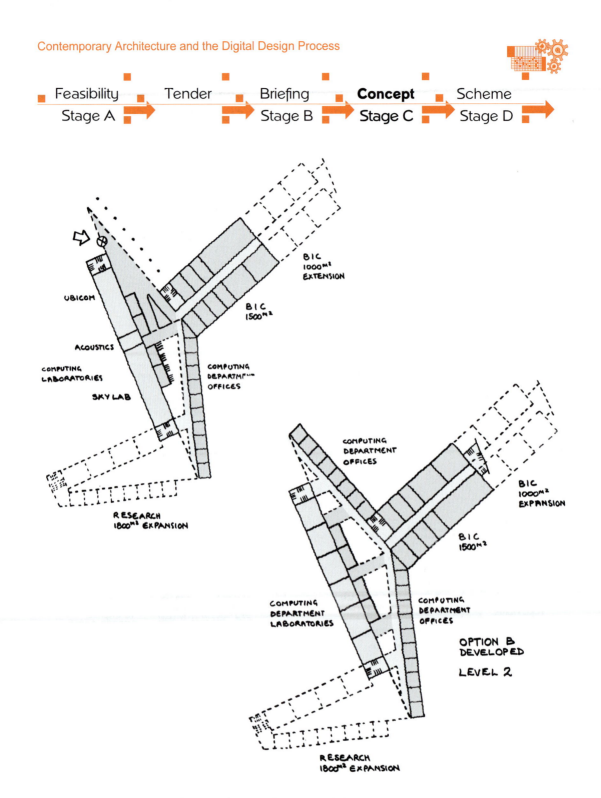

Figure 6.35: Development of design option B.

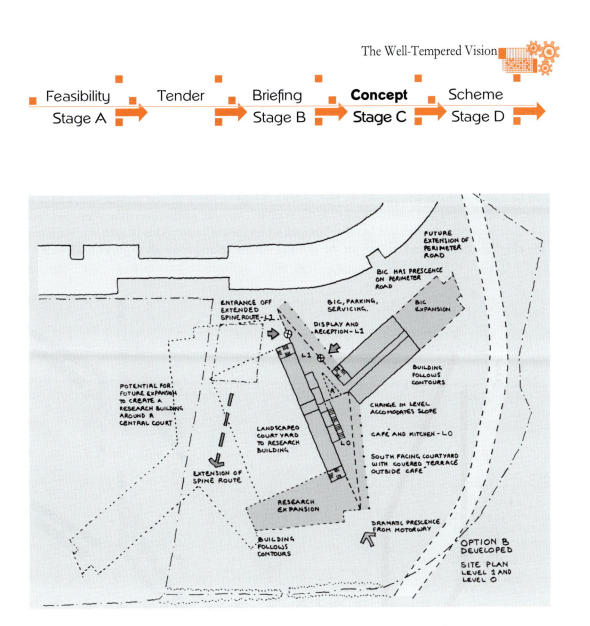

Figure 6.36: Development of design option B with site analysis.

Feasibility   Tender   Briefing   **Concept**   Scheme

Stage A   Stage B   **Stage C**   Stage D

6.6.3   Developing the Brief

The brief was further refined at the concept design stage in order that the ambitions of the project could be met. Emphasis was placed on high quality design within a limited programme, and at a fixed cost. Minimising and controlling risk in the form of exposure to cost overruns, time overruns and loss of quality in the finished building became an important factor. This in turn was reflected in the clear functionality and linearity of the site and building plan proposals (**figures 6.37–6.38**).

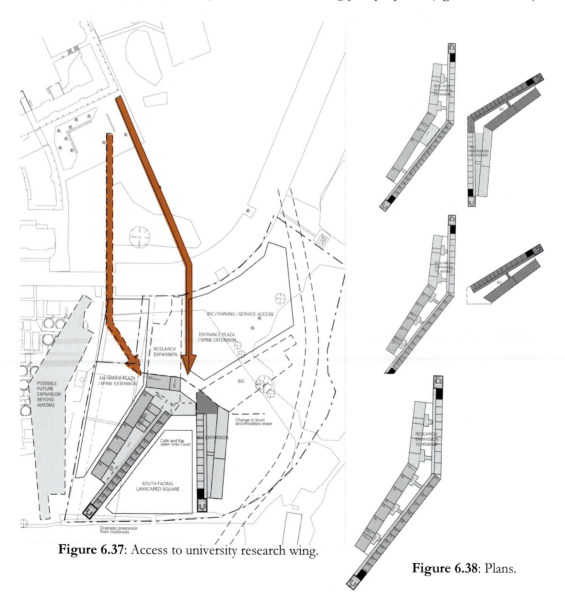

Figure 6.37: Access to university research wing.

Figure 6.38: Plans.

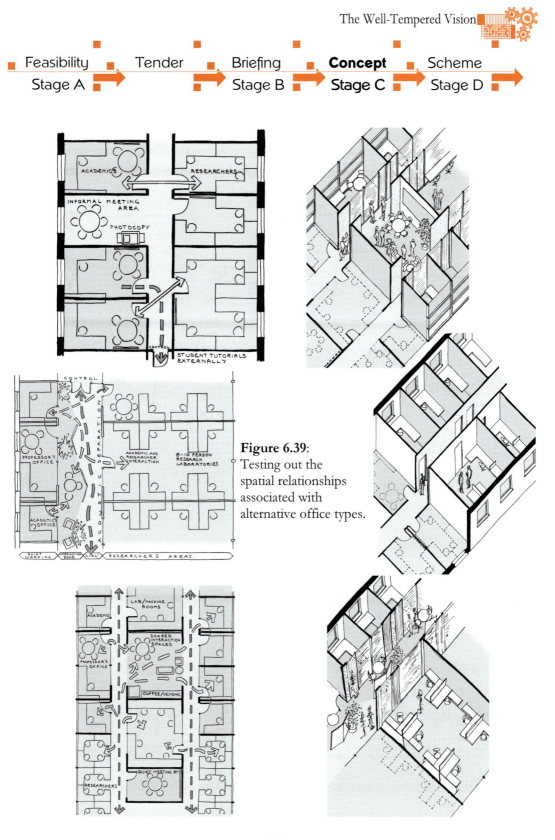

Figure 6.39: Testing out the spatial relationships associated with alternative office types.

Feasibility — Tender — Briefing — **Concept** — Scheme

Stage A — Stage B — **Stage C** — Stage D

6.6.4 Environmental Analysis

Even at early concept design stage, the architects tested out environmental and orientation considerations with the goal of developing proposals that would be environmentally responsible.

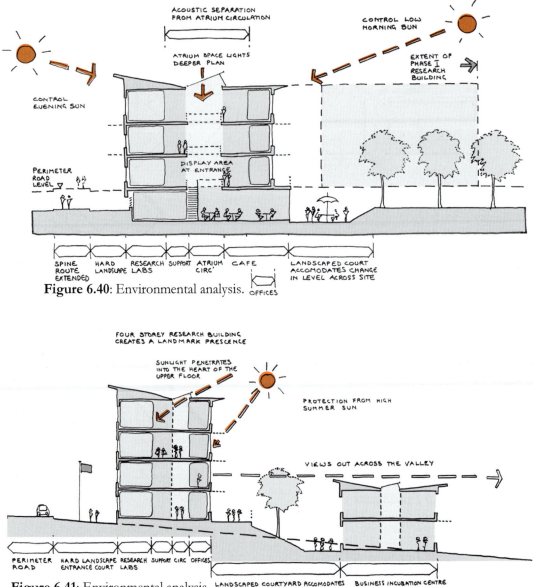

Figure 6.40: Environmental analysis.

Figure 6.41: Environmental analysis.

■ Feasibility ■	Tender	■ Briefing	■ **Concept**	■ Scheme
Stage A ➤		Stage B ➤	Stage C ➤	Stage D ➤

FaulknerBrowns' commitment to environmentally sustainable design led them to become one of the first UK architectural practices to register as ISO 14001 compliant with BSI. As part of developing the office-wide business systems and processes that form the basis of ISO 14001 registration, considerable research was invested in understanding how to improve the environmental credentials of buildings. A large number of different systems offering environmental design benefits were tested and reviewed: BRE's BREEAM and Envest (together with MOD and NHS bespoke variants), CABE's Design Quality Indicators, Arup's SPEAR assessments, IES virtual Environments, Revit, and Bentley systems BIM, to list a few.

These systems split into two categories: spreadsheet-based scoring and costing processes allowing benchmarked assessment of environmental impact and energy performance, such as BREEAM, Spear and DQI; and virtual building and environment modelling software such as IES, Revit, and Bentley systems BIM. The design team's view was that while virtual building modelling software gives designers freedom to arrive at, visualise and quantify sustainable solutions, they are of limited use on many projects due to the investment of time both in developing the skills to use the packages well, and in developing the building models to the level of detail required to give meaningful results. Consequently, these tools only tend to be used on projects where sustainability is very high on the agenda, or where other factors lead to the development of more innovative solutions to particular environmental problems. For most projects, spreadsheet-based systems with good national benchmarking databases offer a more workable solution to delivering improved environmental performance. These systems are more able to address less tangible design issues such as amenity, transport, health and well-being, building management and ecology, whilst offering hard targets in areas such as energy in use, water usage and embodied energy.

Occasionally, at the level of the final score for a building, the results can appear counterintuitive with apparently more sustainable building designs scoring lower than apparently less sustainable building designs. Often, this is because some of the systems consider aspects of a building's location, such as site contamination or the availability of public transport, outside the designer's control. Nonetheless, the picture given is a more realistic assessment of the relative environmental impact of the building, and if the designer cannot achieve good environmental performance within budgetary constraints, this is some incentive towards greater consideration of sustainability aspects of site selection at early planning stages.

Another major advantage of the spreadsheet-based environmental accounting packages is that their backing by independent institutions such as the Building Research Establishment (BRE) helps them to provide objective judgments as to the relative environmental impacts of the different aspects of a design that underlies the scoring and benchmarking. This is a hugely difficult task requiring a degree of structure, rigor, consensus and peer review way beyond the resources of any single consultant or design practice, and is essential if any objective comparison is to be made of the relative merits of projects with diverse sites, functions and aspirations. These considerations led to FaulknerBrowns developing a slight variation of the BREEAM checklist, modified to take account of the public amenity benefits of projects, in line with the recommendations of CABE. As part of the broader systems ensuring compliance with ISO 14001, this checklist forms a central part of procedures for ensuring that the designs achieve environmentally sustainable credentials.

6.6.5   CAD-Generated Massing Model Studies

The following four images illustrate the use of CAD sketch modelling techniques when analysing the consequences of alternative forms that the proposed new buildings could take. These models were presented to a meeting of the steering group for assessment. At this stage option B had the strongest similarities to the final design scheme.

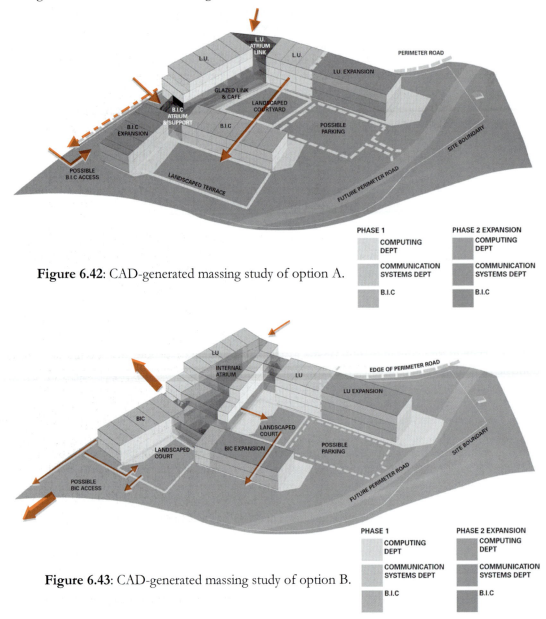

Figure 6.42: CAD-generated massing study of option A.

Figure 6.43: CAD-generated massing study of option B.

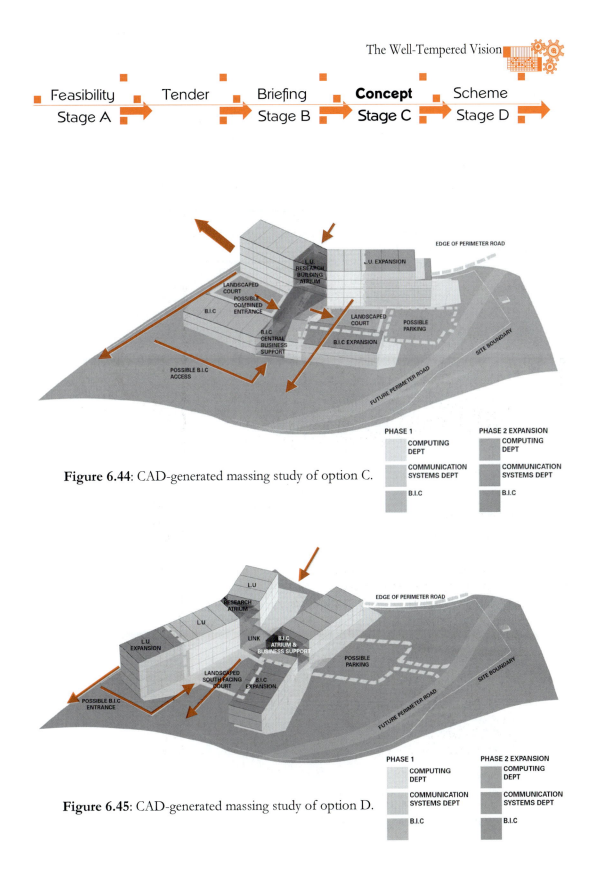

Feasibility — Tender — Briefing — **Concept** — Scheme

Stage A — Stage B — **Stage C** — Stage D

Figure 6.44: CAD-generated massing study of option C.

Figure 6.45: CAD-generated massing study of option D.

Feasibility   Tender   Briefing   **Concept**   Scheme
Stage A   Stage B   **Stage C**   Stage D

6.6.6   CAD Presentation Models

The form of the final design scheme divided cleanly into three sections. An inverted L-shaped four-storey building to the east was to accommodate academics and research groups from the Computing and Communications departments. To the west, a rectangular three-storey building was to contain the Knowledge Business Centre with its Incubation, R&D and support facilities. The two buildings are linked by a three-level glazed bridge containing the entrance and shared facilities.

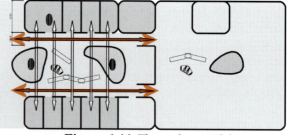

Figure 6.46: Floor plan model.

Figures 6.46–6.48 illustrate some of the digital models produced to indicate more detailed building form as required for Stage C.

Figure 6.47: Curvilinear massing model.

Figure 6.48: Linearised building model.

Feasibility ▪ Tender ▪ Briefing ▪ **Concept** ▪ Scheme
Stage A ▪ Stage B ▪ Stage C ▪ Stage D

6.6.7 Strategic Massing

At Stage C, detailed physical massing models were created with the client in mind. Their tactile quality gave an added dimension to meetings of the steering group, and emphasised the move towards a physical realisation of the initial design ideas.

The models showed how the building was divided into three basic sections in response to the brief. They indicated the pedestrian spine route beneath the link building which is approached by a bridge to the main entrance. Visitors could be directed either left to the university research wing or right into the Knowledge Business Centre.

The physical models in **figure 6.49** were produced as part of the Stage C submission. It can be seen that some of the earlier explorations of curvilinearity have now been resolved into a rational linear form as a consequence of the value management process.

The concept design that was taken forward into Stage D was still insufficiently detailed for a detailed planning application, but allowed the client to agree to and to sign off the general approach.

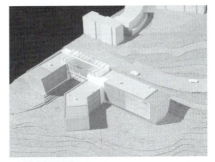

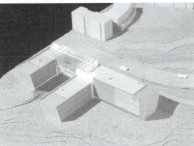

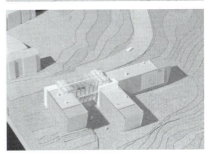

Figure 6.49: Physical models.

Feasibility — Tender — Briefing — Concept — **Scheme**

Stage A — Stage B — Stage C — **Stage D**

6.7   Scheme Design

6.7.1   Structural Analysis

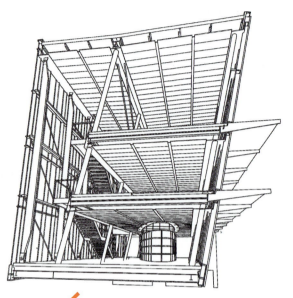

The primary focus of structural analysis at the scheme design stage was to investigate building engineering issues. The architects produced sectional cuts through CAD models such as the one shown in **figure 6.50**.

Details requiring further structural investigation could then be identified and highlighted (**figure 6.51**), and passed on to the structural engineers for more detailed evaluation. The structural engineers developed their own detailed structural digital models to analyse the structural frame and floor technologies.

Figure 6.50:
3-D section cut through CAD model.

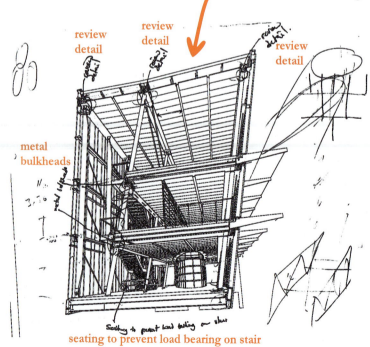

review detail

review detail

review detail

metal bulkheads

seating to prevent load bearing on stair

Figure 6.51: Identification of structural issues for further analysis.

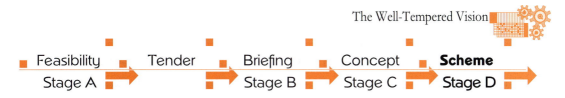

6.7.1 Environmental Services

Issues emerged in considering the relationships between the structural system proposed by the structural engineers (**figure 6.52**), and the provision of environmental services such as ventilation and electrical systems (**figure 6.53**).

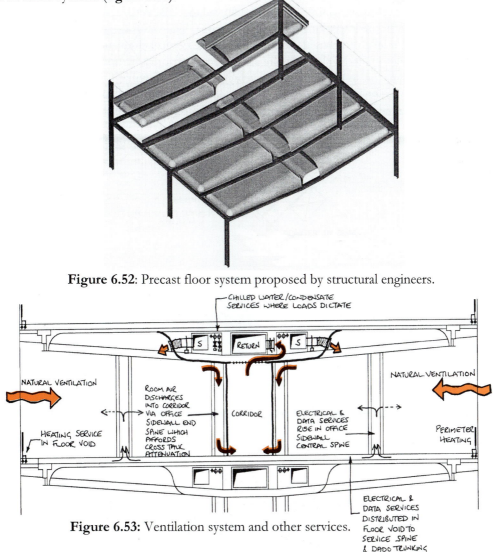

Figure 6.52: Precast floor system proposed by structural engineers.

Figure 6.53: Ventilation system and other services.

The design of the building services also took into account the use of energy efficient systems, selection of appropriate green materials, sustainability, water conservation measures and non-ozone depleting substances. Relevant considerations for energy use included plant efficiency, suitability of plant, plant maintenance requirements, heat reclaim and the efficiency of plant control systems.

Feasibility — Tender — Briefing — Concept — **Scheme**
Stage A —→ — Stage B —→ Stage C —→ **Stage D** —→

6.7.3 External Expression

Elevational treatment and the selection of external materials would produce the flagship building that the university and NWDA were looking for. The strategic massing of two heavy blocks linked by a transparent bridge was clearly expressed, both in the physical and in the digital models. The link bridge was to be encased in double glazed curtain walling. The vertical structure was expressed as a series of ribs, whilst the horizontal joints were silicone. The south facade sloped inwards with balconies on the upper levels to provide solar shading. The vertical circulation shafts to either side of the glass bridge link were to be clad in white architectural masonry. This was to have a split faced surface with a sparkling finish of white dolomite aggregate (a reference to the Ruskin Library at Lancaster University designed by Richard MacCormac shown in **figure 6.54**). This would be more durable and better suited to a high quality building than the render used elsewhere on campus.

Figure 6.54: The Ruskin Library at Lancaster University designed by Richard MacCormac.

The north gable elevation of the Knowledge Business Centre was to be similarly clad in white architectural masonry, but would incorporate larger feature windows, dressed with smooth textured masonry surrounds and quoins. Brightly coloured large-scale building signage was to be designed to accent this entrance facade. Prepatinated copper was selected to clad the university research wing and the Knowledge Business Centre. The copper cladding was to be welted to give a vertical rhythm, which would continue in the mullions of the windows.

Feasibility   Tender   Briefing   Concept   **Scheme**

Stage A   Stage B   Stage C   Stage D

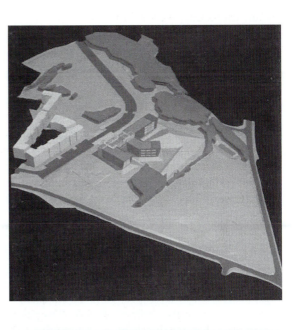

At this stage, agreement was reached on the overall layout of the scheme, as well as on engineering techniques and materials. The proposal outlining the essential form and function of the scheme was now submitted for a planning permission.

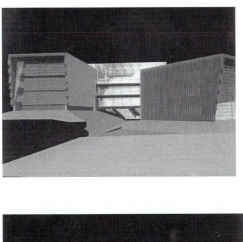

Figure 6.55: Rendered digital models of agreed scheme design.

In this case study, the effort involved in developing conceptual ideas into design proposals was counterbalanced by the project organisation and its emphasis on the management of value. The effect on subsequent design development was to channel the generative and directive force of the initial ideas into focusing on function and costs. The design-driven generation of an effective organisational solution was achieved through a process of selection and development of conceptual ideas that required simultaneous representation and development of alternative proposals.

The process of proposing and refining alternative solutions was supported digitally as well as more conventionally throughout the design stages. In the early sketches, such as those produced for the analysis of office layouts, for example, dimensional accuracy was absent – approximate dimensions were sufficient, with intuitive understandings of scale and spatial relationships being more important. Physical models display similar characteristics, often having incomplete descriptions of elements. Both sketches and physical models are effective tools for an appreciation of spatial relationships. Dimensionless and partial models still pose problems for digital representations, and CAD systems typically require commitment to dimensions from the outset of modelling.

The immediacy of 2-D sketches and drawings was combined with the benefits of analytical 3-D digital models. The latter proved to be especially useful for understanding movement and circulation, as well as for the analysis of views. Diagrammatic 2-D sketches had more importance for the design team than for the client, for whom the 2-D analyses often needed to be converted into 3-D visualisations, both physical and digital. Exploded 3-D CAD-generated isometric views, for example, made some of key design issues and relationships explicit.

Moving into Stage C, the dialogue between design concepts and organisational criteria achieved a level of schematic resolution, albeit with a degree of curvilinearity in the external expression of the form. An important contributory factor at this stage was the analysis and evaluation that was supported through digital massing model studies. A further level of resolution was still needed before progressing to a more linearised detail design of the functional final form.

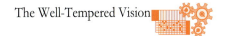

6.8   Summary

The key factors of the case study presented in this chapter can be summarised as follows:

*   The application of digital techniques was set within the framework of the design stages determined by external regulations and the guidelines set by professional bodies such as the RIBA.

*   Digital techniques of representation and visualisation were clearly being applied in early design stages in order to explore and investigate key design issues such as circulation, massing, site relationships, analysis of views, etc.

*   Visualisation techniques were used by the design team not only to develop the scheme, but also to inform and involve the client in the design process. These were particularly important for the analysis of circulation and of views.

*   Consistency of presentations for the client. Once digital techniques had been used in the early stages for something as simple as basic sketch layouts, there was more coherence with the more detailed CAD-generated models later on in the scheme.

*   An enormous amount of design effort was used at the early stage of tendering for the architectural design work without any guarantee of actually being given the contract by the client body.

*   The digital techniques applied include a range of techniques from modelling and visualisation through to costing and testing for compliance with environmental standards. As far as the latter analytical criteria were concerned, systematic assessment was carried out according to established benchmarks. Given an established heat loss level and data on the fabric of a proposal, it was a straightforward task to systematically calculate whether or not the fabric and the proposal achieve the required minimum level.

*   The importance of analysis. Different parts of the scheme were categorised in simplified detail rather than looking at a whole complete building. Analyses of form revealed the design concepts in particular categories, such as structure, for example. Basic analysis using conceptual diagrams and simplified 3-D models was an essential component of the design development of this project.

Chapter 7: Visionary Integration: This Blessed Plot

In the early hours of a May morning in 1994, the best part of a bottle of whisky to the good, we had a concept that, though rough around the edges, excited us. There would be five glass houses, or giant poly-tunnels, linked together for a walkthrough experience. Four would focus on a particular climate region of the world and the fifth would contain a composite of the world's productive domesticated plants. As I recall we suggested rainforest, subtropical rainforest, Mediterranean, and a combination of savannah and desert. At the time we were focused on celebrating the floristic riches and the productivity of the planet, with a nod towards conservation - in essence a large-scale theme park fit for a garden festival that intended to make a case for permanence. (Smit, 2001, p. 33)

The Eden Project emerged out of Tim Smit's visionary idea, which in turn inspired botanists, engineers, architects, artists, as well as public and private financiers. The inspirational effect of the vision undoubtedly smoothed the progression from conception through to design and construction. Eden is now seen as a considerable commercial investment supported by the Millennium Commission, English Partnerships, the European Regional Development Fund, local authorities and other organisations. The use of digital techniques was evident in many aspects of this project including the design, fabrication, structural analysis and environmental controls. Of particular interest is the form itself which has mathematical and structural significance. According to Robbin:

A few dozen engineers and architects share the view, currently considered revolutionary, that geometry drives architecture forward. To be ignorant of complex polyhedra, four-dimensional geometry, fractals, three-manifold topology, and the like – to have the cube and the octatruss the only geometric options – is to restrict structures with a severity that not even nature demands, its stern doctrine of optimization notwithstanding. (Robbin, 1996, p. 81).

In addition to the digital representation of the complex geometric form together with its structural analysis, a range of digital techniques were also applied to the environmental analysis of the functionalities associated with keeping and exhibiting plant life under controlled conditions. The idea for the scheme was initiated by Tim Smit together with Jonathan Ball, who then approached Nicholas Grimshaw and Partners architects and Anthony Hunt Associates structural engineers. The design team also included Land Use Consultants as landscape architects and Ove Arup and Partners provided mechanical and electrical design. Smit's long search for a suitable site culminated with the finding of the Bodelva pit, located about 5km east of St Austell in Cornwall. The design generator for the structure, climate and water control systems was the need to create the correct environment for plant growth using clear span, lightweight transparent structures and minimum water and energy resources. Four key ideas were developed:

- wrapping enclosures around a south-facing rock face to maximise heat storage
- maximising light transmission for plant growth whilst minimising heat loss through the fabric
- controlling indoor climates for plants, matching temperature and humidity with available light
- using, recycling, and treating the rainwater and groundwater, minimising use of new water.

Support for the realisation of these ideas through digital technologies focused on four key areas: digital representation and analysis of the site, computer modelling of the complex form, and structural and environmental analysis techniques.

7.1   Key Issues in the Digital Representation of the Eden Project

The Site

The site in was a china clay pit nearing the end of its working life – the Bodelva pit close to St Austell in Cornwall (**figure 7.1**). The pit covered an area of about 22 hectares and varied in depth from 30 to 70 metres. (Jones, 2000, p. 90)

The visually dramatic landscape presented a substantial challenge to the engineering team. The brief was to preserve as much of the wild, rustic appearance as possible, while creating a safe stable environment for visitors. Digital ground models, or *digital terrain models* (DTMs) as they are sometimes referred to, based on aerial survey data, were used to sculpt the pit. The DTMs were needed in order to simulate in detail the cut and fill operations that were to take place on site. As part of the environmental statement for the project, an undertaking was given that the exporting or importing of fill material would be kept to a minimum.

The Form

The design solution progressed from one in terms of a series of arches to a more structurally efficient one based upon the idea of a geodesic sphere. The undulating ground profile meant that the spheres, known as *biomes*, became more organic and less geometric. Intuitive ideas for the form were influenced by what is sometimes referred to as *biomimetics* – looking at how nature resolves similar problems. The soap bubble studies of Frei Otto referred to in **chapter 4** were a significant factor in this process. According to Barry Johnson, McAlpine's project manager:

> *It's a natural fact that where bubbles intersect they do so vertically in a plane, which means that you can put an arch between the two bubbles and it will automatically be vertical and straight.* (Jackson, 2000, p. 36)

Figure 7.1: The pit before construction.

Figure 7.2: Excavating the site.

Figure 7.3: Physical model of form.

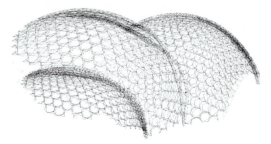

Figure 7.4: Digital model of form.

Structural Analysis

In addition to modelling the form together with its structural detail, computational structural analysis was used to assess intuitive solutions to the problems of *intersecting biomes* of different sizes and frequencies (number and size of panels). The structural resolution of horizontal thrusts needed particular attention, and additional arch elements needed to be modelled where biomes intersected each other.

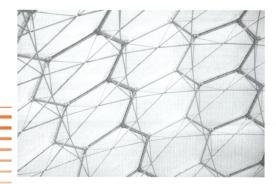

Figure 7.5: Biome structure.

Foundation lines also needed to be identified where the biomes intersected the ground (**figure 7.6**). Since geodesic structures consist of discrete elements, elements can be added or removed depending upon the location of the foundation lines. Hexagonal elements with pentagonal intersections were chosen primarily to maximise the amount of light that could be received into the biome structures.

Figure 7.6: Foundation structure.

Environmental Control

The maintenance of proper temperature and humidity was crucial to this project in which plants were the focus of the whole scheme. Passive heating and natural ventilation were embodied within the design as much as possible, but to accurately determine when additional heating and cooling would be needed within individual biomes, dynamic thermal computer analysis was carried out. Computational fluid analysis techniques produced 3-D graphs showing the speed and direction of the air movement, and the temperature distributions across the internal spaces. The results of this analysis was used to position additional heat input sources, which could then be adjusted for direction and speed to give an even distribution of temperature.

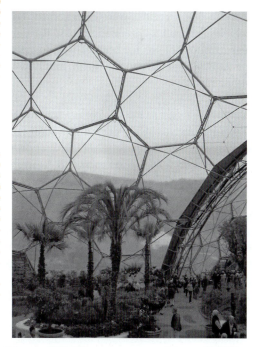

Figure 7.7: Warm temperate biome (WTB).

7.2   The Site

The Bodelva pit was within the eastern end of the St Austell granite in a zone of biotite granite which had become variably kaolinised (Jones, 2000, p. 90). Kaolinisation is the process of chemical alteration of the feldspar component of the granite rock mass. The other components, quartz, tourmaline and mica, remained unaltered. The feldspars were leached of potassium and broken down to a plastic clay known as kaolin or china clay. The rock mass encountered on site was classified into four different grades. Grade 1 – fresh, unaltered rock through to Grade IV – a highly kaolinised plastic material that can be moulded by hand. An option to purchase the pit was negotiated with the owners at an early stage. However, whilst the scheme design progressed and funding was secured, the owners continued to work the pit *winning* china clay from any areas of their choosing.

A digital ground model, based on aerial survey data, was used to sculpt the pit. (loc. sit.). The digital ground models were created using the Microstation system combined with the use of specialised road modelling software (In-roads). The ground models allowed a detailed evaluation of cut and fill operations to take place (**figure 7.8–7.11**). As part of the environmental statement for the project, an undertaking was given that the exporting or importing of fill material would be kept to a minimum. The landscape architect developed his scheme and provided outlines to be input into the model. After several iterations, a balance was obtained. Approximately 800000 cubic metres of material were moved to create the final profiles. No material was exported. The only materials imported were aggregates for concrete, hardstandings and drainage together with organic matter to construct the topsoil and planting medium.

Sculpting of the site included the creation of terraces around the pit rim for parking areas and access roads. Facilities were designed for coaches, visitor land train, taxis and service/emergency vehicles, as well as disabled access. Road modelling software was extensively used to produce reasonable gradients for both vehicle and pedestrian routes. A new access road was created linking the site with the A30 to the north, and new entrances were created for local traffic off the existing public highway.

Water management was also important to the long-term stability of the site. The base of the pit is around 30 metres below the natural water table in the area. During quarrying operations, this water was an essential part of the clay extraction process. High pressure hoses were directed onto the quarry faces releasing the kaolin and creating a suspension, which was pumped onto settling tanks remote from the site. Since the Eden project does not extract water in this way, a new storage and pumped drainage system was constructed. Stormwater runoff was controlled by swales and ditches interlaced with car park terraces and landscaped areas. These store water in the short term and augment the retention provided by a series of storage lakes. The stormwater system was designed to contain a 1:100 year storm event. The final pumped outlet into the Bodelva brook to the south of the site was strictly regulated to prevent flooding downstream in compliance with Environment Agency flow restrictions.

Figure 7.8: DTM model of pit site.

The digital ground model or DTM (Digital Terrain Model) allowed the detailed evaluation of cut and fill operations to take place.

Cut and fill outlines were input into the digital model. Through several iterations, material was removed and the site re-modelled to create the desired profile.

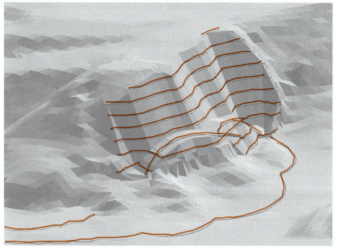

Figure 7.9: DTM lines of cut.

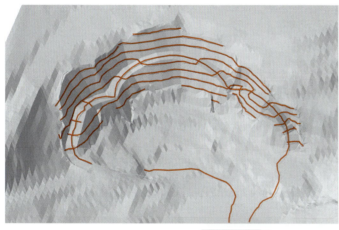

Figure 7.10: DTM lines of cut.

Sculpting of the site included the creation of terraces around the pit rim for parking and access roads. Digital terrain modelling operations generated reasonable gradients for both vehicle and pedestrian routes.

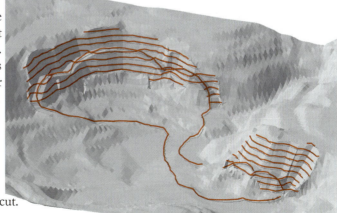

Figure 7.11: DTM lines of cut.

7.3   Site Work

The first operation on site was the construction of structural embankments to support the biomes. To create the new ground profile, up to 15 metres of fill was placed in the base of the pit, in an operation described by the client as *reversing the mining process*. The principal reason for this was to achieve acceptable gradients on paths and access routes down into the pit and to provide level areas for planting within the landscape. At the same time, car parks and visitor access roads were created on the excavated terraces formed around the pit rim. The lower foundations of both biomes were to rest on top of the fill. Without special measures, the settlement under load would have been far in excess of the limits set for the envelope design. There were two separate effects that needed to be taken into consideration:

- undisturbed ground below the fill had experienced pressure relief from the removal of the overburden during mining, allowing it to absorb ground water.
- although compacted in layers, the fill would hold water and would take many months to consolidate without enhanced porewater pressure reduction.

A site laboratory was established to identify and monitor the quality of fill material available on site. The two types were:

- acceptable fill for the embankments and roads
- general fill for other areas of soft landscaping.

A grid pattern of vertical band drains was installed in the virgin ground beneath the structural embankments to a depth of 15 metres before any fill was placed. The horizontal spacing was calculated to achieve an acceptable level of consolidation within 60 days. As the fill was placed and the ground surcharged, the increased porewater pressure forced ground-water up the band drains, into drainage layers incorporated into the base of the fill, before being pumped off site.

Horizontal drainage layers were also laid in the fill material making up the structural embankments to help reduce pore pressure in the embankment itself. A beneficial effect of this groundwater control system was that it created an excellent source of irrigation and grey water. The groundwater is collected in a network of deep drains that are up to 20 metres below finished level before being pumped up into the stormwater system.

Although water conservation was an important issue on the project, available natural resources were more than adequate to provide for all of the project's horticultural requirements, including irrigation and humidification, with emough to service part of the fire hydrant system and for grey water. Water extracted from groundwater and spring sources was collected and stored in a large underground tank before being pumped into the water distribution system via, filtration and ultraviolet disinfection plant. Excess groundwater overflows into the site surface water disposal system.

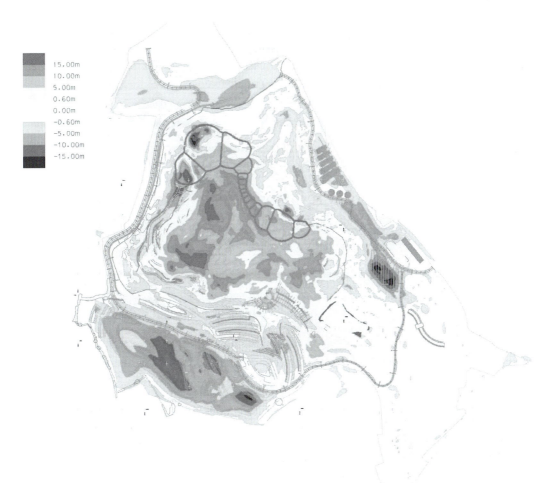

Figure 7.12: Comparison of land use contours with an existing ground survey.

Programme constraints dictated a move away from full-scale laboratory soils tests. These were replaced by continuous in-situ nuclear density gauge testing at each stage of the filling process. Horizontal inclinometers and pneumatic piezometers were installed to monitor settlement and groundwater pressures and to determine when it was safe to proceed with foundation construction. As a final check, dynamic probing was carried out to confirm the effectiveness of compaction. A system of ground anchors was installed, through the foundation strip into the fill, so that the foundation could be preloaded before erection of the envelope commenced. This removed any remaining short-term settlements within the embankments. Consolidation of the fill was estimated to take up to 30 days, but after a three months of wet weather when filling was suspended, the consolidation of both the naturally occurring material and the fill took less time than expected, allowing construction to proceed. Once the embankments had been formed and the consolidation process had commenced, work began on the slope stabilisation and re-profiling of the pit walls.

7.4   Geodesic Geometry

A series of intersecting domes of varying diameter were developed. Once the size and relative position of the domes could be determined, the shape of the pit became a secondary consideration. The structural form of the domes could then be confirmed, and the intersection line between superstructure and ground determined the position of foundations and extent of cladding. This enabled the team to proceed with design development of the biome envelope even before the final survey of the pit was complete.

A principal criterion in the clients' brief was to maintain the transparency of the envelope at a maximum. To achieve this, the cladding material had to provide high levels of light transmission, and structural elements had to be kept to minimum size and number. After a detailed study of various geometrical arrangements for a spherical surface, a geodesic arrangement was selected. By adopting hexagons with pentagonal intersections, an even distribution of structural members could be achieved. Varying the frequency of subdivisions in the spherical elements (**figure 7.13**) gave rise to optimum cladding panel sizes and light levels.

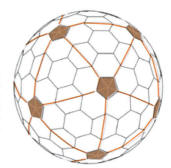

Once the type of cladding and intensity of environmental loads had been established, the design team focused on deriving the optimum geometrical arrangement for the spherical structures. The objective was to use the largest cushion possible in order to maximise light transmission and to minimise cost: large cushions mean fewer connections in the steelwork and reduced length of aluminium framing. Mero, the subcontractor undertook the detailed design of the cladding system. Cushion sizes with side lengths up to 5.5m were possible, but would need cable net reinforcement above and below the cushions. To avoid this added expense, the geometry of the domes was scaled to suit their size – smaller domes incorporating smaller cushions. Only the largest cushions, on dome B in the HTB and dome G in the WTB, required reinforcement.

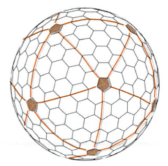

Figures 7.14 and **7.15** opposite give the final geometrical arrangements for the biomes. The lines of intersection between domes posed a particular problem. It was not possible to align the nodes on either side and this was exacerbated as the geometry of each dome had been scaled to give suitable cushion dimensions. Tubular lattice arches were introduced to accommodated this and pick up individual node points. These were fabricated in segments from curved tubes and site welded together.

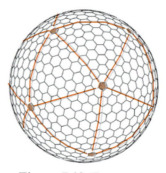

Figure 7.13: Frequency subdivision.

Each sphere was orientated such that one of the twelve principal nodes was at the apex. The geometry determined that a pentagon was formed at this location. The spherical surface was then set out from this point (**figure 7.14**). Repetition within the structure was also important.

The shaded hexagonal areas within **figure 7.15** indicate the hexagons which repeat within each spherical segment.

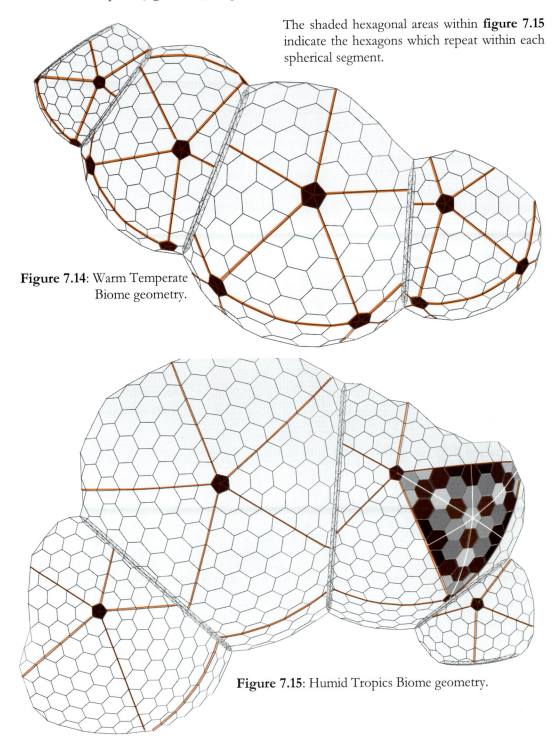

Figure 7.14: Warm Temperate Biome geometry.

Figure 7.15: Humid Tropics Biome geometry.

7.5   Positioning the buildings

The principal buildings were the biomes (**1** and **2** in **figure 7.16**). They were designed to provide two climate zones, one modelled on the Humid Tropics (HTB) and the other a Warm Temperate (WTB) or Mediterranean climate. Each zone required high levels of natural daylight with the Humid Tropics biome being the most critical. In response to solar shading studies carried out by the architects Nicholas Grimshaw & Partners, the HTB was positioned against the north face of the quarry with the WTB curving away to the southeast. In this way, the environmental control system benefited from maximum sunlight and the thermal mass of the rock face. However, this positioning of the buildings led to considerable complexity in the design of the foundations. The HTB is up to 110 metres wide, 55 metres high and 240 metres long. Within its length, it rests on all four designated grades of granite, passing from unaltered rock, across the kaolinised clay materials and back to unaltered rock. At the base of the pit it sits on up to 12 metres of fill material. Slightly smaller in form, the WTB (65m x 35m x 150m) has a similar formation. The visitors centre (**4**) was positioned on the south west face to give views across to the biomes and external landscaping, and sat on a new plateau cut into the side of the pit extended with reclaimed fill material.

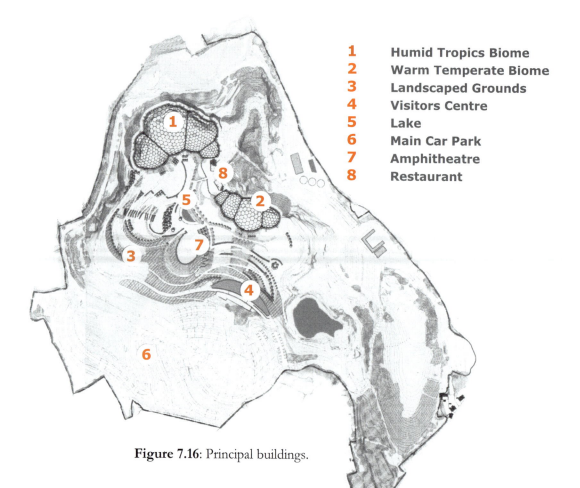

1	**Humid Tropics Biome**
2	**Warm Temperate Biome**
3	**Landscaped Grounds**
4	**Visitors Centre**
5	**Lake**
6	**Main Car Park**
7	**Amphitheatre**
8	**Restaurant**

Figure 7.16: Principal buildings.

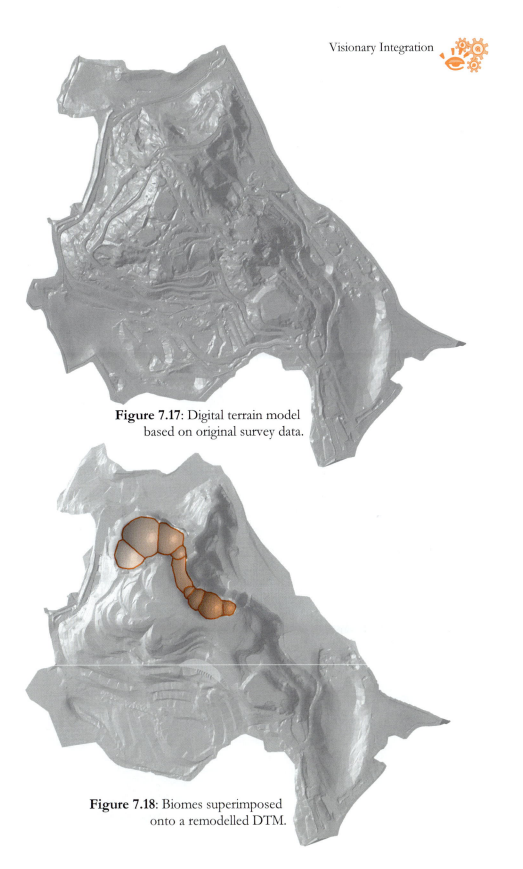

Figure 7.17: Digital terrain model based on original survey data.

Figure 7.18: Biomes superimposed onto a remodelled DTM.

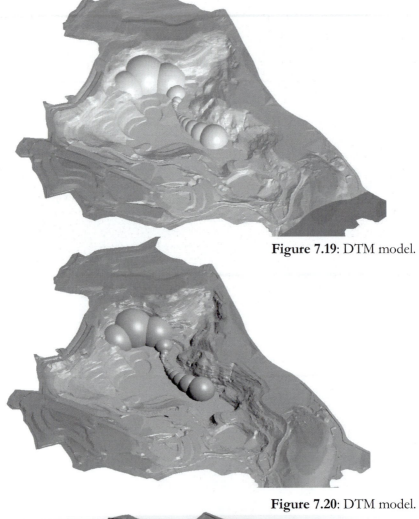

Figure 7.19: DTM model.

Figure 7.20: DTM model.

Figure 7.21: DTM model.

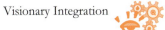

Figure 7.22: Section through DTM model.

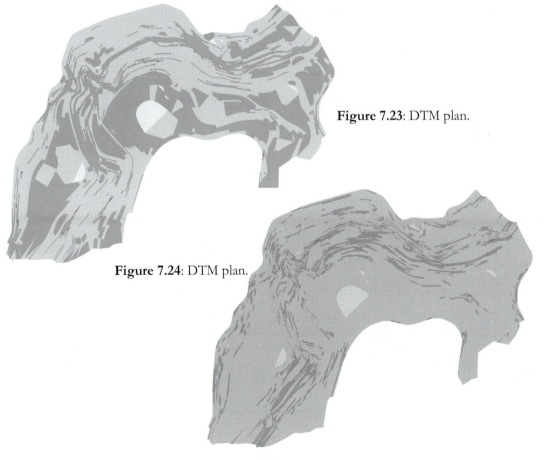

Figure 7.23: DTM plan.

Figure 7.24: DTM plan.

7.6   Structural Form

During early scheme design, it became apparent that the exact profile of the pit would not be known until construction began. Initial schemes for the biomes used curved, arched trusses at regular intervals spanning from the base of the pit onto the cliff face (**figures 7.25** and **7.26**). Each truss had a unique profile and span. For this solution to work, the the pit shape needed to be maintained wherever possible, but even if it was, very little repetition or rationalisation of trusses could be achieved. In this approach, and with the constantly changing topography as mining continued, several redesigns would be necessary before a final geometry could be determined.

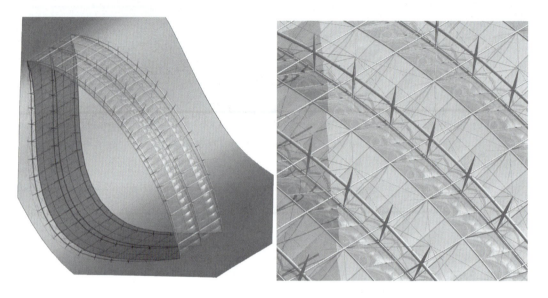

Figure 7.25: Early scheme design.   **Figure 7.26**: Arched truss details.

At this point, the design team proposed a radical change to the basic form of the biomes, and considered the benefits of having an external structure in the form of intersecting domes (Jones, 2000, p. 91). One benefit would be easier access for the application and maintenance of a corrosion protection system. This approach also allowed the possibility of placing the structure *within* the envelope. A twin layer system with sealed skins above and below the structural zone could also provide a *controlled environment*. This solution also offered the possibility of having a fully braced geodesic geometry all in one plane.

After evaluating the practical limitations, a single layer, unbraced, three-dimensional space frame structure with 500mm diameter circular hollow sections was selected. Without triangulated bracing in the spherical plane, hexagonal cladding panels located within structural openings could be used. The envelope was tendered as two packages, steel and cladding. The successful contractor, Mero Gmbh, offered to supply the frame and cladding. Their proposal incorporated a space truss system, developed over many years.

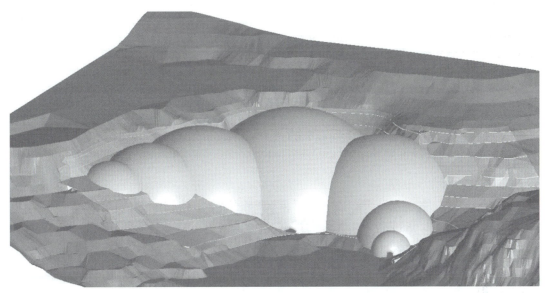

Figure 7.27: Basic form model superimposed over DTM.

After several initial conventional arch-based proposals for the basic form of the Eden biomes were rejected, the geodesic dome solution began to emerge – interconnecting spheres made up of hexagons.

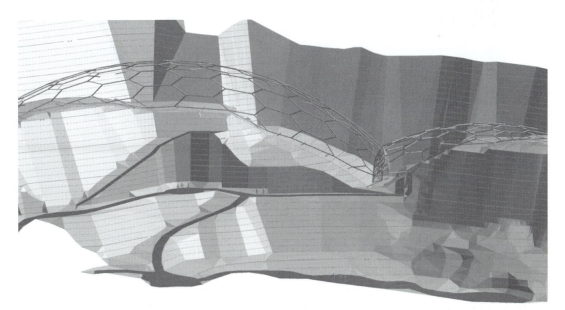

Figure 7.28: Basic structural form superimposed over DTM.

7.7   The *Hex-tri-hex* Structural Form

Grimshaws and Hunts, together with Mero, finalised the design of an efficient two-layer steel space frame structure, which used the geometry given in the tender (hexagonal, with occasional pentagons) for the outer layer, with a combination of hexagons and triangular elements for the semi-braced inner layer. Diagonals connected the node points of the layers together to make the structure rigid. This structure was called the *hex-tri-hex*. The two-layer structural system, the first of its kind on this scale in the world, was referred to as a *hex-tri-hex* arrangement (**figures 7.5**, **7.48** and **7.49**). The series of images in **figures 7.29–7.37** give an indication of both the outer and inner structural elements, as well as their relationship to the connecting trusses and concrete foundations.

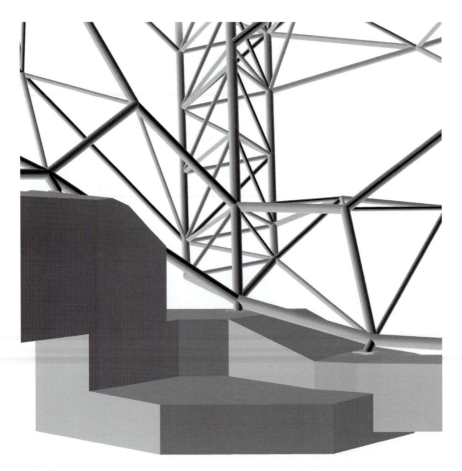

Figure 7.29: CAD model showing concrete base into which structural elements are embedded.

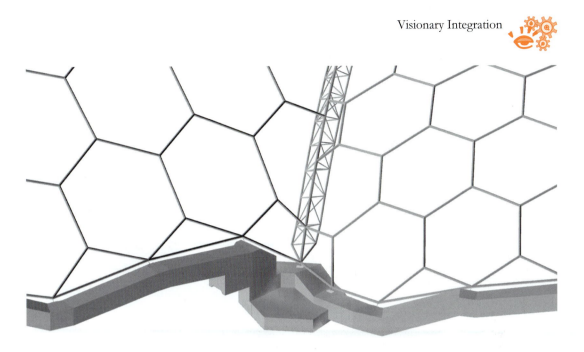

Figure 7.30: Junction detail of Humid Tropics Biome showing outer layer of *hex-tri-hex*.

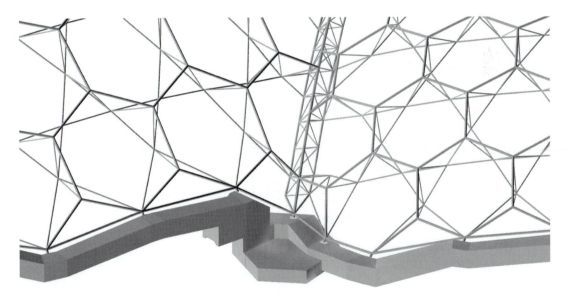

Figure 7.31: Structural detail of Humid Tropics Biome with *hex-tri-hex* system.

In the *hex-tri-hex* structural form, the larger the diameter of the sphere the larger the hexagons and pentagons. The side lengths were fitted together through a series of universal connector ball joints at every node position that allowed for connection in all the different configurations. Side lengths varied from 1m to 5.4m. The largest uninterrupted clear panel was nearly 11m from point to point.

Figure 7.32: Junction detail with truss element.

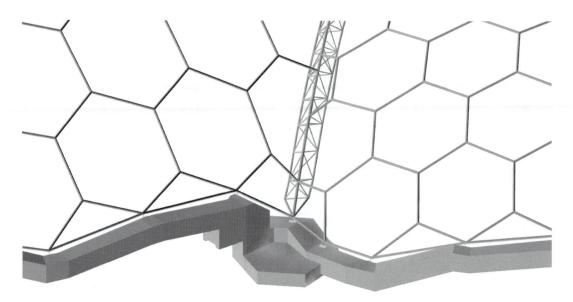

Figure 7.33: Junction detail with outer structural elements.

The inner lighter shell was braced to the main outer frame to give it rigidity using diagonals connecting the node points of both layers. Having two shells connected vertically makes it a curved space frame. This three-dimensional curved space frame acts like a shell, such that wind, snow and other loads are transferred through the shell into the foundations.

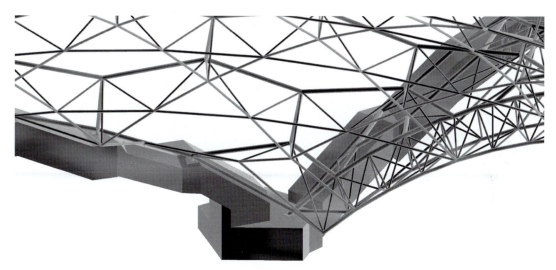

Figure 7.34: Junction detail with truss and outer and inner layers.

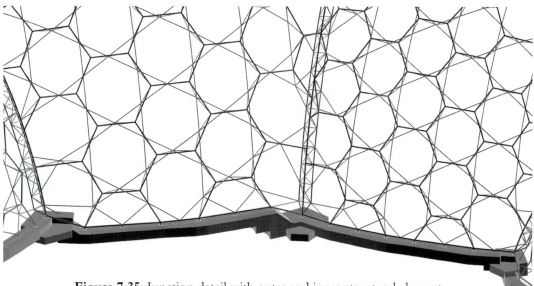

Figure 7.35: Junction detail with outer and inner structural elements.

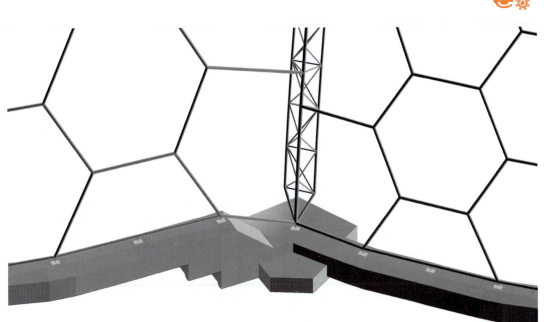

Figure 7.36: Junction detail with outer layer of *hex-tri-hex* system.

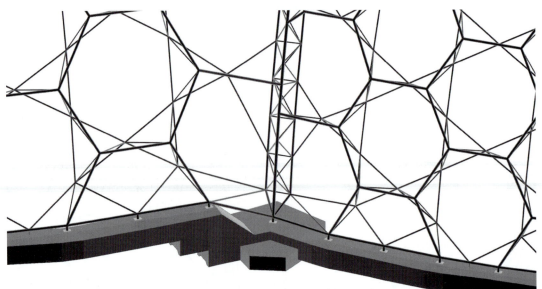

Figure 7.37: Junction detail with both layers of *hex-tri-hex* system.

Around the perimeter of the structure the top and bottom booms of the trusses meet to form true pin-joints to the foundations. This simplifies the forces being transmitted to the foundation strip.

7.8   Structural Analysis

In addition to the succession of digital ground models of the site produced at various stages of its development, a broad range of computational analysis techniques were used by Anthony Hunt Associates for the different types of analysis of the structural form. The design of the biome structures incorporated full *linear elastic analysis* of all environmental loads and combinations of loads. These included wind loads, temperature loads, snow loads, and analysis of the differential settlement of foundations. An important feature was the development of a CAD model specifically for the foundations of the scheme. This model represented the intersection between the structural model of the biomes and the ground model, and required a total of six months' effort for its completion. It is effectively a 3-D concrete *necklace* which follows the perimeter of the buildings and hugs the contours of the site (**figures 7.38–7.39)**. The digital model incorporating the necklace was used as a basis for the generation of all working drawings, as well as the for numerical analysis, such as the computational fluid dynamics (CFD) techniques developed by Arup Associates.

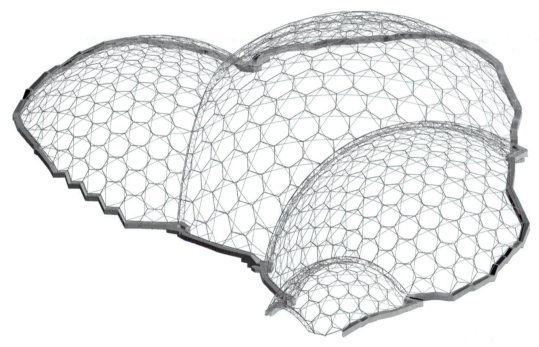

Figure 7.38: Structural CAD model of the HTB with concrete necklace.

The in-situ reinforced concrete strip forming the concrete necklace was generally 2 metres wide by 1.4 and 1.0 metres deep in the HTB and WTB respectively. The 3-D structural analysis model developed to investigate the relationship between the foundations and the rock mass used equivalent spring stiffness to represent the varying soil properties of the four grades of granite. In the HTB, the building passed from Grade I and II granite at the West End, through a band of Grade III and IV and back onto Grade I and II granite at the East End. Predicted settlements were limited to 25mm overall with a maximum differential between adjacent node points of 15mm. These values were incorporated into the detailed design of the superstructure.

When the pit was handed over for construction, a full topographical survey identified the areas most recently worked. The DTM was integrated with the superstructure model to give an intersection line, which formed the setting out for the foundations. At the locations where the foundations passed from the hard granite onto the softer clays, a mechanism to give a smooth transition was required. Articulation joints were introduced to avoid abrupt steps in level and prevent high shear stresses developing in the foundation beam. During the early foundations design stage the final loads from the steel superstructure were not available from the frame contractor. Anthony Hunt Associates constructed a full three-dimensional model of each biome and performed a preliminary analysis to estimate the foundation loads. These loads were used to design the foundations. Once the final loads were available, a further check was undertaken to ensure the foundation design was acceptable. The models created for the superstructure were then used to perform an independent category III check on the subcontractors' design.

The final design of the biome structure incorporated a full linear elastic analysis of all environmental loads and combinations of loads. These included:

- Wind loads derived from the wind tunnel test
- Temperature loads between the extremes of $-10°C$ and $+50°C$
- Uniform snow loads
- Drifting snow accumulating between cushions
- Drifting snow accumulating between spheres
- Differential settlement of foundations.

The structural behaviour of the biomes is a combination of bending stiffness and shell action. Because of this it was impossible to incorporate effective expansion joints even though the largest biome is over 250 metres long. Given the large variations in design temperatures the likelihood of high thermal stresses developing was an important consideration. In practice, the curvature of the frame is sufficient to allow the whole building to breathe, moving out of plane to relieve potential stresses. The asymmetric geometry of the HTB produces a significant imbalance of loads within the structure. The space truss is subjected to out-of-plane bending moments which induce large deflections up 200mm. These are within normal limits when compared with the clear spans of up to 110 metres.

Digital representations of membrane theory combined with bending effects, along with finite element and finite strip analysis (which sum over large numbers of discrete sections) have been in existence since the 1960s (Robbin, 1996, p. 63). In the 1970s non-linear time-dependent analysis was introduced which supported the dynamic representation of structural responses under increasing loads. More recently, structural analysis software has been developed for a wide variety of analyses including load history, creep, shrinkage, aging of concrete, anchor slip, friction and relaxation (loc. cit.). Digital representations of structural topology can support the optimisation of both shape and topology. For shell structures such as the Eden biomes, the goal was to minimise tension and bending forces as much as possible. Once the structural frame layout had been determined through analysis, consideration could then be given to the positioning of the structure relative to the cladding envelope.

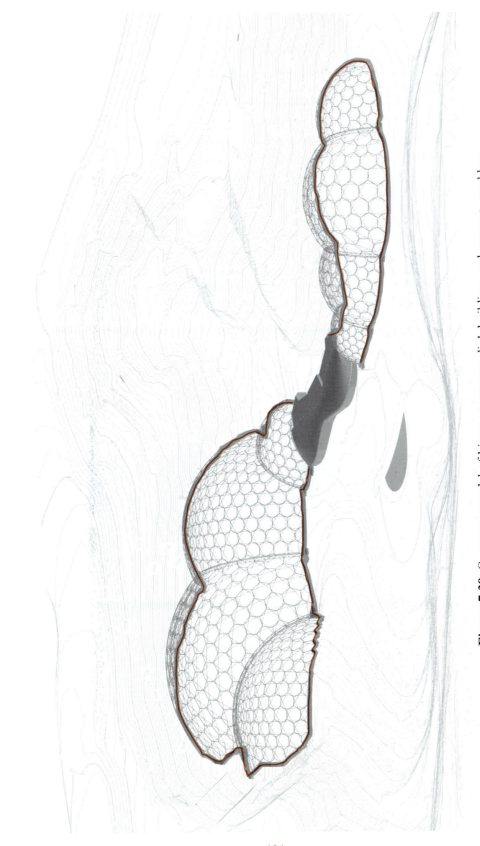

Figure 7.39: Computer model of biome structures, link building, and concrete necklace.

7.9   Cladding design

The design of the ETFE cushions was initially based on theoretical analysis using an iterative solution. The size of the panels was greater than any system previously built by the supplier, so a series of physical tests and mock-ups were included in the contract. As a result of these tests, the degree of patterning used to form the cushion profile was increased, and cable net reinforcement was omitted in favour of a second top layer of foil. Under negative wind pressures, principal loads are applied to the top layer of foil and the load capacity can be increased by either providing thicker material or a greater rise in the profile. The former was not recommended as the foil was already 200μm thick and above this limit it can become brittle and difficult to weld overlapping seams.

The cushion profile was based on a maximum of 10% of the span. Above this, the lateral stability cushions under transverse loads is unpredictable. Hence the adoption of two separate layers of foil. On the inner layer, which experiences principally snow and positive wind pressures but no transverse loads, the load capacity was achieved by increasing the patterning of the profile to give a rise of 15% of the span under full load conditions. Cable net reinforcement on the inside of the cushions was still required adjacent to the valleys between domes to support the high loads generated by drifting snow. Under normal operating conditions, the cushions would be inflated to a nominal pressure of 250 pascals above atmospheric. In the event of heavy snow, the pressure would be increased to 400 pascals to prevent deflation under sustained load.

Figure 7.40: CAD model of cladding cushions.

Figure 7.41: Exterior view of hex-tri-hex structure with cladding cushions.

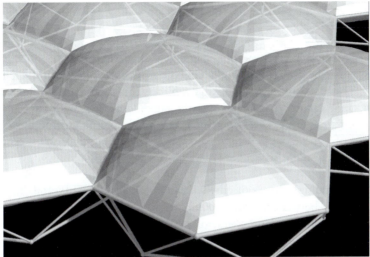

Figure 7.42:
Cladding Model.

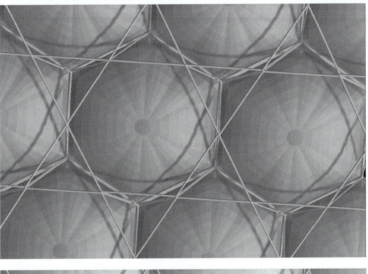

Figure 7.43:
Cladding Model.

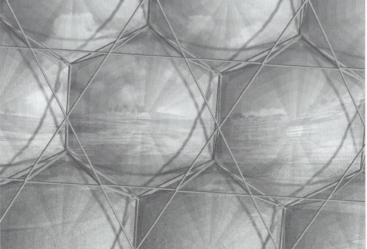

Figure 7.44:
Cladding Model.

7.10   The Cladding System

The performance criteria developed for the cladding system were extensive. The size of panel was very important, and glass would be limited to double glazed panels no greater than 4 x 2 metres weighing up to 75 kg/m². The installation, cleaning and replacement of large glass units requires careful planning and large crane capacities to reach over the buildings. The system chosen to clad the biomes was a pneumatic structure of *cushions*. Each cushion was contained within one module of the structure in the form of a hexagon, pentagon or triangle. On the largest domes, hexagonal cushions up to 10.9m across were used.

The panels were formed from multiple layers of ethyltetrafluoroethylene (ETFE) foil. The foil is extremely thin, each layer being between 50 and 200µm thick, giving very high levels of light transmission in both the visible (94–97%) and ultra violet range (83–88%). The cushions are held in extruded aluminium perimeter frames using a *luff* groove and bolt rope type detail, known as a *keder*, derived from sailing and fabric structure technology (cf. ideas from Gehry's work in **Chapter 8**). The frames are in turn bolted to brackets on the tubular steel structure at regular intervals. Even with such large panels, the whole cladding system only weighs around 15 kg/m² – a considerable weight saving on the equivalent glass envelope. Thermal insulation values (U=1.95 w/m²°k for a triple layer cushion) are better than triple glazing when used horizontally. The ETFE is a modified copolymer which is extruded into a thin film. This means the surface is extremely smooth and when coupled within the anti-adhesive properties of the material, gives a self-cleaning surface. Dirt such as bird droppings is washed off by rain and the requirement for regular cleaning is minimal. The material is unaffected by UV light, atmospheric pollution or weathering and extensive testing has been shown to give an anticipated life expectancy in excess of 40 years. The foil panels themselves only weigh up to 50kg making replacement a much easier operation than glass. It is also possible to effect short-term repairs in-situ using adhesive ETFE tape. The system is considered to be environmentally friendly. The inflation units consume energy to maintain the air pressure within the system, but the increased light transmission compensates for this in reduced artificial lighting requirements.

Figure 7.45: Cushion encased braced structure.

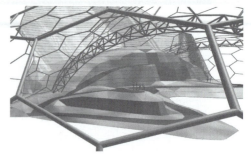

Figure 7.46: Transparent structural system.

In the hex-tri-hex structural system, the outer members were 193 mm diameter circular hollow sections with semi-fixity at the nodes, whilst the inner members were 114 mm diameter circular hollow sections with pin ended connections from the Mero system. This alternative offered considerable reductions in the weight of steel although fabrication complexity and the number of nodes increased considerably so the tendered cost was generally in accordance with the anticipated budget. The number of nodes in the system has a significant effect on cost, as does the size of the cladding panels. The larger the panels, the lower the number of nodes and generally, the cheaper the cladding. Hence the objective was to develop the largest possible cladding panels.

Cushions were installed from the perimeter up to the apex. The inflation system for the cushions consisted of a single flexible connection feeding into each cushion. Once in place the cushions were inflated immediately to ensure structural integrity. Any flapping in windy conditions would inevitably lead to damage.

A further aspect of the structural analysis was the checking of exceptional loads such as rainwater ponding in deflated cushions in the event of a long-term power failure. Back-up pumps and power supplies were set up for the inflation system. Air can also be diverted from one pump unit to the next thus taking several hours for the cushions to deflate.

Calculations indicated that the steel frame was capable of supporting up to six flooded cushions without any predicted failure. Further investigations using non-linear techniques showed that the risk of progressive collapse in this condition was acceptable.

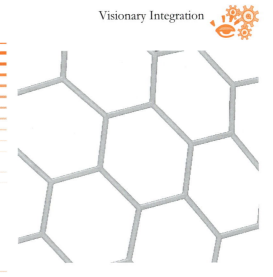

Figure 7.47: Single layer geometry.

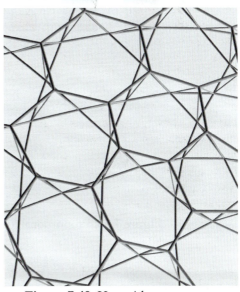

Figure 7.48: Hex-tri-hex geometry.

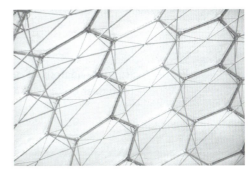

Figure 7.49: Hex-tri-hex with cushions.

7.11   Environmental Loads

The combination of a lightweight steel frame and cladding system (with an average combined weight of around 40 kg/m² of surface area) meant that the effect of environmental loads on the structure was very critical. To achieve the most efficient solution possible, snow and wind loads were assessed in detail according to proportional loading characteristics (**figure 7.50**). The consequences of drifting snow accumulating between cushions, or in the valleys between domes were evaluated, with particular emphasis on the arch between the two biomes (**figure 7.51**).

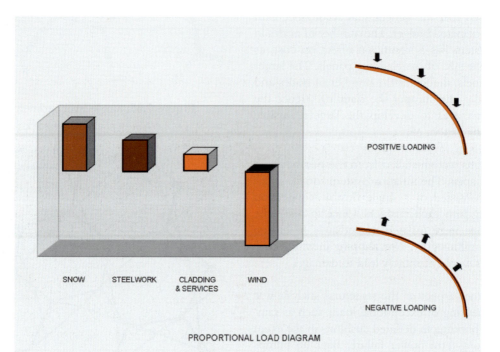

Figure 7.50: Proportional loading of structural and environmental factors.

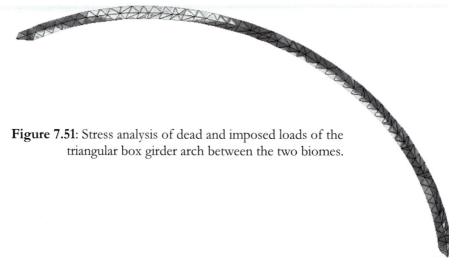

Figure 7.51: Stress analysis of dead and imposed loads of the triangular box girder arch between the two biomes.

Accurate wind loads were impossible to assess from the standards because of the unique topography of the site and the complex geometrical shape. A detailed study was conducted using a 1:300 scale model of the biome complex and surrounding quarry in the *wind tunnel* at British Maritime Technology Ltd. (**figures 7.52–7.54**) (Jones, 2000, p. 94). The biomes were instrumented to measure the surface pressures at 300 locations.

The wind tunnel tests demonstrated that the profile of the pit sheltered the buildings from the extremes of wind, but with strong fluctuations in surface pressures due to unsteady wind flow in the quarry. As the pit is over 60 metres deep and the highest biome is only 50 metres to the apex, the whole development was considered to be below ground level. The results of the tests supported this, giving design wind pressure values well below those initially predicted.

Figure 7.52: Wind tunnel testing of physical model.

Figure 7.53: Wind tunnel testing of physical model.

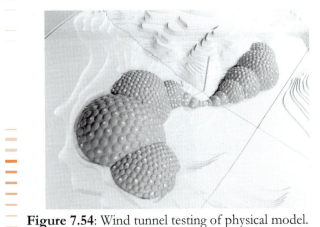

Figure 7.54: Wind tunnel testing of physical model.

Figure 7.55: Aluminium cladding frames.

Figure 7.56: Aluminium cladding frame.

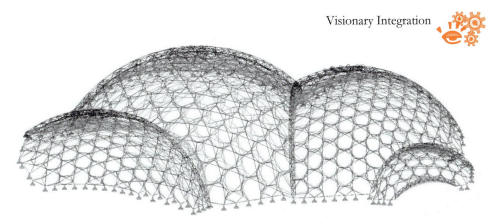

Figure 7.57: Deflection diagram for snow loading on HTB.

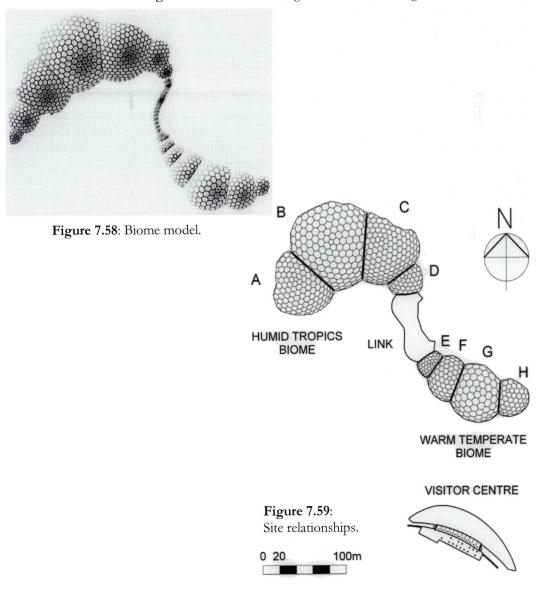

Figure 7.58: Biome model.

B   C

N

A   D

**HUMID TROPICS
BIOME**   LINK   E F   G

H

**WARM TEMPERATE
BIOME**

VISITOR CENTRE

Figure 7.59:
Site relationships.

0 20   100m

7.12   Thermal Performance of the Biome Environment

The rock faces were an important part of the climate control strategy. When the sun heats up the biome enclosures it also heats the rock inside. Heat is stored, daytime overheating reduced, and heat is put back into the space as the enclosure cools. To make the most of this natural energy storage system, the critical factor was the performance of the enclosure skin. The triple layers of ETFE have an insulation value of $1.9w/m^2$ °C. This reduces the heat loss at night, and in winter it increases the performance of the rock storage, thus reducing the amount of additional heat energy required. The skin also reduces the length of time for condensation to occur.

The horticultural team identified the environmental conditions required in each of the biomes; in particular the maximum and minimum temperature and humidity. This resulted in a temperature and humidity chart for each biome showing acceptable variations. Applying this information to the geometry of the enclosures, a computer simulation model was developed to predict the thermal performance of the spaces to determine how the natural storage system could best be exploited.

A number of schemes were considered early in the design process to provide additional heat. These ranged from combined heat and power (CHP) systems, to active solar collectors, to biomass boilers. However, funding pressures meant that gas was used as the source of additional heating. This heat is put into the biomes by jets of warm air that induce air circulation currents throughout the biomes maintaining the temperature. These jets come from large fans, which are supplied with hot water from the energy centre, by an underground heating main. To engineer the correct position of the jets within the irregular shapes of the biomes, a *dynamic thermal computer analysis* was carried out to calculate and visualise the airflows and air temperatures throughout the space. The computational fluid dynamics (CFD) analysis produced 3-D graphs showing the speed and direction of the air movement, and the temperature distribution across the space. Using the results of this analysis, the air jets and fans were positioned and adjusted for direction and speed to give an even distribution of temperature, and to check that the airflow would not create unnecessary draughts for the plants.

The environmental control systems were based on a combination of natural ventilation and blowers. Consequently, the hexagons at the apex of each dome were subdivided into triangles to form opening vents. Air is introduced at the base of the domes via louvered panels in hexagonal openings. These panels also allow the passage of air ducting from the air-handling units through the envelope. The internal environment of the biomes can generate temperatures as high as 50°C and relative humidity of 95%. With such extreme environmental conditions, corrosion protection and future maintenance needed serious consideration.

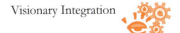

It was also necessary to consider what happened in the summer when the enclosures could overheat with the sun. Automatically controlled openings are located at the top and bottom of the biomes. These are opened in stages, letting hot air out at the top and drawing replacement cooler air in at the bottom.

The areas and locations for these were designed using the CFD computer simulation model in *summer mode*. Plants give out moisture as they grow, and the ventilation system is controlled to reduce this moisture build-up if it gets too high. On the other hand, it is often necessary to increase the humidity, particularly in the Humid Tropics Biome. This is achieved using fine spray misters.

With all these systems installed, the automatic control has to ensure that they all work together to achieve the right temperature and humidity. Unlike normal air-conditioned buildings, these conditions vary continually. For example, when there is no sun in winter, the temperature is allowed to drop to a daytime minimum before the heating jets are turned on. Conversely when the sun comes out, the temperature is allowed to rise, storing heat in the rock face until the maximum temperature for the season is reached, and then the ventilation openings are activated.

Since the relative humidity depends on the temperature, the misters need to respond to changing conditions to keep the humidity within the right band. This will then provide the best conditions for plants with a minimum consumption of energy.

Figure 7.60: Exterior view.

Figure 7.61: Exterior view.

Figure 7.62: Exterior view.

7.13 Landscape and Construction

Slopes in the Grade III and IV granite up to 50° were created by battering the profile and spraying on a mix of grass, shrub seed and fertiliser in a hydrated adhesive gel, to bind the surface. Using a similar technique, slopes up to 35° could be achieved in the fill material. In the Grade I and II granite, some blasting was required. Because of discontinuities in the rock, rock anchors were used to prevent toppling of large segments and to create a safe rock face. In the Grade III and IV granite, the faces steeper than 50° were also reinforced with self-drilling grouted anchors, which were then used to restrain a sprayed concrete facing. As this produces an unnatural finish that is difficult to plant, the landscape architects preferred to minimise its use wherever possible. In visually sensitive areas, for example inside the biomes, the anchor heads were pre-tensioned and sprayed over using a special technique of precracking the sprayed concrete backing.

Once slopes had been stabilised and when settlement monitoring indicated that the consolidation of the fill had effectively ceased, the construction of the foundation necklace began. The complex geometry made conventional drawing methods insufficient as a form of communication with the contractors on site. 3-D co-ordinate data was provided for the contractors, providing them with alignments similar to those used in road construction. These were fed directly into electronic distance measuring equipment and set out point by point. Despite access problems on site, the foundations were constructed in twelve weeks. This was followed by the assembly of a vast birdcage scaffold used as temporary support for the erection of the biome frames.

The reuse of rainwater was another interesting aspect of the Eden project. The horticulturists wanted pure water for humidification in the biome providing a tropical environment. Water purity is important for the prevention of mineral deposition on plant surfaces. The best source for this water was considered to be the rainwater collected from the surface run-off of the biomes. The rainwater is collected via a drainage system located at the base of each of the biomes, using a proprietary enclosed channel drainage system. The channel system is linked to hoppers located at the base of each of the biome main gutters. After collection, the rainwater is subjected to coarse filtration in a gravity system and discharged to underground buffer tanks before it is pumped via fine filters into three existing concrete storage tanks. At the top of the pit, the static head is sufficient to pressurise the distribution system serving the tropical biome without additional pumping, where it is used to maintain the required humidity via a high-pressure misting system. The cleanliness of reused rainwater is ensured by disinfecting stored water after collection, and again before distribution.

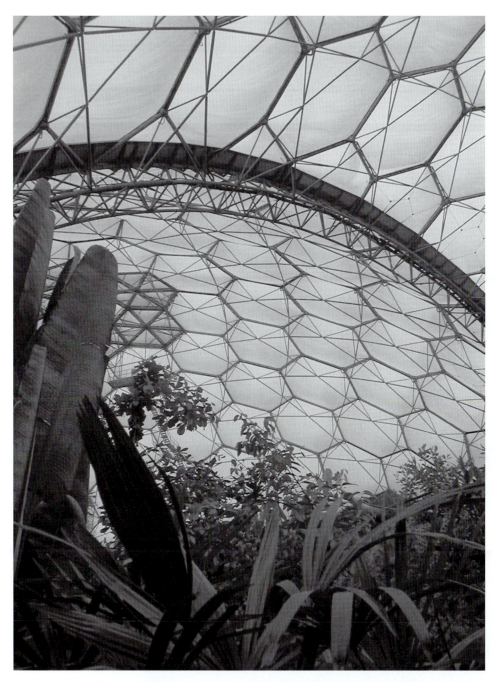

Figure 7.63: Internal view of Humid Tropics Biome (HTB).

Figure 7.64: Interior view of the Warm Temperate Biome (WTB).

Figure 7.65: Interior view of the Warm Temperate Biome (WTB).

7.14   Future Use and Maintenance

The buildings were designed for a 50 year life span, and the galvanised finish to the steelwork should last this long without major treatment or repainting other than areas of damage. The cladding system will require regular maintenance of seals etc., but the basic components were expected to last longer than the stated life span. Replacement of cushions can be carried out in a similar way to their installation. Internal gantries hang from the steel frame below the apex of each dome to allow access roof vents. The building management team is required to undertake regular inspections of the cushions to identify any damage or air leakages. Any necessary repairs need to be carried out promptly to ensure the integrity of the envelope.

Figure 7.66: Interior view of the Warm Temperate Biome (WTB).

Figure 7.67: Interior view of the Warm Temperate Biome (WTB).

7.15   Architectural Qualities of the Biome Form

- **structurally efficient**: maximum size and strength with minimum steel.

- **energy efficient**: maximum volume within a minimal surface area, thus minimising heat loss.

- **adaptable**: structural form configured to the shape of the site.

- **transparent**: it lets through more light (including UV light) than glass.

- **lightweight**: weight of the steel structure is similar to the weight of air enclosed by it.

- **spacious**: spans 110m at its widest point with no internal supports, thus allowing unrestricted planting and landscaping.

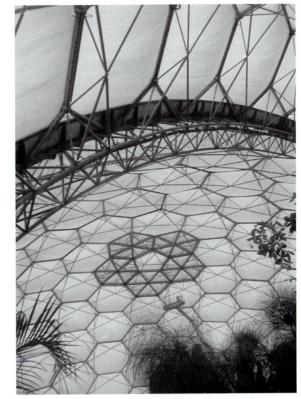

Figure 7.68: Interior view of the HTB.

Figure 7.69: Interior view of the WTB.

7.16   CAD/CAM Technology

CAD software is primarily concerned with geometric modelling techniques, along with varying degrees of analysis and optimisation functionality. Computer-aided manufacturing (CAM) is the technology concerned with the use of computer systems to plan, manage, and control manufacturing operations. Integrating these two processes aims to make the product cycle more efficient, and therefore more cost-effective.

The complex structural design of the Eden steelwork was digitally represented using 3-D CAD/CAM modelling and structural analysis software developed jointly between Grim-shaws, Hunts and Mero. The digital data was exported to a machine shop where a computerised production line automatically cut components to the precise specifications provided. The many thousands of individual components were individually numbered, so that when fitted to their unique positions, matching elements could be accommodated with minimal tolerance values.

Figure 7.70: Interior view of the HTB.

Beginning with dome A of the HTB in the west and dome H of the WTB in the east, a space frame was assembled from a kit of individually labelled parts. Primary elements were shipped to site prefinished by hot dip galvanising. Nodes were prefinished with a zinc rich paint system. Elements were lifted into position by mobile crane and on the larger dome in the HTB, a tower crane on piled foundations was used. Aluminium cladding frames were bolted to the top boom elements on the ground before erection, leaving only the corner units to be installed at high level. As each dome and parts of adjacent domes (to ensure stability) were constructed, the pneumatic cushions were installed.

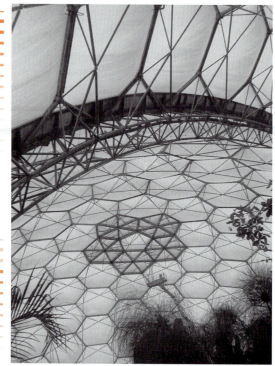

Figure 7.71 : Interior view of the HTB.

7.17 Procurement process

The whole project was driven by the many funding initiatives required to raise the £75 million total cost. The initial programmes were amended repeatedly by revised applications for grants and sponsorship.

The tender was issued using a preliminary design in late 1996 and the constructors were invited to assist with funding. The successful tenderer, a joint venture between Sir Robert McAlpine and Alfred McAlpine was given preferred contractor status in early 1997. The form of agreement used was the Engineering and Construction Contract Option C target contract with activity schedule, amended to make it a Guaranteed Maximum Price (GMP), with profit sharing. The latter was split 50/50 between client and constructor, which is considered to be extremely beneficial to the client.

A period of protracted negotiation followed, during which the design was modified on numerous occasions to bring the cost plan/GMP into line with the target figures. The McAlpine joint venture led the tender process for the envelope and mechanical and electrical services and negotiated the final contracts. Both of these major packages were let as contractor designed works with detailed design being the responsibility of the works package contractor.

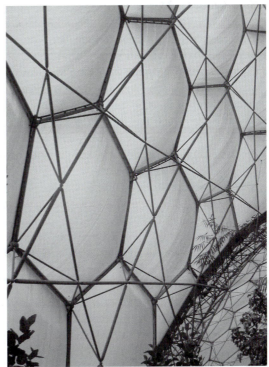

Figure 7.72: Interior view of the HTB.

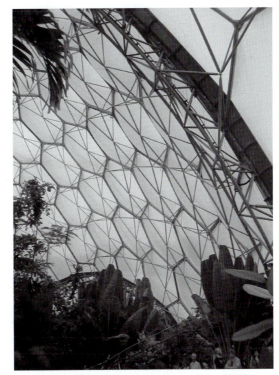

Figure 7.73: Interior view of the HTB.

7.18   Geodesic Domes

Design concepts based upon natural forms helped the design team on the Eden Project to explore new and innovative solutions. Natural forms are concerned with efficiency, minimising use of energy and maximising use of resources. Geodesic domes have the appearance of a sphere, yet all the surfaces are planes and all edges are straight lines. A geodesic line is the shortest distance between two points on a sphere and is always part of the circumference of what is called a *great circle* – a circle which has its centre at the centre of the sphere. A *great circle* on a sphere is the intersection of that sphere with a plane passing through the centre of the sphere. Examples of great circles include the equator and the lines of constant longitude.

Given any two non-antipodal points, there is a unique great circle joining those two points. Given that three non-collinear points determine a plane, these two points and the centre of the sphere thus define a plane. The intersection of the plane determined by these points and the sphere is the great circle joining the two given points. If great circles are to be lines, then we can measure the angle between two intersecting great circles as the angle formed by the intersection of the two defining planes with the plane tangent to the sphere at the point of intersection. A geodesic line is the shortest distance between two points on a curved surface. By drawing geodesics on a sphere and connecting the points at which they intersect with *straight lines*, a geodesic structure is produced. Forces within a geodesic structure are uniformly distributed, and natural forms indicate that hexagonal structures are an extremely efficient way of absorbing stress.

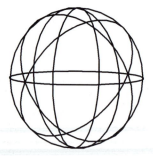

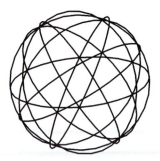

Figure 7.74: Six great circles.   **Figure 7.75**: Eight great circles.

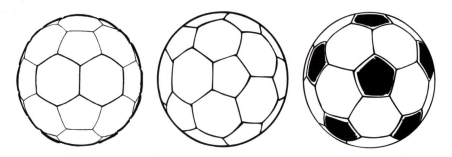

Figure 7.76: Emergence of geodesic dome idea for basic form.

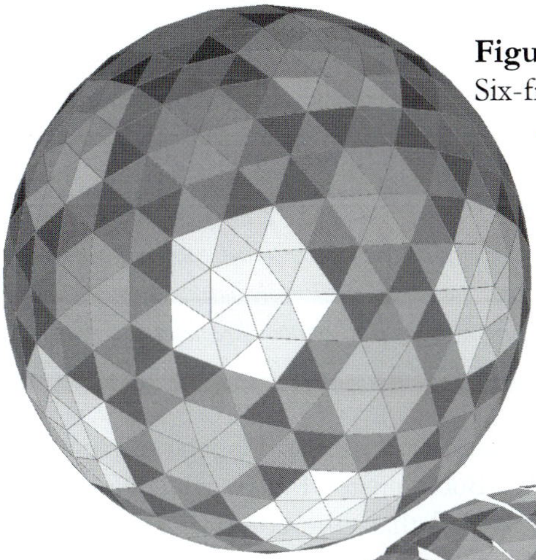

Figure 7.77:
Six-frequency icosahedral geodesic sphere.

7.19   Unfolding Geodesic Spheres

The process of unfolding moves towards more basic shapes, whereas folding complicates the shape. Unfolding structures are objects that smoothly transform in size and shape.

Figure 7.78:
Unfolding of six-frequency icosahedral geodesic sphere.

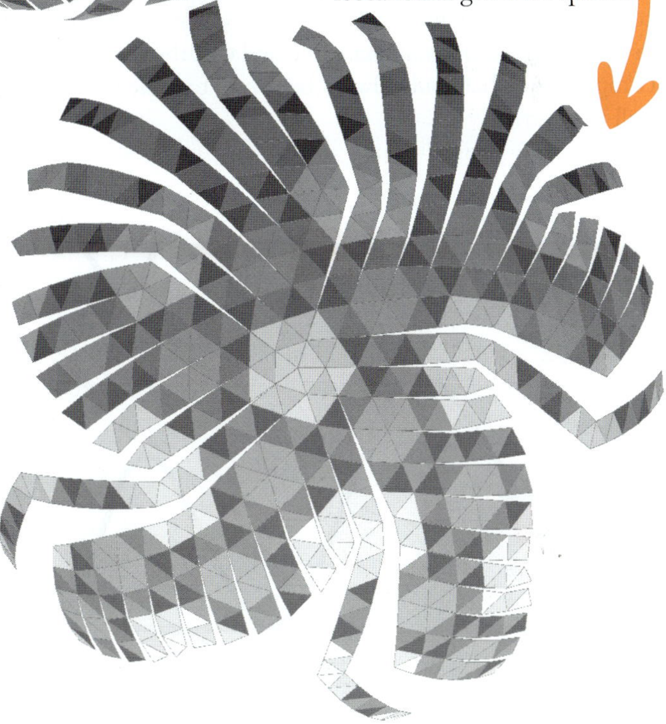

Figure 7.79:
Unfolded six-frequency icosahedral geodesic sphere.

The unfolding of a geodesic dome is based on the idea that three-dimensional polyhedra can be formed by the rotation and displacement of two-dimensional polygons. Each of the triangular elements in **figure 7.77** is considered to be *developable*. In the Eden Project these parts were hexagonal, but developability was still an intrinsic property of the geodesic structure, i.e. component parts could be fabricated essentially in a flat plane. The important idea of developabilty will recur in the following chapter, and has implications for ways in which digital manufacturing processes might be used to fabricate structural components off-site before reassembling whole structures on site.

7.20   Tensegrity

The word 'tensegrity' is an invention: it is a contraction of 'tensional integrity'. Tensegrity describes a structural-relationship principle in which structural shape is guaranteed by the finitely closed, comprehensively continuous, tensional behaviors of the system and not by the discontinuous and exclusively local compressional member behaviors. Tensegrity provides the ability to yield increasingly without ultimately breaking or coming asunder. (Fuller, 1975, p. 372)

The history of geodesic spheres goes back to Walter Bauersfeld's Zeiss Planetarium in Jena, Germany in 1926 (Whalley, 2000, p. 79). In the 1950s, Buckminster Fuller, an engineer and architect, further demonstrated their capabilities. He observed that the compression forces in conventional masonry structures were always balanced by an equal amount of tensional force – masonry walls have a tendency to arc outward. The under-exploitation of tensional forces in conventional architecture led Fuller to develop geodesic structures. His Dymaxion House was a prototype structure that led to investigations concerning co-ordinate systems and their relation to naturally efficient structural systems. Fuller's exploration of spherical geometry led him to build the spherical structures that he considered to be the most efficient means of construction. His initial dome models were merely spheres constructed from crisscrossing curved pieces of material (each of which represented an arc of a great circle) that formed triangles. Later, he developed this concept and formed more complex curved pieces from tetrahedrons or octahedrons, which were then joined to create spherical structures. The simple triangulation of struts formed geodesic domes.

It is important to remember that Buckminster Fuller considered *tensegrity structures* to be a generalisation of geodesic domes. Tensegrity is the pattern that results when push (compression) and pull (tension) are in equilibrium with each other. The pull is continuous and the push is discontinuous. The continuous pull is balanced by the discontinuous push producing an integrity of tension and compression. Push and pull are commonly encountered in everyday experience as forces working in opposite directions. Fuller explained that these fundamental phenomena were not opposites, but complements that could always be found together. He further explained that push is *divergent* while pull is *convergent*.

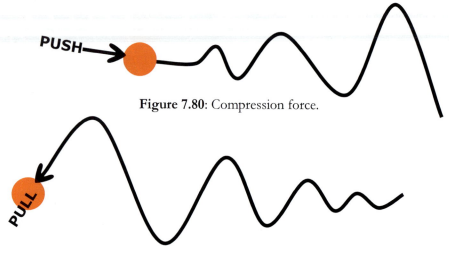

Figure 7.80: Compression force.

Figure 7.81: Tension force.

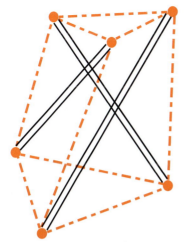

Figure 7.82:
A tensegrity structure of order 3.

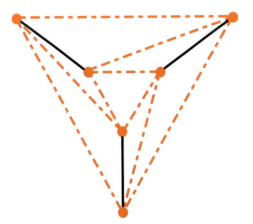

Figure 7.83: Graph representation
of an order 3 tensegrity structure.

Physically, a tensegrity structure can consist of a pin-connected truss. Since the connections are frictionless pins, the elements of the truss pivot freely upon them, and so the elements carry only forces parallel their length. The elements of the truss may be either bars, which carry either tension or compression and which can neither extend nor contract, or cables, which carry only tension and which cannot extend, but may contract. The mathematical literature often introduces another sort of element, a strut, which may endure compression but not tension and cannot contract, but can extend (fall out of the structure). These rigid *struts* interact with more elastic *tendons*, and an intriguing length ratio of 1:0.6124 exists for the relationship between struts and tendons in a non-redundant tensegrity structure (Kenner, 1976), which is remarkably close to the golden ratio referred to in **chapter 3**.

Mathematically, a tensegrity structure can be described as a *connected bigraph* together with a specification of a set of edge-lengths (Williams, 2003). A graph consists in a set of edges E and a set of nodes N. In the engineering literature, authors frequently consider all or some of the elements to be elastic. Mathematicians also use elastification as a relaxation method to arrive at stable positions of tensegrity structures (**figure 7.85**).

Figure 7.84: Rigid.

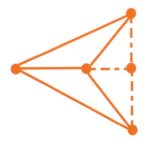

Figure 7.85: Stable.

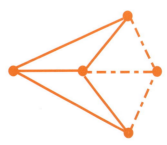

Figure 7.86: Unstable.

Figure 7.87: Exterior view of the HTB.

7.21   Summary

The key factors of the case study presented in this chapter can be summarised as follows:

- Extensive computer-based site modelling techniques were needed to model the shifting context of the site based upon available survey data. The continual remodelling of the site was needed to determine the necessary cut and fill operations, as well as to visualise the locations of the biomes in the landscape.

- Structural modelling and analysis software was used particularly to model and analyse the effects of horizontal thrusts at the intersections of biomes, and also for assessing the structural properties of the geodesic structural elements along with their environmental loading characteristics.

- Computer-based environmental simulation and control models were used to anticipate required heating loads and cooling controls for the completed structure.

- The role of the client was an important factor in the process, contributing to the development of a structural system that achieved the required levels of lightness and transparency.

- The lightness and toughness of the biomes arose out of the tensile properties of geodesic structures, which were highly suited to the functionalities required in this project.

- The mathematical basis of geodesics and tensegrity underpins the architecture of organic dome structures, and needs to be understood by architects wanting to build geodesic structures that do not necessarily have to be spherical.

- The CAD/CAM fabrication of parts enabled efficient production of complex elements.

Chapter 8: The Exuberant Vision: Throwing Off the Bowlines

When I was working on Disney Hall I got excited about movement. I got into sails and the luffing of the sails. When you're sailing, the wind catches the sail and it's very tight, and it's a beautiful shape. Then, as you turn, the wind is coming at you when you're going forward – the wind is actually coming at an angle. When you turn into the wind slightly, the wind is on both sides of the sail. At that moment, the sail luffs – flutters. And when it flutters, it has a beautiful quality that was caught in the seventeenth century by Dutch painters such as the van de Veldes. But I didn't have the guts to do it. So everything is tight in Disney Hall. Later, when I saw Sluter, it was luffing all over the place; it was very much like Greek drapery. It gave me courage. (Gehry, 1999, p. 43).

Frank Gehry's creative use of state-of-the-art CAD technology to design and develop innovative yet well-planned buildings has realised ambitions in CAD that have lain dormant since the 1970s, the central principle of which was that of the integrated CAD system. This radical and ambitious concept first arose in the early days of CAD when computing power was comparatively weak, but expectations high for digital-based design. The aim was to be able to describe a design from inception through to production entirely within a digital environment. The emphasis was less on specialised design functions and more on the expression and manipulation of design information, at that time associated with rectilinear building geometries, to serve all possible functions.

Gehry's projects demonstrate that a point has now been reached in which complex free-form building geometries can *only* be analysed and resolved, structurally and otherwise, through the application of computer applications which in many cases have been appropriated from engineering disciplines such as hydrology and aeronautics, for example (Lyall, 2002, p. 9). Frank Gehry's design process is heavily dependent upon the use of such software, for initial explorations of form, for structural analysis, and for digital fabrication. The relationship between modelling and construction is especially strong and important. Schemes such as the Walt Disney Concert Hall, der Neue Zollhof in Dusseldorf (**figures 8.1–8.4**), and the Stata Centre at MIT all demonstrate the prevalence of digital technology. The latter project also happens to be a set of buildings for research into digital representation, with connections between some of the research activities that take place there and new construction industry technologies.

Much of this chapter is again concerned with investigating the whole design process in order to contextualise the digital methods. Some of the more significant techniques used within Gehry's office include extensive use of large-scale physical models, fast and accurate 3-D digitising processes, surface regeneration, and the identification of control surfaces and setting out points. The complex geometries that emerge from these processes may appear to pose problems for fabricators and contractors, but the office has been able to exploit fabrication methods from other industries (aircraft and shipbuilding in particular) that enable them to realise designs in an effective way. Design development in Gehry's office is predominantly three-dimensional, though the office still generates technical drawings for construction. These drawings include reference to node intersections, clearances and interferences for all layers of construction. The ways in which digital technologies are being used in Frank Gehry's office has immense significance for the future directions of architectural practice in general. For this reason we need to investigate not only the working methods of the office, but the future directions of the technologies themselves.

In the 1980s, Gehry became disappointed with the consequences of having to contract out construction documentation to executive architects. Having middle-men between himself and his own contractors and clients led to misunderstandings, errors in construction, and increased costs (Gehry, 1999, p. 15). The worst case scenario, and the trigger for change in his office structure was the Walt Disney Concert Hall project, which was effectively stopped because of cost overruns arising from the organisational structure. The way out of this impasse was to develop in-house technical expertise that would allow the office to develop projects from initial design right through to fabrication and construction. The following quote by Gehry himself is very revealing:

> *Our office structure and working method have changed a lot in the past ten years: staffing, computers, clients. It all has to do with people. Earlier, I could not get experienced managers and systems experts (the Randy Jeffersons and Jim Glymphs of the world) to work with me, because they could be paid better in other places where there was more predictability for them in their work and in their lives. People who worked here in the mid-1980s would freak out when I would re-design something, because that meant their bonus was out the window (if the client wasn't paying). That was the period when I ran into technical problems. We couldn't do working drawings for large projects; we had to farm them out.*
>
> *When Jim Glymph joined us (in 1989) I pointed out that we drew curves like those on the Vitra Museum using descriptive geometry. I said, 'I want to go into more complex shapes now'. He said, 'That's no problem; we'll do it with the computer'. He went to the aerospace industry and had meetings and discussions about it. From those we got the CATIA program and several new people, including the computer expert Richard Smith.*
>
> *Jim developed the computer thing slowly, and that was expensive. But he does make it work for us. That's how we controlled the costs of Bilbao, and how we can do those curves now. Consequently we have a lot of freedom. I can play with shapes. When I create the curved shapes on all the little models, we have a gadget that digitizes them. It's becoming quicker and quicker. With our new equipment, shapes can be transferred to the computer in fifteen minutes, and now we know how much it's going to cost per square foot to build those shapes, because we've had the necessary experience. Now we can budget jobs in the earliest design phases. Also, we know that if we use flat materials it's relatively cheap; when we use single curved materials it's a little more expensive; and it's most expensive when we warp materials. So we can rationalize all these shapes in the computer and make a judgment about the quantity of each shape to be used. It's not possible to know this by looking at the completed building. The most important thing is that the computer gives us a tool we can use to communicate with the contractors.*
>
> *Because we can figure the cost, the subcontractors are starting to trust us. We have a whole group of people who know we mean it. At first, when they saw it, they thought we were crazy, and they said, 'The client's not going to let you do it anyway, so why should we take it seriously?' Now they believe in it, and they want to be part of it. We have a large group of contractors in Europe and America who will work with us now. In the last few years we've been pushing the frontiers that we normally wouldn't push into, because we're afraid to do it! But there's a lot more flexibility out there than we realized.* (Gehry, 1999, pp. 48-50)

In other words, Gehry's office wanted to use computers to get buildings built. One consequence of this was that the office had no rendering software for a long time, and consequently no pretty pictures to look at. This is in marked contrast to commonly encountered preconceived views of CAD in architectural practice and architectural education, which is to emphasise the importance of highly rendered images of 3-D models – images for magazine architecture.

Instead, the role of computing in Gehry's office was, and still is, to realise Gehry's own exuberant sketch designs by first transforming them into topological digital representations that can be directly manipulated and analysed, and then combining the resultant digital models with innovative construction and fabrication processes.

One recent project in which digital fabrication was an important part of the process was a set of three office buildings in Dusseldorf, der Neue Zollhof. The undulating walls of a part of this office complex were clad in stainless steel (**figures 8.1–8.4**). The walls themselves consist of pre-cast concrete blocks that were molded using Styrofoam formwork cut by milling machines using digital model data.

Most proprietary CAD software to date has been implemented in direct response to the needs of large architectural and engineering offices, where the emphasis is on drawing output and on the organisation of the drawings themselves. For a relatively small office such as Gehry's which has a radically different, but very effective design process, with a greater emphasis on 3-D modelling and fabrication, using the same commercial software as everyone else would have had a negative effect on their own design process. According to Jim Glymph:

Figure 8.1: Der Neue Zollhof.

> *If the big companies get there first, they will set the standards and we'll be back with the old divided process again – what Frank wanted to get away from.* (Gehry, 1999, p. 17).

Unlikely as it may seem, the Gehry office is trying to create a model for small offices, particularly as software becomes more affordable. In addition to the core modelling activities, CAD is used in Gehry's office to anticipate construction problems and to calculate quantities and costs. Furthermore, Gehry's working methods haven't changed because of the computer. Instead, it has made it easier for his collaborators to realise his most eccentric forms. He still develops his ideas slowly, from sketches through a long series of physical models.

> *I sit and watch and I move things. I move a wall, I move a piece of paper, I move something, and I look at it – and it evolves.* (Gehry, 1999, p. 17).

Figure 8.2: Der Neue Zollhof.

In Gehry's design process, curvilinear forms are transformed through a series of well-planned steps into constructional information. During the course of this process, there is invariably a transformation of fluid design forms into economically viable technical specifications. The end result is the construction of forms previously thought to be impractical and unbuildable, e.g. when Massimo Colomban's Italian firm Permasteelisa initially applied conventional techniques (2-D drawings of structural form) to generate a full-size 3-D mock-up of Gehry's Barcelona Fish. (Novitski, 1992).

In Gehry's scheme for Der Neue Zollhof in Dusseldorf, the most fluid buildings are the central ones shown in **figures 8.1–8.4**. According to Randy Jefferson:

> *The wall of the center building has a surface whose shape is much like that of folds of hanging fabric. This undulating wall is clad in polished stainless steel, with pre-cast concrete creating the complex shape. For the first time we're using computer data to mill large blocks of Styrofoam that are 2.4 meters wide by 3.4 meters high, by 0.6 or 0.9 meters thick, to create the shape of the building full-scale in Styrofoam. Those pieces of Styrofoam become the forms for the concrete. The products of this construction process are pre-cast concrete panels that have the exact shape of the design model transcribed into real life through computer data. They fit together perfectly. This system is more expensive than constructing a flat wall using wood forms, but the contractor is able to recycle the Styrofoam, and the pre-cast concrete pieces fit exactly, even though they're complex in shape.* (Gehry, 1999, p. 188)

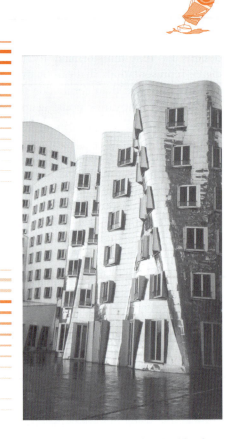

Figure 8.3: Der Neue Zollhof.

CAD-generated models were used for a wide variety of purposes, e.g. structural layout, cladding specifications, surface models, and models for CNC machining which in turn generate new physical models for further design and analysis. Modelling directly in three dimensions is absolutely central to the representation of forms of this complexity. Any plans and sections necessary for construction can be generated routinely from the 3-D models. According to Jim Glymph:

> *We were asking basic questions: what would the process be if you didn't divide projects up into the compartments that have evolved over the last half of the twentieth century? If you just tried to do what was necessary to get the job done, how would you conceive of carrying out the process?* (Gehry, 1999, p. 17).

Figure 8.4: Der Neue Zollhof.

8.1   The Importance of the Sketch

As soon as I understand the scale of the building and the relationship to the site and the relationship to the client, as it becomes more and more clear to me, I start doing sketches. (Gehry, 2003)

A central characteristic of Gehry's design process is his direct expression of design ideas through sketching. The sketches invariably consist of complex curves that express the intention to develop fluid 3-D building forms. They are not ephemeral precursors to optimisation procedures that will straighten out some or all of the curvilinearity. The curves when built will contribute to the intended emotional experience. When Gehry sketches he means it. Gehry's sketches are always:

. . . returned to, through the laborious and iterative process of designing the building. This is a kind of 'reverse engineering', where as more becomes known, and more problems are addressed, the conceptual clarity and energy of the initial gesture must be continually recaptured (Lindsey, 2001, p. 52).

Projects such as the Guggenheim Museum, Bilbao have demonstrated how the final built form resembles Gehry's initial sketches, as indicated by the wire-frame CAD model shown in **figure 8.5**.

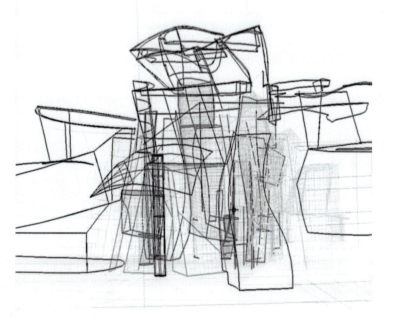

Figure 8.5: Digital model as sketch of the Guggenheim Museum, Bilbao.

The complex curvilinearity of the initial sketch was ultimately transferred into a digital representation, manipulated, detailed and then constructed, all according to Gehry's views on form generation:

I try things on, like I used to when I was a kid. I do it all the time. I get to know it. I assimilate it, and then it comes out some other way – translated. I used to be a symmetrical freak, a grid freak. I used to follow grids, and then I started to think and realised that those were chains – that Frank Lloyd Wright was chained to the grid, that grids are an obsession, a crutch. You don't need that if you can create spaces and forms and shapes. That's what artists do. They don't have grids and crutches – they just do it. (Merrick, 2003, p. 4).

8.2   The Realisation of the Sketch

The key to Frank Gehry's architecture is in his drawings. A Gehry building begins with a sketch, and Gehry's sketches are distinctive. They're characterized by a sense of off-hand improvisation, of intuitive spontaneity. The fine line is invariably fluid, impulsive. The drawings convey no architectural mass or weight, only loose directions and shifting spatial relationships. (Knight, 2000)

Gehry's intuitive sketches cannot be viewed as a design language in which symbolic representations can be interpreted according to decompositional rules. Instead their emotive qualities have analogical characteristics. Digital representations, on the other hand, are essentially discrete and symbolic. The realisation of these sketches in digital environments, therefore, inevitably depends upon interpolation and approximation.

Gehry seems to get more out of dissolving the grid in the interests of the programme, that is to say, than Eisenman does from making architecture that is about exposing it. If you dissolve it then you've dissolved an idea and replaced it with tangibilities, forces that reflect or contain it but need not be tied to it. If you expose it, all you've done is make an idea into a thing.

Gehry's work has always been about materials as appearance and movement rather than things – i.e. about those aspects of things that exceed them as the thing itself exceeds the drawing of it – which is why his architecture is always more than a structure. (Gilbert-Rolfe and Gehry, 2001, p. 114)

The traditional way of approximating curves has been to use spline tools to connect known points. The digital approach is referred to as *interpolation*, and is used to generate curves from known data points, either from sketches or from physical models. It is often the case that small adjustments need to be made after the initial interpolation curve is produced, and the best way of achieving this is to manipulate the control points of Bezier or B-spline curves rather than using mathematical spline curves (**figure 8.6**). The disadvantages of spline curves are that vertical tangents are problematic, distortions can arise between data points, and local modifications require re-computation of entire splines (Faux and Pratt, 1979, p. 162). The latter can be problematic when dealing with complex curves, but can be avoided with B-splines.

Figure 8.6: Curve obtained by interpolation of known data points with B-splines.

The same principle applies when scanning 3-D physical models to generate digital surface representations. Clouds of points in 3-D space can be converted into surfaces through interpolation algorithms. The digital surfaces can then be manipulated interactively so that the surfaces are pushed and pulled into positions that reflect the dynamic nature of initial sketches. With environments such as the CATIA system, surface manipulations can be associated with real-time structural analyses that indicate induced stresses when loads or other constraints are applied.

> ... *the computer is not used as a generative device but as an instrument of translation: thanks to the computer we can, within the limits of materials and gravity, now build any shape. But the computer also provides another liberation. Secure in the knowledge that anything can be produced, drawing – sketching – is itself emboldened, offering a license that gives the sketch validity not simply as a source but as the final technical authority. The computer enables the representation and manipulation of that which cannot otherwise be drawn.* (Sorkin, 1999, p. 30)

An early but very influential development in graphical user interaction was Ivan Sutherland's TX-2 Sketchpad system (developed incidentally at MIT), which was the first computer system to allow users to display, manipulate and copy images using a light pen input device (Sutherland, 1963). Although research into sketch recognition and graphical input devices has made some progress since (see section **8.13**), there is still some way to go before 3-D digital models can be derived directly from sketches such as the one shown in **figure 8.7**. The lines in this type of sketch convey shape primarily through the expression of selective and suggestive contour information. If this information is known, then non-photorealistic digital renderings that look like sketches can be produced (DeCarlo, Finkelstein, Rusinkiewicz and Santella, 2003), but recognition is a much harder issue.

Consequently, Gehry's sketch ideas are transferred into the digital environment primarily through the digitisation of physical models. This only used to happen after a long and laborious process of physical modelling had resulted in the production of a final design model. More recently, however, this digitisation has taken place at a much earlier stage within the cyclical process of design model development. Physical modelling typically begins with simple *block models* that explore the building programme, and these models then evolve into *design process models* that reflect the development of the scheme (see section **8.8**). Another role of digital modelling has been for the verification of the digital models against the final design models to produce *check models*. For der Neue Zollhof, laminated-paper verification models were produced using CNC milling machines. Nowadays these check models are more likely to be produced using rapid prototyping technologies such as stereolithography, for example (see section **8.19**).

It should also be noted that design development through model-making on all projects is very much a collaborative process with project architects and with clients. The relationship between sketches and models, physical and digital, varies from project to project. The Stata Center project was one in which sketches played a major role before the physical modelling took over. Gehry produced over fifty drawings himself, and hundreds more were produced by the design team (Lindsey, 2001, p. 55). The subjective and provocative sketch remains the driving force behind most design development.

> *In Gehry's practice, much weight is put on the sketch, on the spontaneity of impulse and on an essence of ineffable character to which all obeisance must be paid. For Gehry, (...), the next step is an inversion. The sketch, which defies conventional geometrical organization, must be translated into a system of precise co-ordinates and known structural properties, all of which depend upon an undergirding Euclideanism. The forms are derived after the fact.*
> *This act suggests a constant tension – constant relationship – between a system of familiar Platonic solids and a set of spontaneous forms that riff but do not ape this set of familiars, ...* (Sorkin, 1999, pp. 28-29).

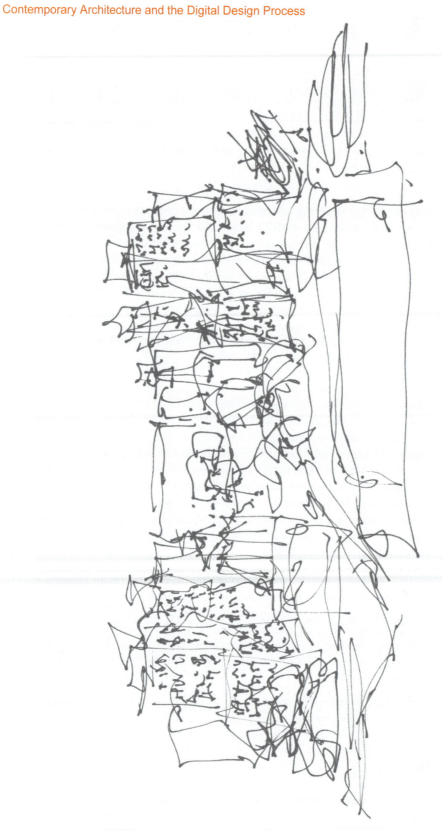

Figure 8.7: One of Frank Gehry's sketches for the design of the Stata Center.

8.3   The Ray and Maria Stata Center at MIT

What excites me about the project is dealing with the scientists. Also it's a piece of MIT that has historical significance. It is the replacement for building 20, which the scientists loved because it was like a warehouse; they could do anything to it. The users want that to happen again, and I want that to happen. The university set up criteria to prevent that from happening again because they say that the building is only on loan to these departments, and twenty years later somebody else may be there.

Anyway, it's going to be fun to work through. How to attach it to the MIT system, how to solve the problems of the scientists, how to deal with the quadrangle of MIT in a way that represents a different way to look at it than the stodgy old way. They have this thing called the 'Idea of the Infinite Corridor'. All of their buildings are connected underground; you can move internally through the whole campus. There aren't very many distinguished buildings on that campus. They want this one to be special.

Before they hired me, I predicted they'd all want what they had, and that's exactly what they said in the first meeting. They said, 'How do you break out of what we're used to?' We said, 'Well, you try things, you start things'. They said, 'Like how?' So that's when we said, 'Let's try a number of ways to organize the staff offices and the shared spaces'. And we did, and got them involved. Some of them hated it and they sent us email. Some of the ideas really bothered them.

One lady was all over me at one of the meetings saying you can't do this and you can't do that. I said to her, 'If you think I'm here to take you out of your banal office, which is poorly lit, poorly furnished, has poor acoustics, and poor natural light – if you think I'm here to take you out of that in order to put you into something that really works, with user-friendly furniture, nice light, and a better relationship to your staff and your colleagues – if you think I'm here to do that, you're crazy. I wouldn't do that to you'. Finally, she laughed.
(Gehry, 1999, p. 226).

The brief for the Stata Center was for it to house the Laboratory for Computer Science (LCS), the Artificial Intelligence Laboratory (AI Lab), the Laboratory for Information and Decision Systems (LIDS) and the Department of Linguistics and Philosophy (L&P). According to Gehry himself, the programme was a complicated one. Each of the departments was autonomous, but they were looking for a way to create synergy between departments (Gehry, 2002, p. 25). They wanted a building that would create more interaction between people. The solution was to provide two C-shaped buildings with communal activities in between. The C-shaped buildings consisted of the Gates building (for the LCS) and the Dreyfoos Building (for the AI Lab, LIDS, and L&P) (**figure 8.10**), separated by a warehouse space on the lower two levels (**figure 8.11**). The centre was to accommodate flexible research facilities, a large auditorium for high-tech presentations, experimental teaching spaces, distance learning projects, and amenities such as restaurants, parking, sports facilities and other services.

The inspiration for Frank Gehry's proposal was building 20, which has been associated with many innovative developments in areas such as computing, communications science, linguistics, nuclear science, cosmic rays, dynamic analysis and control, acoustics, food technology and stroboscopic photography. It was originally constructed as temporary laboratory space during World War II, but lasted for a further 55 years. Stewart Brand gives an insightful description of this scruffy and old, yet flexible and user-friendly building (Brand, 1994). According to Heather Lechtman:

The building is full of small microenvironments, each of which is different and each a creative space. (op. cit., p. 28)

The brief for the Ray and Maria Stata Center was to emulate some of the characteristics of building 20, and thus to stimulate innovation through intellectual and social interaction.

8.4   The Laboratory for Computer Science (LCS)

An illustration of the interdisciplinary connections between LCS and the AI Lab occurred when John McCarthy (based in the AI Lab) defined the high-level language LISP in 1958. The big problem at that time was not the software development, but access to scarce and expensive computer resources. This led McCarthy and others to invent time sharing in 1959. A group of MIT graduate students based in building 20 developed time-sharing minicomputers, and formed the Digital Equipment Corporation (DEC) which went on become the world's second largest computer manufacturer. MIT's Project MAC, originally suggested by J.C.R. Licklider, was a research programme that led to the development of an operating system called MULTICS. Project MAC was a large and well-funded research programme that began in 1963, with as many as 400 research staff by 1967. MULTICS was later developed by Bell Labs into UNIX.

Project MAC was later renamed the Laboratory for Computer Science (LCS) to reflect its widening involvement with computer science and information. Other innovations at LCS have included full-page text editors, the directory system of organising computer files, spreadsheets, ethernet and local area networks (LANs), internet protocols, public cryptography for computer security, X-windows, Project Athena, the NUBUS, data flow processing, data abstraction, which in turn led to object-oriented programming.

LCS is now an interdepartmental laboratory undertaking broad-ranging research in computer science, with a strong focus on communication technologies. Current research focuses on the architecture of information infrastructures: human computer interaction (HCI) through speech understanding and advanced graphics/rendering approaches; new computers and operating systems; communications architectures; automation of information-intensive human tasks; finding and organising information. Researchers are also exploring the boundaries shared by computer science, biology, and medicine.

The World Wide Web was invented by Tim Berners-Lee before he joined LCS. Current research includes the development of new types of man-machine interfaces. LCS is developing speech understanding systems, and interactive graphics systems. Other research areas include electronic bulldozers: computational support for low-level mental work e.g. the automation of office-level work; and electronic proximity: support for shared interaction between users in remote locations.

For LCS to be more effective than a collection of isolated research groups, it aims to build on helpful interactions among groups, linking theory to infrastructure systems and human interfaces when possible. LCS also interacts with research groups in the AI Lab and other MIT labs and centres. The need for such interactions has inevitably impinged upon Gehry's thinking for the spatial relationships that need to be expressed. The complex of buildings provides the physical space which makes these interactions possible. In the past, such relationships have often led to great innovations. The LCS building in MIT's new complex aims to create an environment in which people will be able to link their own research efforts with those of their peers.

8.5   Artificial Intelligence Laboratory (AI Lab)

The AI laboratory carries research into human intelligence, which includes reasoning, perception, language, planning, knowledge representation, learning, and social interaction. Robotics and computer vision have been major strengths of the Lab. AI vision research involves the development of computational representations to enable the recognition of distinct objects from bit-mapped images. Vision researchers talk of different levels of object representation that can be extracted out of lower-level images. Possible higher-order levels include: *primal sketches* (containing brightness/contrast information), *2 1/2-D sketches* (containing surface information), and *world models* (containing volumetric information) (Winston, 1984). Computational vision systems may be structured in bottom-up, top-down, or middle-out fashion, and these applications typically explore the effects of specific visual constraints such as shading, textures and vertex information. David Marr, a leading scientist at MIT in the 1970s, focused AI vision research on the constraints imposed by nature (Marr, 1982). In the AI and psychology literature, these constraints are sometimes referred to as visual *cues* (Boring, 1942), and knowledge arises as a consequence of the interpretation of the sensory information associated with these cues. An important representational idea used by Marr and others was that real-world objects could be represented in terms of *generalised cylinders* (Winston, 1984, pp. 338-340). In CAD terminology, a generalised cylinder is simply an extrusion of a closed 2-D cross-sectional profile of any shape along a 3-D axial line of any shape. The size of the shape can also vary as it is extruded along the path. Complex shapes can be defined as Boolean compositions of generalised cylinders. Generalised cylinders is one example of attempts to represent the sensory data upon which human perception is based. Other important researchers in the fields of computer vision and robotics were Rodney Brooks, currently the director of the AI Lab at MIT, and Mike Brady, formerly senior research scientist at MIT, and now at Oxford University. According to Brady:

Computer vision and robotics are ideal subjects in which to develop Information Engineering, since (a) they are replete in challenging practical applications; (b) they are equally replete in unsolved, basic scientific problems that combine mathematics and computing; and (c) they continually push technology to its limits as they are demanding on storage and computational time, yet to be useful systems must operate in real time. (Brady, 1999)

Another revealing quote, however, was given by Brady in relation to the frustrations of bottom-up approaches to computational recognition:

Increasingly, I was frustrated by the failure of 'low level' image processing operations such as edge detection, localised landmark detection ('corner finding'), image de-blurring, segmentation of an image into 'homogeneous' regions defined for example by their textures, and the computation of visible motion. I still am!! (Brady, 1999)

Brady continued to work on a range of topics in image processing and analysis, and believes that a great deal more can be extracted from images than is commonly thought; but that to do so requires modeling of image formation, and the mobilisation of knowledge about what the images depict (Brady, 1997). The current trend in AI is that intelligence depends upon self adapting perceptual systems, motor systems, and language related modules. A current research area at the AI Lab involves the development of intelligent offices within the new complex; enabling researchers to get away from the traditional window-icon-mouse-pointer, or *wimp*, interface, and move towards a more natural form of interaction with computers.

8.6   Laboratory for Information and Decision Systems (LIDS)

LIDS is concerned with the science and technology of systems, communications, control, and signal processing. In communications, research includes information theory and heterogeneous broad band communication networks. Other research areas include nonlinear systems and their control, identification and adaptive control, and the control of hybrid systems. Signal processing is concerned with image processing and vision, as well as with very large signal processing problems. The laboratory is interested in complex systems problems arising in technological contexts which involve communications, control, and signal processing, as well as problems of optimisation, scheduling, and decision-making under conditions of uncertainty.

Since theoretical aspects of this research impinge strongly upon practice, the department has strong contacts with industry. Historically, LIDS was involved in original research work on the development of the digital control of machine tools, an area of application that has increasing relevance to the construction industry, and with particular relevance to Frank Gehry's office. In many modern industries, complex geometric shapes can be directly machined by using 3-axis or 5-axis machines, combined with CAM software which converts CAD parts data into NC instructions. Since parts often have complex geometries, the mathematical functions used to describe the shapes of parts can be complex. Surfaces can be partitioned into smaller areas, called *patches*, each of which is described by means of polynomial functions. On 3-axis machines, such shapes are machined by first generating the profile of the part along layers at different depth values. Parts are machined by cutting the profile at each layer, then proceeding to deeper layers. The geometry of each layer is described by a sequence of complex mathematical functions. An NC controller works with data expressed in terms of straight lines and arcs. This is called *linear approximation*, which can result in moving the machine tool along many linear segments in each layer. Since NC routines for linear approximations can be quite large, computer numerically controlled (CNC) machines typically process spooled sequences of machining instructions. Computer control of a set of CNC machines allows different parts to be machined on different machine tools. This is known as direct numerical control (DNC), and is used in advanced manufacturing systems.

In communications, work on coding, decoding, modems, data networks, and on the OPNET simulation program has also been influential in an industrial context. In automation, LIDS has played an important role in theoretical and algorithmic development, model-based signal processing, image analysis, and vision. The study of heterogeneous communication networks, perceptual systems (character recognition, speech recognition, image analysis, vision), and how these technologies might be used within distributed controlled systems are areas of important research. Other current areas of research include: the study of optical broadband networks, the development of distributed algorithms and protocols in the area of networks, recognition of targets in cluttered environments, computer vision, and very large signal processing problems, the algorithmic development of the theory of nonlinear systems to solve major nonlinear problems such as those in process control, conceptual developments in such areas as identification, adaptive control, and systems learning.

The Exuberant Vision

8.7 Department of Linguistics and Philosophy (L&P)

Linguistics combined with philosophy in 1976 to form the Department of Linguistics and Philosophy. The MIT linguistics group has been engaged in the study of language since the 1950s. In the early years, research focused primarily on phonetic and phonological problems. Noam Chomsky joined the staff of MIT in 1955, and in 1961 was appointed full professor in what was then the Department of Modern Languages and Linguistics. His ideas on the innateness and universality of language structures has had a massive impact on a wide range of academic disciplines beyond linguistics. His book *Syntactic Structures* (Chomsky, 1957) not only addressed issues of linguistic creativity, but also introduced a theory of *transformational grammar* that was formal enough to be programmed. There is also a close relationship between Chomsky's theory of language and his political philosophy that stems from his attacks on radical behaviourism. According to Lyons:

> . . . he claimed that the behaviourists' impressive panoply of scientific terminology and statistics was no more than camouflage, covering up their inability to account for the fact that language simply is not a set of 'habits' and is radically different from animal communication. It is the same charge that Chomsky has made in his political writings against the sociologists, psychologists and other social scientists whose 'expert' advice is sought by governments: that they 'desperately attempt . . . to imitate the surface features of sciences that really have significant intellectual content', neglecting in this attempt all the fundamental problems with which they should be concerned and taking refuge in pragmatic and methodological trivialities. (Lyons, 1970, p. 14)

Early work on *knowledge representation* was related to linguistics research which in turn was connected with work on the philosophical analysis of language (Russell and Norvig, 1995). AI and linguistics intersect in a research field known as *computational linguistics* or *natural language processing*. Within this field, there are strong divisions between semantic and syntactic applications, as well as other approaches and associated formalisms.

By the early 1990s, psycholinguists interested in language acquisition, sentence processing, phonetics and neuro-imaging found themselves working on many of the same topics as linguists. Linguists, in turn, began asking questions that could only be answered using the research tools of modern psycholinguistics. The research conducted by the MIT linguistics programme aims to develop a general theory that reveals rules and laws that govern the structure of particular languages, and the general laws and principles governing all natural languages. The core of the programme includes most of the traditional sub-fields of linguistics: phonology, morphology, syntax, semantics, and psycholinguistics, as well as questions concerning the interrelations between linguistics and other disciplines such as philosophy and logic, literary studies, the study of formal languages, acoustics, and computer science. The current Dean of MIT's School of Humanities and Social Science, made this observation about the new complex:

> The new facility should prove a stellar opportunity for faculty in the Department of Linguistics and Philosophy to interact in new and exciting ways with faculty from EECS and brain and cognitive sciences around the subject of language and mind. This will help to foster MIT's international leadership in teaching and research at the intersection of linguistics, neuroscience, cognitive science, and artificial intelligence. (Khoury, 1999)

219

8.8 The Role of Physical Models

It's like watching paint dry. I stare at it for weeks It's not mathematical, it's intuitive. We made hundreds of models for the Disney Concert Hall, hundreds. (Merrick, 2003, p. 4).

The initial use of physical models for the development of the Stata Center scheme was as a vehicle for client participation and involvement in the project. Because of the emphasis on emulating the desired characteristics of the earlier building 20, a whole series of very sketchy models was used to ascertain clients' responses to proposals for a loosely structured group of buildings between the two towers containing the main academic departments. **Figures 8.8–8.9** show just two of many models proposed in this pre-schematic phase. They were very loosely based on the programme, and were very experimental. Each one was shown to the client committee, which consisted of professors from several academic disciplines. The reactions obtained from these presentations affected subsequent model proposals, culminating in a more discrete and less amorphous group of buildings. The final design models are shown in **figures 8.10–8.11**.

Figure 8.8: An early design process model.

The schemes are all based on different cultures, different human or animal cultures. We started with a Japanese house that had sliding screens. We told them that we were talking about flexibility, and in the Japanese traditional house you can open up all the doors and have a big public room, or you can divide them up so that no one knows what anyone else is doing. They hated it. It was too much decision making, too many choices, too much neatness required on everyone's part. They didn't identify with that at all. The scheme that did get a positive reaction was the orangutan village. They would live in little nests in the trees. Each person would have one. And then they would come down onto the Savannah in the daytime, and work collectively. That made a lot of sense to them. There's a division in their lives between the private inward routine and the collective lab work that they do in big groups.

People don't understand the importance of the involvement of the client, which is huge. That was not true of beaux arts architecture at all, but it is very true of Frank's architecture. It's important to understand that these things don't happen by magic; they happen because the client wants them to; it's not an accident. (Allen, 1999, p. 230).

Figure 8.9:
A design process model.

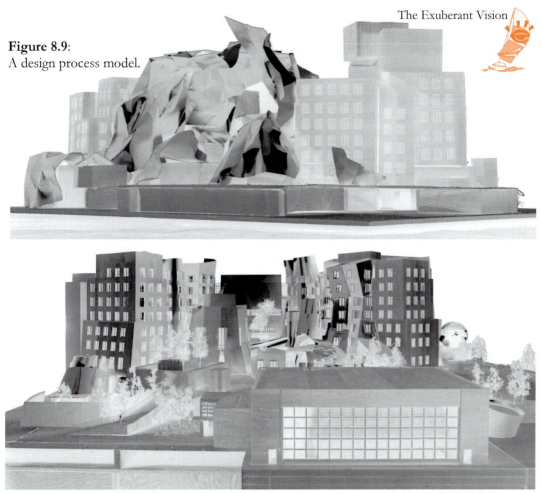

Figure 8.10: A physical model showing the orthogonal pool building in the foreground. The Center is organised internally as a connected set of spaces up through the fifth floor, topped by two isolated towers. The Dreyfoos Tower, holding AI, LIDS and L&P, is on the left, the Gates Tower, holding LCS, is on the right. Each tower appears to consist of a number of separate shapes from the outside, though its floor-plan and space are unified inside.

Figure 8.11: A detailed physical model looking onto Vassar Street. The two lowest floors visible from the Vassar Street side (which are the 2nd and 3rd floors) is tall *warehouse* space intended to provide easily reconfigurable laboratory space to increase flexibility of the building in the future.

In addition to the physical models, coloured diagrams were used as a medium for interaction with clients. Blue represented the underground service tunnel system used by MIT students to move around in winter; red represented public access; and yellow represented shared circulation space. The same colour scheme was applied to early design process models. Just as sketches have an immediacy and conciseness for designers, so diagrammatic presentations of complex arrangements have a similar effect for clients. Diagrammatic presentations are very effective in the communication of logical and temporal relationships, as well as of abstract concepts. This was evident in the case study described in **chapter 6**, particularly at the feasibility stage. The interactive role of diagrams in the design process allows both designers and clients to think through the consequences of design decisions.

The way in which artificial intelligence (AI) researchers treat diagrammatic reasoning is by means of an information-processing approach based on Cartesian dualism i.e. that minds can be disembodied. Numerous computer applications exist in which diagrams are processed in various ways (Sowa, 1984; Glasgow, Narayanan and Chandrasekaran, 1995). However, treating diagrams as mere inputs to computer systems completely misses the point of diagrammatic reasoning in architectural design. The interactions that take place between designers and clients through diagrams are part of the interpretation of the diagrams themselves. Furthermore, the human body is such a fundamental aspect of architectural design that it can rarely be excluded from the interpretation of diagrammatic presentations of architectural concepts. For these reasons, it appears that a more useful way of thinking about architectural design diagrams is in terms of concepts derived from social psychology (Vygotsky, 1962; Vile and Polovina, 1998). Just as thought and speech interact in the field of verbal thought, so visual thought and graphic languages (diagrams) meet in an area referred to as graphic ideation (**figure 8.12**) (McKim, 1980, p.142). Design diagrams, therefore, can be used to influence and expand visual thinking processes.

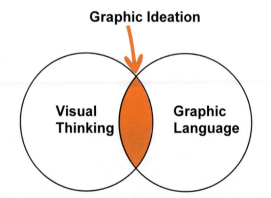

Figure 8.12: Graphic ideation: the interaction between thought and language.

It's a dollhouse thing. The clients love that because they can understand what's happening. They are surprised at the box shape, but they don't believe that it's really going to be a box. They know better. We tell them that it's not going to be a box for long. There are four departments that are divided into two main categories. The laboratory of Computer Science is the highest tower, and the lower tower, which is connected to an existing building, is the Artificial Intelligence Lab, which has all the robots. The Linguistic Department is connected to the Computer Science department, through the notion that computer language is a language in the first place.

We've lifted up the grade about twenty feet and put a main lobby on the campus side. When we lifted the grade we created a plaza area for the students. The lower quadrant is public, and the upper terrace is a more private sort of Philosophy Garden for the scientists. All the colored blocks represent different conference rooms for the different departments. And the red block is the cafe. It's a quiet dining terrace. The circulation between the two towers is connected through and around the public pieces at the terrace level. There is also an education center which will be in the later phase. It will have classrooms and a cafe. A small amphitheater will be an outdoor classroom. We thought that the smoking professors would like that, because they could smoke and teach at the same time. But the amphitheater is another way of transitioning from grade up onto the plaza. (Allen, 1999, p. 227)

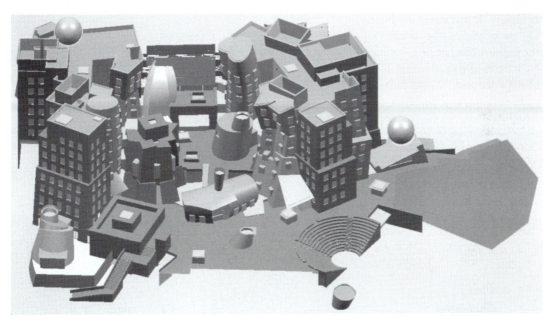

Figure 8.13: An aerial view of the CAD model of the Stata Center.

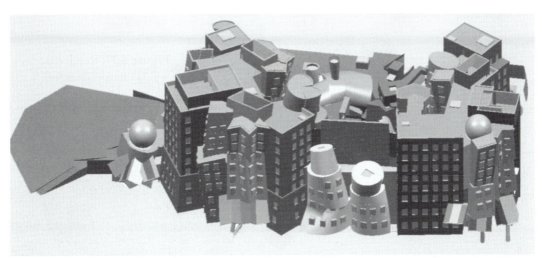

Figure 8.14: An aerial view of the CAD model of the Stata Center.

8.9   Value Engineering

Value engineering is a process of rationalisation used in Gehry's office in order to reduce costs, with some similarities to the value analysis and value management processes described in **chapter 6**, but only comes into play once the design work is complete. It can affect the building programme, the quality of the architecture, or its complexity. It is used to rationalise form relative to cost, taking into account complexity, material, and structure.

According to Lindsey:

The process involves translating the architectural elements, skin panels, beams, columns, etc., into the following hierarchy:

- *straight,*
- *flat,*
- *curved,*
- *doubly curved,*
- *and warped (highly shaped),*

each representing a higher cost.

The translation continues through the following syntax:

- *repetitive,*
- *similar,*
- *and unique,*

again each representing a higher cost of manufacture and assembly. (Lindsey, 2001, p. 71)

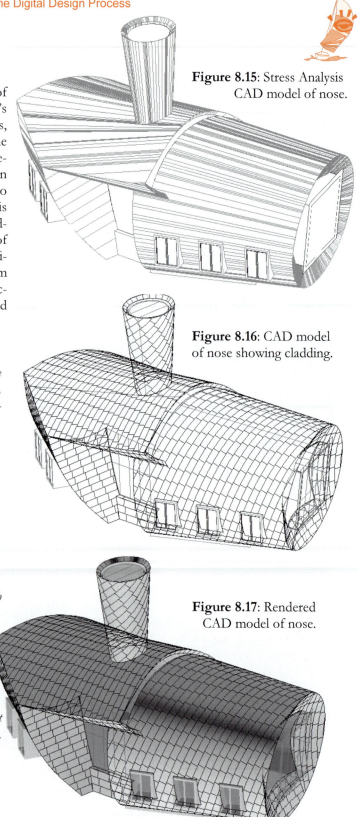

Figure 8.15: Stress Analysis CAD model of nose.

Figure 8.16: CAD model of nose showing cladding.

Figure 8.17: Rendered CAD model of nose.

8.10   Gaussian Analysis

. . . all the infinitely varied curved surfaces we can ever find in nature or imagine belong to only three categories, which are domelike, cylinder, or saddlelike. (Salvadori, 1980, p. 188)

Karl Gauss's discovery of categories of curved surfaces has significant implications for the fabrication of curved elements. Domes and saddle-shaped surfaces are *non-developable* i.e. they cannot be made by folding or bending flat surfaces (see section **8.17**). On the other hand they are stiffer than *developable* surfaces, and have been used as roof forms because of this.

Gaussian analysis is used in Frank Gehry's office to evaluate the degree of compound curvature of building components, particularly surface panels and skins. Curvature equations are used to calculate the rates of change of surface tangents to normal lines at each point on any given surface. Degrees of curvature along with the properties of materials, are represented as 3-D surface models allowing problem areas to be identified. Colour coded digital models can indicate the bending limitations of materials used on a scheme (Lindsey, 2001, p. 71). Gaussian analysis may indicate that material curvature is within tolerance limits, but expensive to fabricate.

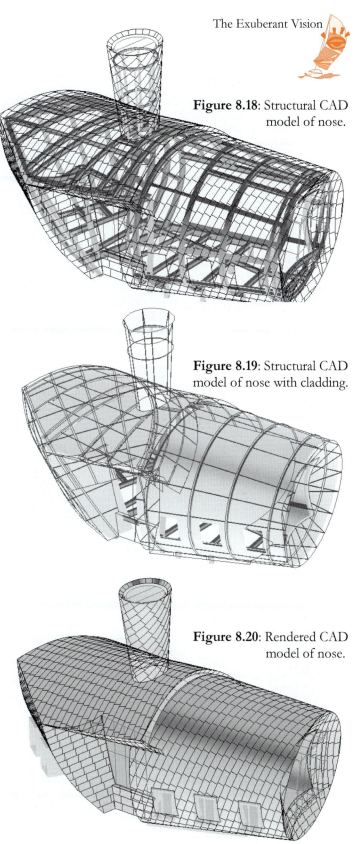

Figure 8.18: Structural CAD model of nose.

Figure 8.19: Structural CAD model of nose with cladding.

Figure 8.20: Rendered CAD model of nose.

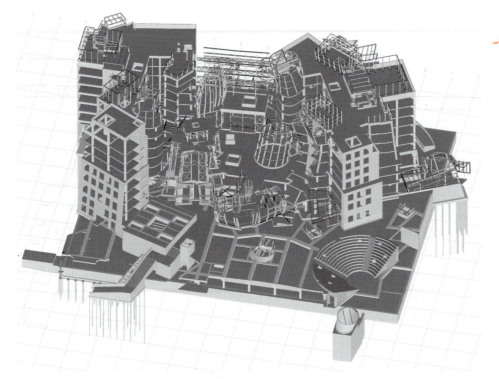

Figure 8.21: CAD model of the whole structure.

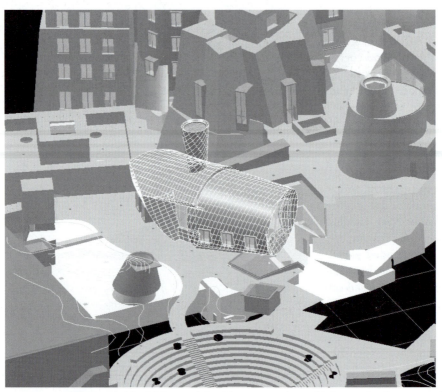

Figure 8.22: CAD model with nose and amphitheatre in foreground.

Figure 8.23: A part of Vassar Street. The two short white circular sections in the centre of the CAD model hold the reading room and a cafeteria common to the entire Center. The flat structure behind and above these is an unoccupied windbreak which separates the Dreyfoos tower from the Gates tower.

Computer glare was an important issue since all the research labs were filled with computers. Because the light was more diffuse on the north side of the building, more of it could be let in to the labs without affecting computers. One idea at this stage was to open up the north side with a curtain wall, and to close up the south side with punched windows to control the light. Small skylights would bring light in without wasting too much space. The warehouse space had a similar programme to that of the towers, a mixture of office and lab space, but with a higher floor-to-floor ratio, because of special height requirements.

. . . shape and movement have a differential relationship to one another. Each operates within the terms of the other: shape shapes movements and movements move shapes. Gehry moves shape through three dimensions . . . He does this in two ways at once: up and down, and across, but always through space where the (. . .) surface describes a shape that ends but does not conclude when it meets other shapes or the ground or the air, because it is a singularity made out of only two edges, and therefore a plane. (Gilber-Rolfe and Gehry, p. 111)

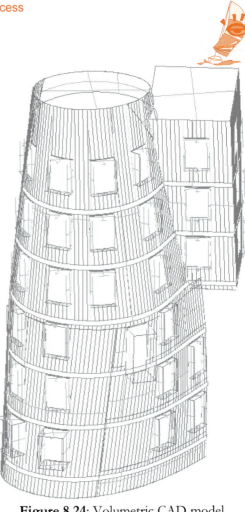

Figure 8.24: Volumetric CAD model of the Buddha building.

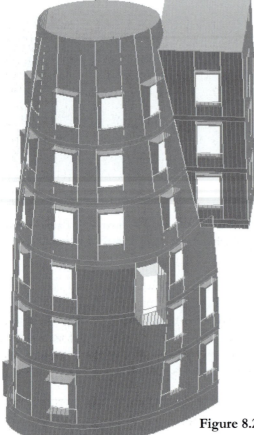

'To say that a building has to have a certain kind of architectural attitude to be a building is too limiting, so the best thing to do is to make the sculptural functional in terms of use. If you can translate the beauty of sculpture into the building . . . whatever it does to give movement and feeling, that's where the innovation in architecture is.' (van Bruggen, 1997, p.119)

Figure 8.25: Volumetric CAD model of the Buddha building.

Flat pieces cost one dollar, single curvature pieces cost two dollars; double curvature pieces cost ten dollars. The good thing about the computer is that it allows you to keep a close control over the geometry and the budget. It was not just speculation; it was real.' (Zaera, 1995)

Figure 8.26: Volumetric CAD model of the Achilles building.

'I look at old buildings, at Erich Mendelsohn's Einstein Tower [Potsdam, 1917-21]. I speculate that if Mendelsohn were still alive today he would have done all the things I've done and I would have had to go somewhere else. Can you imagine Corbusier with a computer?' (Worsley, 2000).

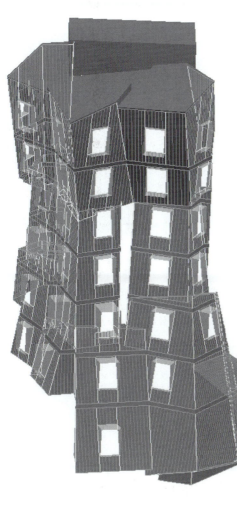

Figure 8.27: Volumetric CAD model of the Achilles building.

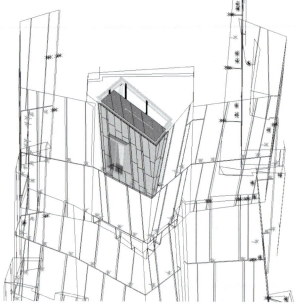

Figure 8.28:
CAD model with
insertion of
glazing element.

Figure 8.29: Structural CAD model
of the Star building.

Figure 8.30: Structural CAD model of the Stata Center exterior.

The strength of Gehry's practice is in the pragmatic integration of the analogue with the digital. The transfer of information from the digital environments of design to the digital technologies of construction in a seamless manner is re-establishing the architect as master builder. This reversal of the trend towards the separation and isolation of the design, engineering and construction professions is a positive step enabling a more integrated approach to professional practice. Once the benefits of this approach are fully realised and adopted more widely, it is quite likely that the nature of professional roles will change dramatically.

We're the only firm in the world doing what we're doing, and I think we're on the verge of revolutionizing the way architecture is practiced. . . .

The new computer and management system allows us to unite all the players – the contractor, the engineer, the architect – with one modeling system. It's the master builder principle. I think it makes the architect more the parent and the contractor more the child – the reverse of the twentieth-century system. It's interesting because you wouldn't think that would happen with something as technical as the computer but, in fact, it has. And you wouldn't think that an office like ours would lead it. Nobody else does it yet. But they will.

In Europe there's a person called the metteur who takes off the quantities of a building. We don't need him any more. The computer does that in an instant. So as we are designing the building, we have an instant metteur that takes off as we go. Consequently, I'm designing with specific conditions and I don't go out of bounds. Because you know, when you design without knowing the boundaries, you find a form and you become enamored with it. It crystallizes. It's a fixed image. It's really hard once it's a fixed image to go back and cut, cut, cut. But if you're cutting as you go, you don't get fixed until you know you can do it. When you're fixed, you're fixed. You know you can afford it. (Gehry, 1999, p. 50)

8.11 Architectural Planning

Intuitively, Gehry succeeds in combining the conscious with the unconscious, schematic planning based on the preliminary program and circumstance of the site with semi-automatic scrawling/writing. (van Bruggen, 1999, p. 40)

Architectural planning, sometimes referred to as space programming, concerns responses to the functional requirements of the brief. As in the briefing stage of the Faulkner Browns case study in **chapter 6**, basic spatial relationships and adjacencies together with corresponding area approximations are often investigated at this stage.

Much has been made of the sculptural characteristics of Gehry's recent projects. It should be borne in mind that his current expressions of form, which may appear to magazine architects as merely sculpting from the outside in, have evolved over many years. During this time his ability to plan from the inside out has never lost its importance. The plan is still essentially a generator of form. This was apparent in his sketches for the Guggenheim Museum Bilbao (van Bruggen, 1999, pp. 68-69). Just as in his Santa Monica house, the sculptural form is on the periphery of and peripheral to the plan. According to Gehry himself:

Solving all the functional problems is an intellectual exercise. That is a different part of my brain. It's not less important, it's just different. And I make a value out of solving all those problems, dealing with the context and the client and finding my moment of truth after I understand the problem. (van Bruggen, 1999, p. 95)

The plans of the Stata Center in **figures 8.31–8.39** are the result of intuitive responses to the functional requirements, developed through interaction with clients, and represented through sketches, physical and ultimately digital models.

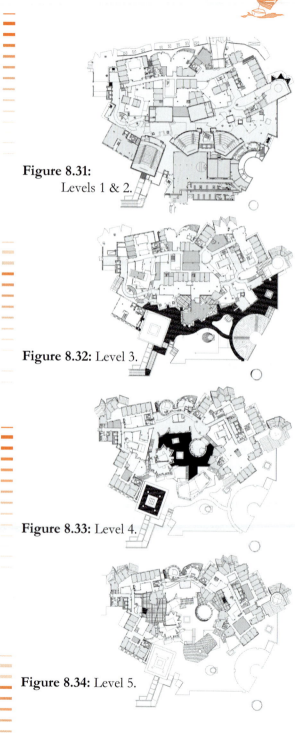

Figure 8.31: Levels 1 & 2.

Figure 8.32: Level 3.

Figure 8.33: Level 4.

Figure 8.34: Level 5.

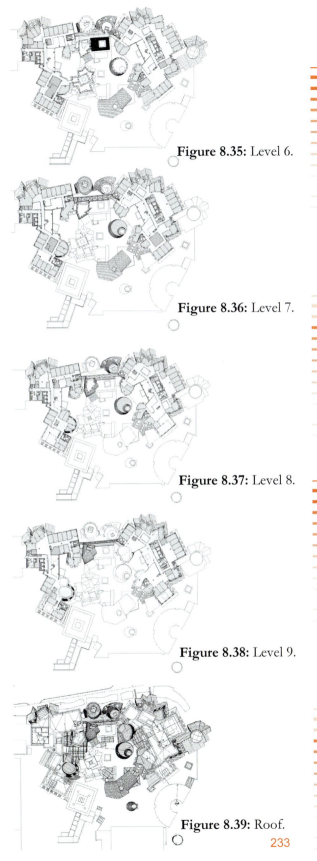

Figure 8.35: Level 6.

Figure 8.36: Level 7.

Figure 8.37: Level 8.

Figure 8.38: Level 9.

Figure 8.39: Roof.

Computational support for the analysis of planning issues is still very limited. CAD software such as Vectorworks, for example, allows basic data related to a building programme to be entered into a spreadsheet (Khemlani, 2002). On the basis of this data, three kinds of graphical information can be derived:

- adjacency matrices corresponding to spreadsheet information,

- stacking diagrams showing floor levels and areas, along with areas of individual spaces,

- bubble diagrams showing spaces as basic shapes with proportional areas e.g. circles, and connections between spaces as lines of varying thickness, depending upon the degree of connectivity (**figure 8.40**).

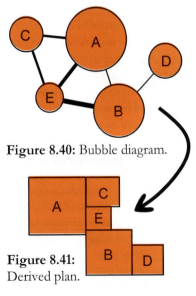

Figure 8.40: Bubble diagram.

Figure 8.41: Derived plan.

Although plans can be derived from the manipulation of bubble diagrams, it is clear that these digital space planning techniques are still a long way from competing with intuitive processes in the generation of optimal layouts.

8.12   Dialogues with Jim Glymph

Some of Jim Glymph's observations of the digital processes used in Gehry's office now follow:

JG: *More than a decade ago when we first looked at this process, basically based on what Frank was doing without computers, we determined that what we needed was a really good geometric modeller. We arrived at CATIA at that time because it was it was simply the best geometric modeller that we could find. It was capable of dealing with almost everything that we wanted to deal with. We used the model at that time, based on all the technology, was primarily based on having this robust, very scalable modeller as a geometry modeller, parametrics wasn't even around, as a product anyway. And so, a whole lot of our process for a long time simply had to do with exploring how much you could develop in a three-dimensional environment, what the advantages were in it, throwing out a few kind of old rules about drawing not to scale, working to scale, and providing the kind of data that created enough geometric modelling that fabricators who were moving into various forms of software that worked in 3-D and worked with CAD/CAM applications and had immediate 2-D drawing production capabilities, things like that, could wind up with a model from the architect where they could transfer data and really take advantage of the tools that they already had, or were just emerging, but were not really working for them because they usually had to build the building from the ground up to make them work. So our focus was primarily on geometric modelling. That is still the heart of what we do.*

With the emergence of competition in the market when the first parametric modellers came out, CATIA went into a process of rebuilding their software from the ground up, and so there really are two different stories here: one that is, and its culmination, and Disney represents that, which is a pure geometric model that's annotated, and drawings are extracted from it, information is transferred to other users during the entire lifecycle of the project. So that was the downstream intent. The cycling of models became an obvious front-end offshoot. So Frank working on a sketch model, us digitising into 3-D, building a 3-D model for a couple of purposes: one purpose would be to do measurement, to support estimating, to do analysis of various forms; and the other would be to template or to fabricate the next scale model or the next version of a physical model that would go back to Frank, and be dealt with in the physical environment – either CAD/CAM fabricated in a variety of ways, or depending on the nature of the model, simply templated out of the 3-D model such as lofted models in house and out house outsourcing. And of course that got us involved in virtually every kind of CAD/CAM fabrication of model scale, which was really good for the staff here because it made them better appreciate what contractors and fabricators could do at full scale. There are some synergies between those two processes. That was an interesting feature in itself.

The parametric modeller for CATIA is what they call V5 in the new version. We did a lot of different things with V5, including making it PC-based, and a lot of things we've been hoping they would do for a decade to actually create pricing structures that would allow this to be more broadly broadcast across projects. Our own process has been to use CATIA as a sort of receptacle for all of the work done in other software, and as a co-ordination tool to bring three-dimensional shop drawing work back into this environment to do entrance checking and those kinds of things, and to review and to develop in 3-D. There is where the efficiency in the process was, and still is when the players along the food chain are sophisticated enough to deal with this. Now in that environment, and with the new version of CATIA V5 which is a parametric modeller and object modeller, we began looking at parametric applications on a variety of projects, and MIT was one of them. We were working primarily at the fabricator level, where shop-drawing production of multiple panels of a project in which the geometry was constantly changing, could be developed into a parametric model, which was useful and created direct productivity gains. We also have learned a lot, and this is ongoing right now, at least from our point of view, where applying parametrics doesn't work too early in the project, where relationships are changing based on far more complicated issues than appear in the geometry of a computer screen – everything from the aesthetics to the politics of a project, and changes of programme direction.

I think there is limited potential for parametric applications in the early stages of designing complex buildings.

PS: Is this because users need to understand the mathematics of parametric relationships?

JG: *No, no, no, no, I don't think so, because actually establishing parametric relationships in V5 is really, relatively simple. It's that you're investing time when you don't have the rules of the project from a studied or technical standpoint, well-enough understood, for the investment, however easy it may be, in establishing parametric relationships to be worthwhile. There's a learning curve, which in terms of being able to use parametric design tools in the real-world environment, outside the academic environment, you're really only talking about the last couple of years. The proper positioning of that tool, which I think is across the entire design process, but understanding where it has to apply and where it doesn't, where you're really going to get real productivity gains and enhancements to the design process, and where you're not (then you're going to find you've invested a lot in a model that has the wrong underlying relationships), is a question that we're still trying to figure out. Obviously if you make a mistake you waste a lot of time, and when you get it right you gain a lot of time, or quality, or there's something to be gained.*

The other side of this, if you can jump out of that design world of institutional landmark buildings, and shift over to say a chip manufacturing plant, I know of a number of people who have created phenomenal parametric models for specific, for example, manufacturing buildings, which are driven by such strong underlying logic that they can create just breathtaking gains across the entire lifecycle of a project. So if you're dealing with a building type that is engineering driven, which means not particularly humanistic, not particularly artistic, not particularly urbanistic, or not necessarily not, but it's machine-like, then the potential for radical improvements in the process all the way across the board, right through the bidding and even into the construction speed, time for acquisition and everything else. The potential is almost limitless. When you're talking about creative one-off buildings, the same parametric features have huge gains if applied in the right place in the right way, and are overly complicated unless used in the right way in the early front-ends of a project. This is the proper place for parametrics to fit in this world, at least in our world. This is something that is still an ongoing discovery process. The further you get down into the design development and the technical development of a project, the more powerful the tool is.

Architects who operate from a design standpoint might be interested in shape grammars and all kinds of other computer-generative design issues, will I'm sure find these capabilities incredible enhancements to the design process. That's simply not the process that is used here in terms of generative design. For us it's a bit of a curiosity as to why the designer would give up design to a machine anyway.

PS: A lot of people in academia still believe in that kind of approach. I gave up on that some time ago. It doesn't make any kind of sense to design from categorisations of known architecture.

JG: *It's the one thing in the process that you wouldn't want to take over! Basically, if you're really talking about looking at us historically, you'll see that parametric design emerges as a useful tool in the process in very recent projects. With Zahner, the fabricator of the exterior metal panel system for the MIT project, they actually switched from Pro-ENGINEER which was a parametric modeller earlier than CATIA, to CATIA. They worked with us in Pro-ENGINEER before. And there in the final detailing shop drawing and fabrication, which includes some CAD/CAM fabrication, parametrics were a big, big thing. Projects starting up now are using parametrics in a much more robust way. MIT is at least a real-world example of the use of parametrics. It fits into a broader context of everybody working in this 3-D geometric model. One of the advantages of having a cross-section of the team working in 3-D, in at least something through translation, if not directly, creates a single model database. The more trades you can get involved in that process, the more gains you see on the co-ordination side of the construction process.*

Figure 8.42: Sketch CAD model with shaded surfaces of the Walt Disney Concert Hall.

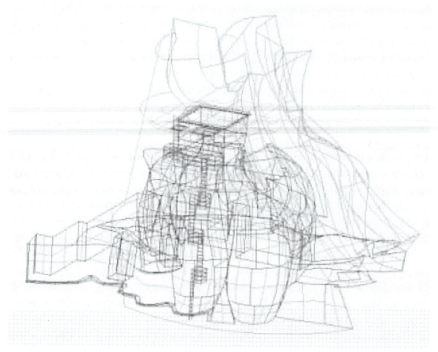

Figure 8.43: Wireframe CAD model of the Founders' Room in the Walt Disney Concert Hall.

JG:　　On the MIT project there is a steel fabricator who worked in SDS, which is similar to X-steel and BoCAD. It's software developed for 3-D steel detailing, specifically with automated 2-D shop drawing output. We did translation back and forth with X-steel from CATIA and attempted to do paperless steel construction on the MIT project, which was an interesting story in itself for two reasons. One is that translations between trades that are concerned about one element, steel, and models that are concerned about all elements that the steel is interfacing with – we found a lot of holes in translators and those kinds of things. Part of this was the identification of where fixes needed to take place. This caused us to write translators. What caused us to use paper was the weight of tradition. The SDS detail model is sophisticated enough to have every weld and bolt in it, and is annotated, and has all the data and more than a 2-D document has. Shop drawings were reviewed in that environment and approved.

At the end of the day, the traditional bureaucracy still insisted on some hard copy paper that was chasing the whole process. Sometimes this was to support the inspectors in the field who were not ready to buy into this global change, or certainly aren't going to for a single project. Sometimes it had to do with the kinds of documents that building departments require. The real issue underlying all these projects (I think we've become more sophisticated about this), is the route to a paperless process. It's a pretty clear and open route, and while the technology to support it is certainly available, the process of bringing people to that technology is a business proposition issue, in terms of when is there enough critical mass for people to make that kind of move. A probably even more daunting problem is that it's a cultural issue. You have embedded cultures throughout the tens to hundreds of organisations that are involved in the construction approval review, design and engineering a building. You can see this in these projects if you get very close to them. You can see the people working with the technology who've actually crossed the line and bought in, seeing the paper as a nuisance. You can see the people who are unprepared to buy in, whose organisation or agency or whatever is not prepared to buy in. They just see the world in the opposite way, that the computing is a nuisance.

This led us to a newer schtick. Basically when we go down this road on a project, we wind up doing double work, building these large 3-D databases and models, but we're still producing the traditional documents, except for certain sub-trades. Even in the sub-trades where the technology exists across the entire lifecycle, there is still oversight of one form or another that still requires paper.

It convinced us that one of the issues we need to focus on, which is what our current projects do, is automating the 2-D drawing process so that we could continue to invest more and more in the virtual model. The requirement for paper is going to be around for decades culturally. In order to pursue the obvious advantages of working in these more robust, both geometric models and data models, meant that one thing or the other had to give, because you weren't showing the capital or productivity gain if the 2-D process remained independent of the 3-D process. There's a lot of software at the component level that deals with this already, so it's not a huge problem. The steel detailing software, for example, has pretty much established views on cuts and annotation standards that can be extracted with varying degrees, and in some cases very impressive degrees of automation. We're developing in the CATIA environment a similar capability which we now have, to start to get substantial portions of documents, if not entire documents as extractions from the 3-D model. That's a real important thing for productivity. It's not the most exciting thing that we're doing, but it's the obvious thing that allows the implementation of everything else. That is something that did not happen on MIT, but is beginning to happen in the shop drawing process on MIT as the project comes to conclusion. Our drawings are abstracted from the computer model on MIT, but without the degree of automation that we have today. The problem there is if the paper documents are an independently developed database, then tracking changes, keeping the two databases co-ordinated can become overwhelming. So one of the keys here is if you're going to leave the paper world, you can't just walk away from it, you have to automate the dinosaur, so that it can run in the background while you move forward where the technology can really take you.

PS: What is interesting is that what you're describing is driving the design process, at least in your office, if not in the way that other practices are progressing. Certain things need to be put into the background in order to focus on what you think is more important.

JG: *We've been experimenting and pioneering for a long time, some of it out of necessity, just because of the kinds of buildings we're trying to build. We always have this healthy disrespect for the standard approach to buildings. I suppose it's got us into trouble sometimes, but it certainly has lead to some pretty big breakthroughs in terms of real efficiency gains. So you've got glass and metal and concrete and steel all fully controlled in 3-D at MIT. MIT is now looking at whether it's the largest, most complicated project they've ever attempted, having the lowest change order rates, the fewest R5, the fewest construction problems they've ever experienced. These kinds of things are really important to promoting this process, when you're on a going boat, something's going to happen there.*

PS: What about future maintenance of the building?

This is the big PLM thing. Obviously it's something that the IBM souls of the world have promoted and developed extremely successfully for things like the automotive and aerospace industries, or shipbuilding, where you're dealing with a computer model where any modification that is made lives on in the model. If any modifications are made, they're made in a very serious documented way. If you modify a car, an aeroplane, a product, there's an approach there where you can show real value to the model going forward. The level of modelling we do from a maintenance standpoint obviously has some value. If you're retrofitting a building and you have a 3-D model of a steel structure, then this is certainly nicer than having to go through drawings. The problem with buildings is that buildings are maintained and modified without the discipline of a car, so people who have attempted, for example, to put together 3-D models that deal with chemical and electrical systems, those models are only usable and valuable if every electrical and mechanical retrofit of the building is loaded into that model. Buildings tend not to be remodelled that way. People tend not to track that level of detail in the remodelling, and so the models which are absolutely reliable when the building is finished, become unreliable extremely quickly because they are not updated. You can see where something like dealing with a structure which has the rigour of the engineer and everything else being involved, would have the discipline and the process. The real future in terms of a robust maintenance model for 3-D computer models, I think lies in only certain building types. Hospitals may be one of them. Certainly for something like a nuclear power plant or refinery, it makes a lot of sense. For common buildings – who's going to maintain the database to make it reliable? I haven't yet heard a good answer to that.

By PLM, Jim was referring to product lifecycle management, a technical concept associated predominantly with manufacturing processes, but also closely associated with PDM, product data management. PDM is concerned with controlling and distributing data as and when users need it, and places emphasis on data storage and access.

JG: *There is certainly a lot of research on this. There are people who are actively pursuing this, from airports to power companies, where it looks like a good idea. There are organisations like hotel chains that have looked very seriously at this, in terms of the value that this kind of database would have. For the most part they find that it's really hard meet the cost of maintaining the databases' power. Even if cost weren't an issue, the discipline, the cultural change that needs to take place isn't there. If this weren't to happen then there would be more limited applications. So I guess that the other reason I'm waving the issue is that there's a lot out there about what buildings could be. I guess I'm in the real world about what's really happening, not what will happen next. I do think that there's a future there, but you have to understand that a lot of where we come from has to do with what's happening in manufacturing, because that where the stuff's really happening, not architecture. Most of these ideas have not only been thought about, but have actually been implemented, and have succeeded or failed in the manufacturing environment, or are evolving there. That environment is a completely different environment than both the way we design or build buildings. Some of what's successful in that manufacturing environment, which is where PLM is really from, and where it is really a hot concept that is showing massive payback. Whether that's transferable today to the building industry I think is an open question and in my own view is limited to very few building types today. Where it'll be in a decade? That may be another issue. I think that a certain level dealing with code-related firewalls, sprinkler systems – a lot of the things that should never be modified on an ad-hoc basis. There's real value in the investment that the owner would have to make, even in major plant design and major principle mechanical systems. There's a limit where you stop on a building in the product design or the automotive/aerospace/shipbuilding industries, manufacturing industries, where you would not stop. You would keep going right down to the detail. And so a lot of these ideas that are coming out of manufacturing have to be viewed very, very carefully in terms of whether there's the value for the investment today in the AEC industry. You have incredible proven values in the manufacturing field. And of course where the lines all cross is at the fabricators. So where you can make the most rapid strides forward, where you can show the greatest paybacks are at the fabricators who are in the manufacturing process. The difficulty for the industry means that you're asking an architect or engineer to invest more in the front end for a payoff that's the fabricator and the pay on to the process.*

Some ideas to emerge from Jim Glymph's remarks are as follows:

- a good geometric modeller is crucial to exploratory design processes

- digital modelling can play an important role in the early stage cycling of sketch models

- relating digital models to CAM fabrication can have a dramatic effect on the design process

- parametric representations are useful for constantly changing geometries

- parametric representations are not so useful in early project design, where changing relationships are based on more complicated issues than geometry

- paperless design processes are feasible provided the 2-D drawing process is automated, thus freeing up more time for the virtual model

- manufacturing processes should be examined closely for relevance to architecture.

8.13   Creative Expression in CAD Environments

In Frank Gehry' office, 3-D digital input devices are used to accurately digitise model data, thus generating a virtual building model. The use of other kinds of graphical input device, in conjunction with CAD environments, can potentially benefit many areas of design. Creative design exploration involves the generation and manipulation of conceptual and schematic objects, typically externalised as sketches or dimensionless objects. Furthermore, these conceptual objects are invariably viewed differently depending upon which member of a design team is looking at them. Any generation and manipulation of schematic objects, therefore, needs to be *user-defined* within an environment that supports the expressions of different design team members. New developments in graphical input device technology can support the expression of conceptual and schematic design thinking in intuitive ways (i.e. through sketching and flexible manipulation of design objects). Such environments can potentially be used as user-definable interfaces to existing, proprietary CAD systems, where more detailed design can then take place by experienced CAD users. Alternatively, CAD generated drawings may be used as a starting point for the *superimposition* of conceptual design schemes.

In any form of digital interaction through sketching, it will always be the case that user-defined mappings will need to be established between digital sketches and the objects that these sketches are intended to represent. Rather than considering how the computer recognition of sketches might be exploited (an unresolved issue in artificial intelligence approaches to design), a more modest objective is to consider how designers might describe their own intentions for the sketches they produce, particularly in the light of recent developments in graphical user-input technology. In design, the problem of sketching can be viewed as a step-by-step resolution of the mismatch between users' intentions (of which they themselves may not be aware) and their graphical articulations. In a design context, therefore, the convergence to a match between the meaning and the graphical statement of that meaning is complicated by continually changing intentions that result from users viewing their own graphical statements. Sketching can be considered both as a form of communication with oneself (introspection) and as a form of communication with others (presentation).

To date, research and development of CAD systems has focused predominantly on facilities that aid the production of detailed design drawings. This involves the exact positioning and dimensioning of predefined design objects, which are then perceived through realistic rendered and animated images. The operators that support this approach are often complex and difficult to use, and this interferes with the *reflection-in-action* (Schon, 1983) that is crucial in the early stages of design. A central issue here concerns the extent to which we can preserve this way of working in order to maintain design creativity, whilst at the same time allowing designers to progress from sketch ideas through to more detailed design objects. Once 3-D CAD models have been generated, it is commonplace nowadays to set up VR walkthroughs of 3-D scenes for presentation purposes. The critical literature should be borne in mind (Woolley, 1992; Markley, 1996). Mainstream VR technology, apart from being very expensive, relies upon immersion in 3-D environments for the duration of design development, and places little emphasis on interaction through 2-D sketching as an intuitive way into 3-D modelling. There is still to some extent, therefore, a separation between the viewing of a model and its generation. Increasingly, however, various types of 3-D positioning and orientation input devices are becoming available, incorporating hand and body motion allowing interaction with 3-D scenes.

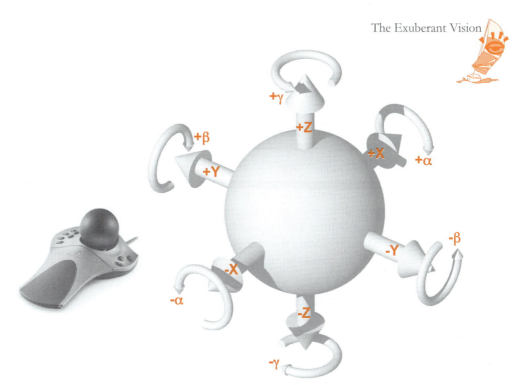

Figure 8.44: 3-D interaction with six degrees of freedom

Spherical 3-D graphical input devices allow users to interact in 3-D space with six-degrees-of-freedom as shown in **figure 8.44**. Electromagnetic sensors mounted inside provide accurate orientation in 3-D space. Switches provide both tactile and audible feedback for positive actuation and control. Such 3-D graphical input devices are simpler to use and less expensive than datagloves and other immersive VR input devices. They can be used as part of a strategy for design development based upon direct 3-D manipulation.

What appears to be emerging from the innovative working practices of architectural design offices such as Frank Gehry's, is that the intuitive interface offered by 2-D sketching, supported by new and inexpensive types of graphical input devices, can be combined with developments in knowledge engineering to produce environments ideally suited to architectural applications. Gehry's methodology is pointing the way forward for a greater involvement by the architectural profession in the use and evaluation of new digital technologies, instead of being passive recipients of inadequate, outdated, and overpriced systems.

Contemporary research in the field of computer supported co-operative work (CSCW) that has taken into account the design of 3-D forms, has also focused on the conventional (i.e. virtual reality) sharing of views of a common scene using 3-D pointer and stereoscopic devices; as well as on the presentation of conventional multiple views of an object based upon a common data model. An ambition of creative design expression through the use of new types of graphical input device, therefore, is to support design development in the context of multiple views of multiple types of objects without necessarily involving the use of expensive VR hardware. Not only is the exploitation of new kinds of graphical input device important, but also the computational representation of the contexts in which this graphical interaction take place.

8.14 Human-Computer Interaction

The name 'human-computer interaction' is in some ways a misnomer because it focuses on the fact that you have a person using a computer. The fact that the person is trying to do something means it's really 'human-work interaction' with the computer as an intermediary. So I think for me the focus isn't on interacting with the computer, but interacting through the computer. (Winograd, 1994, p. 53)

Design work centres on yet to exist artefacts not inherently connected to drawing activity. In practice, however, it is difficult to separate designing from drawing, particularly for the development of preliminary design schemes. The structures of design artefacts emerge from interactions between people, which in turn condition the communication and collaboration processes amongst designers. The following observations can be made:

- communication between designers is often through drawings whose meanings need to be interpreted and understood regarding their function and context

- communication between designers and computer systems is through digital interaction, which should support natural and fluent gestures, without distractions interrupting the flow of thinking and the development of ideas

- the digital representation of complex design information requires a great deal of geometric and topological data requiring frequent user interaction for its unambiguous description

- the structuring of digital design object information requires the expression of constraints or parametric relationships.

Digital interaction currently takes place through a range of hardware devices and software mechanisms. Interaction between users and CAD systems typically involves a range of processes such as scanning, digitisation, the definition of graphical objects in terms of co-ordinate values through modelling operations, the selection of predefined objects from libraries and menus, and the declarative decomposition of existing objects through sequences of graphical interactions. Most CAD commands and operations are directly accessible within the screen interfaces provided, and interaction typically proceeds through menu selection combined with sequences of mouse and keyboard operations. Custom shortcuts may speed up interaction sequences when commands are being used frequently and repetitively.

Just as with keyboard shortcuts, there is no reason in principle why designers should not be able to customise graphical input devices to their own needs. This would allow the creation of personalised tools relevant to the working contexts of individual design practices. Graphical input devices should allow users to specify and instantiate classes of objects together with their associated attributes. This information can then be used to establish relationships and rules over and above those already existing in specific software applications. These rules can then be used not only to control common tasks, but also for more domain-specific functions.

8.15 Digital Sketching

The most common input device in HCI, the mouse, reduces digital design interaction to a succession of selection actions. Single selection actions are insufficient for digitally capturing the richness of sketching activity. Sketching is a design activity that can be considered as a form of communication in which the sketches themselves are the traces left by communicative acts (**figure 8.45**). Shared perception and understanding of the traces, and thus of communication, is conditioned by a shared understanding of drawing actions that produce and use the traces.

Figure 8.45: Sketches reveal traces of drawing actions.

In order to progress beyond the purely geometric line-based drawing functions offered by most digital imaging and modelling software, interest has been growing in the use of interaction devices with increasing degrees-of-freedom that are now widely available. This has led to new HCI approaches in which designers have the opportunity to express their ideas with more gestural forms of interaction (Bosvieux Coilliot, Szalapaj and Boissier, 1995). A promising development in this area has been the introduction of stylus devices allowing several degrees of freedom via input parameters, as well as the standard x-y selection of objects (see following section). Dynamic variables can be associated with parameters such as speed of movement, angle and pressure, for example, each of which is instantiated by stylus movements. The user is able either to associate a significance to some or all the input parameters, varying continuously with the movement of the stylus, or to associate significance only to the variation of one or some of the parameters in a limited area of application.

New graphical input technologies are enabling the definition of new models of digital interaction which are intuitive to use, as well as being responsive and precise when needed for specific applications. The development of new forms of interface that exploit such devices focus on problems of *multi-parametric capture* and to aid their interpretation. Proposed interaction strategies will enable designers to specify which of the available parameters they wish to use, and how to connect one or several of them to the data needed in the process using a menu of dependency links.

A stylus is essentially a pencil-like device with an integral switch that permits users to quickly and accurately capture x, y and z co-ordinates of real objects. Digital styli also include contoured switches with tactile feedback so users know when they have captured particular points. Applications involving the use of digital styli can exploit a range of parameters which include the width of the stylus, as well as the pressure and tilt with which the stylus is being used. They can be parametric, chosen from a menu, a set of values, shapes, or qualifications. They can be static or dynamic variables that depend on one or several gestures, and on all the parameters provided by control values associated with rules and constraints. Generally, design process variables can be instantiated by input data, according to user preference. Personal constructions will help users build their own tools and personal preferences (Bosvieux Coilliot and Boissier, 1992).

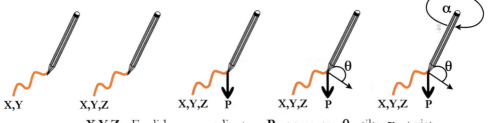

X,Y,Z - Euclidean co-ordinates; **P** - pressure; θ - tilt; α - twist.

Figure 8.46: Increasing degrees of freedom for a graphical input device

The tools needed for particular design applications have specifications that can be customised to the application in question, e.g. for orientation of the pen as in **figure 8.46** above. For tasks that involve drawing and painting, a multi-parametric stylus device can potentially increase expressiveness, and encourage a feeling within users that their own gestures generate feedback. In the free creation of shapes and volumes, by distortion, or by composition, sensitive gestural input is important. The extra parameters allow the addition of values or qualifications that can be used in the decoding of design information. Attempts have been made to predict the performance of direct manipulation interfaces using various input devices combined with a range of tasks (MacKenzie, Sellen, and Buxton, 1991). Dragging turns out to be a variation of pointing, and performance can be predicted with Fitts' Law, a robust model of human psychomotor behaviour developed as long ago as 1954. Fitts' Law is based on Shannon's theorem 17 (Shannon and Weaver, 1949), a formulation for the effective information capacity of a communication channel:

$$C = B \log_2((P+N)/N)$$

where C = effective information capacity, P = signal power, B = bandwidth, N = noise power

In movement tasks, the channel through which information is transmitted is a person. The difficulty of movement tasks can be measured by various information metrics. Fitts' law attempts to establish the information capacity of the human motor system, and is given by:

$$MT = a + b \log_2(2A/W)$$

where MT = movement time,
A = distance of movement from starting point to centre of target,
W = width of target; a and b are regression coefficients.

The study noted that the performance of devices differs between pointing and dragging, and that the index of performance is higher when pointing than when dragging. One conclusion was that:

It is felt that a stylus,.............., has the potential to perform as well as the mouse in direct manipulation systems, and may out-perform the mouse when user activities include, for example, drawing or gesture recognition. (MacKenzie, Sellen and Buxton, 1991)

Stylus devices have been found to be more intuitive to use than spaceballs because they are *displacement-based* rather than *force-based,* so that there is immediate tactile feedback from the device itself. Rigid force-sensitive devices are more likely to lead to repetitive strain injuries.

In addition to developments in graphical input technology, important parallel developments are taking place at the software level. Recent developments of object-oriented standards such as InkML (Chee, 2004) are beginning to have an important effect on graphical user-interaction in digital sketching applications. Object-oriented computer programming techniques are particularly suited to the representation of dynamic and evolving processes, and hence to design applications. Standards such as InkML provide support for the development of stylus functionalities by specifying activities that exploit pen activations. InkML describes the syntax and semantics for ink markup as a basis for a common data-exchange format between components such as handwriting and gesture recognisers, signature verifiers, and other pen-based modules. Facilities for detailed recording of time information and trace data can be associated with the corresponding input devices.

MathML is an XML application (see below) for describing mathematical notation and capturing both its structure and content (Carlisle et al., 2003). The aim of MathML is to enable mathematical expressions to be served, received, and processed on the World Wide Web, just as HTML has enabled this functionality for text. MathML formulas can be linked with and triggered by ink traces described in InkML. By exploiting these object-oriented software standards in the development of interfaces for digitising and manipulating design information, it becomes possible for software applications to be tailored to the uses and intentions of individual design practices. Pen-based interfaces generating digital ink marks on computer screens can be processed by recognition software, so converting the digital inputs into user-defined digital actions.

The Extensible Markup Language, or XML (Bray et al., 2004), is a technology for web-based applications. InkML, MathML and XML are all officially defined and recommended by the World Wide Web Consortium (W3C). XML is derived from the Standard Generalized Markup Language (SGML), a markup standard that allows individual users to create their own formatting codes known as *tags*. Many HTML tags have been implemented differently in different internet browsers. The significant difference between HTML and XML is that HTML tags describe how to depict things on a computer screen, whilst XML tags describe the structures of objects as users under-stand them to be. Again, the latter concept fits in with the need for designers to be able to define their own working preferences and practices.

8.16 From Sketches to Models

The following images show one possible way of quickly progressing from the kinds of 2-D marks produced by stylus devices to the generation of 3-D forms. Marks interpreted as Bezier curves in 2-D (**figures 8.47–8.48**) can be swept (**figure 8.49**), rendered (**figure 8.50**) and distorted (**figures 8.51–8.55** opposite). In principle, these further operations can be instantiated and controlled by the graphical input device.

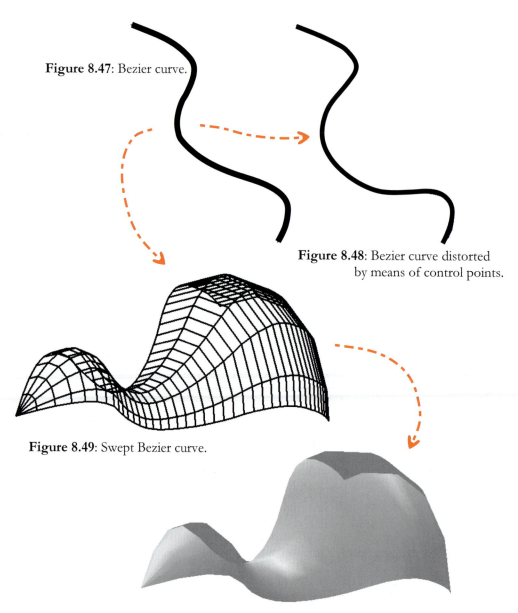

Figure 8.47: Bezier curve.

Figure 8.48: Bezier curve distorted by means of control points.

Figure 8.49: Swept Bezier curve.

Figure 8.50: Rendered sweep.

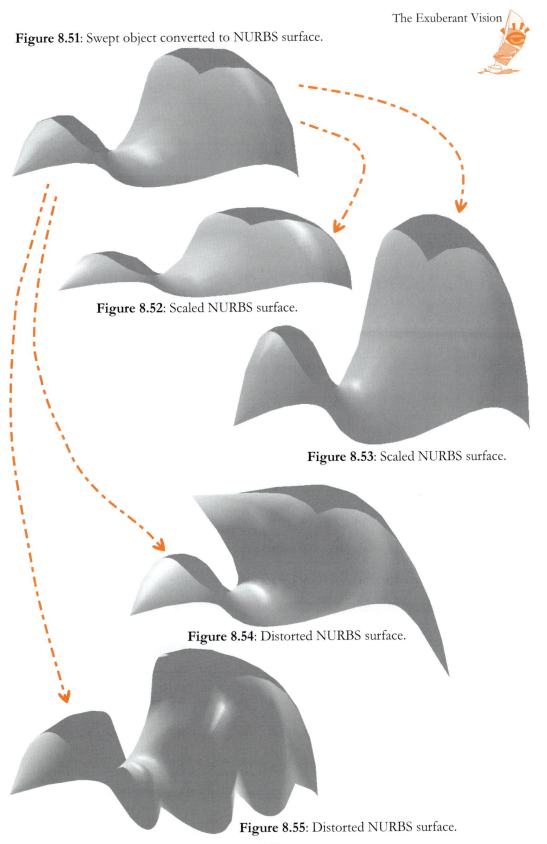

Figure 8.51: Swept object converted to NURBS surface.

Figure 8.52: Scaled NURBS surface.

Figure 8.53: Scaled NURBS surface.

Figure 8.54: Distorted NURBS surface.

Figure 8.55: Distorted NURBS surface.

8.17 Developable Surfaces

Developable surfaces are used in many areas of design; in naval architecture for designing ship hulls (**figure 8.56**), and in the design of aircraft fuselages and wings in the aerospace industry. These applications are in turn based upon the sheet-metal and plate-metal industries. A developable surface is an *intrinsically flat* surface in that it can be unrolled or unfolded into a flat sheet. Think of the developable surface as a piece of paper. You can role a sheet of paper into a cylinder or a cone, so both cylinders and cones are valid developable surfaces. Any other shape you can think of that can be unfolded or unrolled into a flat sheet could also be used as a developable surface. However, some shapes can't be unrolled or unfolded into flat sheets, and these shapes cannot be used as developable surfaces. For example, it isn't possible to unroll a spherical surface like the surface of a spheroid, an ellipsoid or a geoid, into a flat sheet, so these spherical surfaces cannot be developable surfaces.

Figure 8.56: Surface of Ship's Hull.

A developable surface can be defined as a surface which can be unfolded onto a flat plane without any distortion, stretching or tearing i.e. no folds and no generators crossing. Developable surfaces are a subset of *ruled surfaces*. A ruled surface is generated by sweeping a straight line through 3-D space. These straight lines on the surface are known as *rulings*. Mathematically speaking, these surfaces can be mapped *isometrically* onto the Euclidean plane. In general the tangent plane to a ruled surface changes along a ruling. If the tangent plane is constant along any given ruling, the surface becomes developable. Thus, mathematically, a developable surface is defined as the envelope of a single family of planes. Developable surfaces can take the form of planes, cylindrical surfaces, conical surfaces (**figure 8.57**), surfaces composed of tangents to a curve (**figure 8.58**), of surfaces made of some combinations of these. In the latter case, algorithms exist to ensure that when surfaces intersect, no gap is created and a tight fit of the surfaces can be constructed.

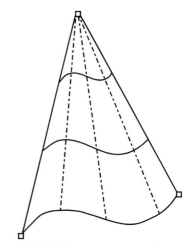

Figure 8.57: Conical ruled surface.

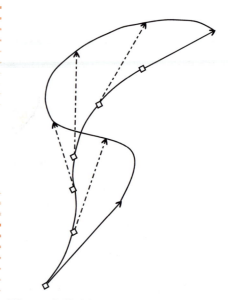

Figure 8.58: Tangential ruled surface.

Developable surfaces in current CAD/CAM software are represented as NURBS surfaces, and one way of representing developable surfaces in such applications is by using a parametric vector-based solution such as that described by Konesky (Konesky, 1993) which creates a developable surface in terms of a *directrix*. The directrix contains the generators defining the developable surface (**figure 8.59**). A directrix-based developable surface has three governing constraints which define it. The first is that the tangent and the generator must be perpendicular. The second is that the generator must be of unit length. And third, that the vector normal is invariant along a generator. With these three governing equations holding a differential equation is derived which defines the next consecutive generator located along a directrix.

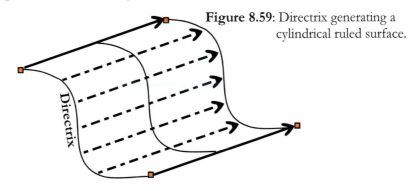

Figure 8.59: Directrix generating a cylindrical ruled surface.

Directrix

Unique tangent planes can be associated with the lines on ruled surfaces thus forming the developable surfaces as shown in **figure 8.60**.

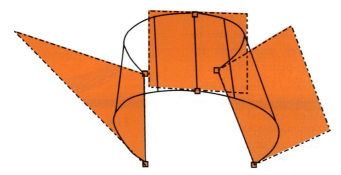

Figure 8.60: Tangent planes form developable surfaces.

Parametric vector equations can be linked together give adjacent intersecting developable surfaces. Applying these to various applications has its success dependent upon the complexity of the surfaces involved. Also, for simple surfaces the concept of phantom surfaces similar to phantom points used in splines are needed to ensure adjacent tightly closed intersecting surfaces. When drawing CAD/CAM models and using splines, the end conditions are solved using a phantom point with the end tangent passing through the phantom point, the last point and the second to last point. End phantom surfaces can be created as extra surfaces in order to solve the equations which relate to all of the surfaces.

8.18 Modelling with **NURBS** surfaces, phantom surfaces and directrices.

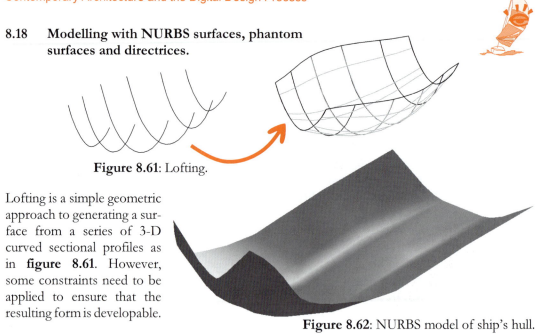

Figure 8.61: Lofting.

Lofting is a simple geometric approach to generating a surface from a series of 3-D curved sectional profiles as in **figure 8.61**. However, some constraints need to be applied to ensure that the resulting form is developable.

A basic NURBS-modelled form for the lower portion of a ship's hull is shown in **figure 8.62**. The corresponding plan, elevation and rear views of this model are shown in **figures 8.63–8.65** respectively.

This model will subsequently form the basis for a single chine hull i.e. one having a single extreme outside longitudinal member. The upper portion of the hull will be modelled later. Usually a vessel like this has the bow region as the hardest area to make into developable surfaces, since there are large changes to in and out-of-plane curvature of the hull lines resulting in large twisting of each surface. More complex hull designs often cannot attain complete developability around the bow location. Major twisting of the hull surface results in many developable surfaces programs failing, becoming unstable or show that no solution exists in this region. Often the designer will break that region down into more strips to get a working solution. This is also more expensive in terms of construction and requires more welding and fitting, etc.

Figure 8.62: NURBS model of ship's hull.

Figure 8.63: Plan view of hull.

Figure 8.64: Elevation view of hull.

Figure 8.65: Rear view of hull.

Figure 8.66: Phantom surfaces.

Figure 8.67: Plan view of phantom surfaces.

Figure 8.68: Elevation view of phantom surfaces.

Before completing the hull model, therefore, it is necessary to constrain the NURBS surfaces by means of phantom surfaces in order to ensure that the end product is developable.

Simple adjacent phantom surfaces can be created by following the axes pointing in the same direction as the length of the hull. By keeping a convention when designing objects such as ship hulls, phantom surfaces can be easily constructed and they can be placed on separate layers within CAD models.

Similar modelling techniques can also be applied to the design of aircraft wing and body shapes, in which many factors contribute to the shapes of these parts. Transonic aircraft, for example, require thin, often swept-back wings and slim bodies. At subsonic speeds slimness reduces drag, and at transonic speeds it becomes even more important to reduce shock waves and shock drag. This is done by keeping the camber of wings low, having wings with a low ratio of thickness to chord, having laminar flow aerofoils, slim fuselages, and smooth surfaces free of bumps and bulges. (Kermode, 1970)

Figure 8.69: Rear view of phantom surfaces.

Once the tangent planes have been identified, these can then be fabricated as plates that can be welded together. The tangent planes are checked separately for *developability* for each surface. Until developable surface analysis is done, there may be too much in and out-of-plane curvature or *twist* resulting in only parts of a modelled surface being developable. When rulings or generators cross, there are no developable solutions in these cases. This is very important to understand since once the plating is cut and manufacturing is started, it becomes very expensive to fix or to *retrofit* a solution when some of the surface is not developable.

Figure 8.70: Hull model with sides.

After using developable surfaces software and plotting the directrix, one can get a much better visualisation and feel for various surface configurations and how close they can be to developable. Absolute certainty of developabilty is only achieved once the developable surfaces applications generate plotted output for the developable surfaces. When designing a ship or small vessel it is very easy to quickly change the hull shape with modern naval architecture CAD software. The user has to make sure that the final design has been checked if it can be made with developable surfaces which should also include the flat plate layouts.

Figure 8.71: Plan view.

Figure 8.72: Elevation view.

Many naval architects and ship builders are often approached by clients that have a complete hull design for a compound curvature hull but they want to make it developable in order to save costs of manufacturing. With existing developable surface CAD/CAM programs one can try *what if* scenarios and try to fit a closest developable hull to the specifications initially given. This is getting to be very common today since there are many existing designs that are proven and many clients still demand them in many ship building markets.

Figure 8.73: Rear view.

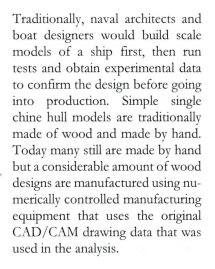

Traditionally, naval architects and boat designers would build scale models of a ship first, then run tests and obtain experimental data to confirm the design before going into production. Simple single chine hull models are traditionally made of wood and made by hand. Today many still are made by hand but a considerable amount of wood designs are manufactured using numerically controlled manufacturing equipment that uses the original CAD/CAM drawing data that was used in the analysis.

Figure 8.74: Hull model with upper and lower directrices.

Figure 8.75: Plan view of directrices.

Figure 8.76: Directrices in elevation.

Traditionally, in architecture the abstract space of design is conceived as an ideal neutral space of equivalent Cartesian coordinates. In other design fields, however, design space is conceived as an environment of forces rather than as an inert neutral vacuum. In naval design, for example, the abstract space of design is imbued with the properties of flow, turbulence, viscosity and drag so that the particular form of a hull can be thought of in terms of its motion through water. Although the form of a boat hull is studied in motion within an abstract space that has properties, there is no expectation that the shape of the boat hull will literally move. Similarly, an ethic of motion neither implies that architecture must be literally moveable, nor does it preclude actual motion. The contours and profiles of form can be shaped by the collaboration between an envelope and the active context in which it is situated. (Lynn, 2001, p. 10)

New techniques for manufacturing ship models are also emerging. Some of the first NC manufactured models were made from solid blocks of polystyrene (the same material used by Gehry to produce digitised models) but were not stable when placed in water. These were mainly used for demonstration purposes. A newer emerging modelling technique is to manufacture models from thin sheet aluminium. Developable hulls scaled down and tested for developability could be manufactured by the same method as the final full scale ship.

Figure 8.77: Rear view of directrices.

8.19   Rapid Prototyping

The most common way of fabricating simple geometric forms is by *subtractive machining* using a CNC milling machine. Subtractive methods such as milling and turning are fast, versatile and cheap. This was the process used to produce the Styrofoam panels for Gehry's Der Neue Zollhof in Dusseldorf, Germany (completed in 1999):

> *The panels were made utilizing CNC (computer numerical control) routers, which cut Styrofoam molds that were then fitted with reinforcing steel and poured with concrete.* (Lindsey, 2001, p. 80).

Even more complex or compound shapes, however, can be fabricated using *rapid prototyping* technology. Rapid prototyping is also referred to as *computer-controlled additive fabrication* – a technique that is used when a complex form is difficult to machine *subtractively*. As well as fabricating complex forms, additive technologies are also useful for fabricating multiple parts into assemblies of components. A component assembly generates a level of geometric complexity that can lead to problems for subtractive machining methods. Rapid prototyping reduces geometries to a series of simple layers, and is therefore a technology with a greater degree of geometric control. The geometric control that comes with rapid prototyping has the potential for more economical manufacturing processes, particularly when only a few specialised component parts are needed.

The process of rapid prototyping builds object in layers, which often leads to a *stair-stepping* effect produced because layers have finite thickness. The technology that produces the thinnest layers is based on inkjets. With inkjet technology, each layer is milled flat after it is deposited, and layer thicknesses can be very small. A slightly less accurate method of rapid prototyping is *stereolithography*. Other rapid prototyping methods produce more pronounced stair-stepping. Rapid prototyping technologies that incorporate some form of subtractive technology as part of the process have greater   accuracy. This is because the subtractive technology can be used to correct the compounded errors made by the additive process. Rapid prototyping is slow. It can take several hours or even several days to fabricate a part. This is still faster than using subtractive CNC, which can take weeks of machining time for complex components.

Methods based on forms of laminated object manufacturing (LOM) are limited by material thicknesses. Methods based on powders, such as selective laser sintering (SLS), or 3-D printing (3DP) are only limited by the size of the powder used. In recently emerging methods of LOM, variable layer thickness is used, followed by a cutting process to reduce the stair-stepping effect. This technique can be used to fabricate larger components made from plastic foam or ceramic materials.

8.20   Summary

The key factors of the case study presented in this chapter can be summarised as follows:

- The ability to sustain the immediacy of sketch design whilst simultaneously digitally representing the sketch proposals themselves in a cyclical design process is a characteristic feature of the working methods of Frank Gehry's office.

- Just as with sketches, physical models are vehicles for developing and assessing design proposals. The role of physical modelling was significant in the evolution of design proposals and as a medium for client interaction.

- A powerful geometric CAD modelling system is central to office practice.

- In order to keep a firm grip on the costs of constructing complex curved forms, the office practices a value engineering methodology that is closely associated with the evaluation of fabrication and construction costs of complex elements. This invariably relates to the curvature of surfaces which can be determined through Gaussian analysis. Developable surfaces are particularly cost-effective.

- In addition to digitisation through 3-D scanning techniques, the technology of digital sketching is evolving to an extent that it is now feasible to generate digital sketches in very direct ways.

- Relating digital models to CAM fabrication can have a dramatic effect on the design process. The output of digital models through milling and rapid prototyping techniques during design development can provide useful checking information and tactile feedback.

- Parametric representations are not that useful in early project design, where changing relationships are based on more complicated design issues than purely geometric ones. Parametric representations are useful when the representation of constantly changing geometries are needed.

- Paperless design processes are feasible provided the 2-D drawing process is automated, thus freeing up more time for the development of the virtual model.

Chapter 9: Conclusions

From the case studies presented in the previous chapters, common threads begin to emerge as aspects of the digital design process are revealed. Some of these connections relate directly to the ways in which CAD technologies are applied to modelling and representational issues, particularly to the modelling of complex forms, such as the Great Court roof, the Eden project, and many of Frank Gehry's schemes. The ability to visualise design proposals by navigating in and around 3-D digital environments is the simplest and most direct way of exploiting digital representations. The relationship between form and circulation in the scheme by Szyskowitz-Kowalski could not have been resolved without the visualisation of digital models. The presentation of similar design criteria to clients in FaulknerBrowns' InfoLab 21 project was achieved through exploded views of digital models. In the Stata Center project, as in most Gehry schemes, many alternative geometric arrangements were investigated by making simple and rapid changes to complex CAD models.

Increasingly, however, architectural practices are using digital techniques and representations for more than just their visualisation potential. The ability to sketch design ideas directly into digital environments was illustrated by the presence of schematic and undetailed digital models in early design stages in several case studies. Developments in digital sketching technology combined with the direct manipulation of 3-D digital models represents an important contemporary trend in the digital input of design schemes. *Immediacy of digital sketch modelling* is achieved at the expense of technical detail and textural information so that spatial design concepts become the focus of attention. Just as sketch models are ultimately developed into more detailed models, so the detailed digital models are reused and extended to form the basis for the fabrication of important elements, particularly structural elements and cladding. To seamlessly achieve these transitions, the emphasis is increasingly on *3-D representation*. Projects such as the Kunsthaus, Graz and the Stata Center at MIT demonstrate the primacy of 3-D digital representation throughout design development. 2-D drawings can always be generated as by-products of 3-D representations whenever they are needed.

Digital design invariably involves the expression of relationships between interconnected and dependent parts of a proposed design scheme. These parts give rise to a requirement for some form of digital co-ordination. One way in which this co-ordination can be achieved is through the computational technique of *parametric expression*. The power of parametric expression is such that this technique can be used to implicitly represent parallel design proposals, thus strengthening connections between sketch and detail design models. Modifications to parametric models result in the propagation of changes throughout the model as a consequence of parametric relationships.

Another important theme has been the way in which the constraints of design practice have affected the role of digital techniques in individual offices. The case studies have highlighted ways in which digital technologies serve to maintain the design vision. They are an important means to an even more important end, and never an end in themselves. The *digital customisation* of office practice can be achieved by configuring digital environments in ways appropriate to the design philosophies associated with particular offices.

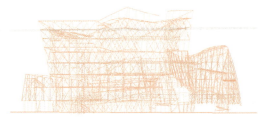

Digital Sketch Modelling

One central thread has been the idea of digital *sketch modelling*, in which the role of digital techniques is to support and preserve key sketch design ideas as they evolve and develop. The immediacy of the sketch (whether paper-based or input through digital stylus devices) is a property essential to the visual evolution of design thinking. Sketching is still done on paper, but increasingly sketches are digitally captured in some way, such as through scanning devices, for example. Detailed CAD modelling is out of the question at the sketch design stage, forcing designers to specify more details than they want or need. The translation of sketches to a digital format is a process that may need to be repeated several times if the design changes. This is illustrated by the way in which initial polystyrene models are generated through 3-D digitising devices in Frank Gehry's office. Designers need tools that give them the freedom to sketch rough design ideas quickly, the ability to test designs by interacting with them, and the flexibility to fill in the design details as choices are made.

The digital sketching tools described in **chapter 8** provide an example of how this might work in the context of sketching directly into computer interfaces. Customisation allows users to associate meanings with data that has been digitally captured. This inevitably implies that there will always be a pre-processing phase in which gestures are associated with meanings, prior to the applied use of the input devices, much as in speech-recognition systems. For designers, information is significant as soon as it is captured (i.e. there is an intuitive meaning of the gesture within the mind of the designer, but outside of the digital environment), and coherence of this information with existing information needs to be supported. Current applications do not fully exploit multi-dimensional graphical input devices. Means for their integration with modelling sytems are presently still missing, but when developed will bring new design possibilities. Offices such as those of Frank Gehry are developing their own strategies for integrated design, in which new types of graphical input device are incorporated into creative software environments.

Design intentions and ideas, expressed through digital sketch modelling and object manipulation, allow designers to sketch ideas as propositions into digital databases. Physical models continue to be useful for initial form studies due to their tactile value. They provide a means of communication between members of the design team and clients. The generation of physical prototypes from digital design processes is becoming increasingly feasible. In future, designers may choose to work with other emerging forms of digital media that also do not require precise dimensioning, such as digital painting, for example. Emerging techniques, such as directly drawing surfaces in 3-D space through semi-immersive virtual environments, may offer new forms of interaction at the sketch design stage (Schkolne, Pruett and Schroeder, 2001).

These imprecise and intuitive forms of digital input all aim to support and stimulate designers' creativity. The emphasis is on expression and communication allowing fast exploration of multiple design solutions. Digital sketch design environments, therefore, rather than simply being drafting accessories which are used after designs have been developed (much as conventional CAD systems are used), will instead become widespread working tools for the creation of early stage design proposals.

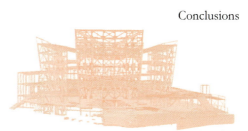

Digital Visualisation

Another important thread concerns the need for 3-D computer visualisations to generate insights into evolving design processes. This was evident in particular in the Szyskowitz-Kowalski case study, and again in Frank Gehry's work. The presentational advantages of 3-D visualisation was illustrated in the FaulknerBrowns case study, in which a combination of conceptual spatial models and more realistic models produced informative presentations for clients who were central to the design process. 3-D computer visualisation techniques can often reveal unique relationships between spaces and the objects contained within them. This again re-emphasises design-theoretical ideas in which visual analysis clarifies formal design relationships and the specific architectural conditions that give rise to them (Baker, 1989; Clark and Pause, 1985; Ching, 1996).

Most CAD systems are based upon representations in which objects and spaces are defined in terms of line-based models (i.e. lines define the edges of objects). Gehry's office has moved towards the use of surface-based models, but there are also potential advantages to be gained by the use of more volumetric or spatial modelling techniques. Spatial models can potentially give more intuitive visual feedback, particularly if they can be presented dynamically as a series of changing viewpoints, yet they appear as yet to be relatively under-exploited as a representational mechanism in design practice (Szalapaj, 2003). According to Bacon:

> *the basic ingredient of architectural design consists of two elements, mass and space. The essence of design is the interrelation between these two. In our culture, the preponderant preoccupation is with mass, and to such an extent that many designers are 'space blind'.* (Bacon, 1974).

Within any CAD environment, models of the various volumes of a design scheme can be constructed in order to analyse the spatial conditions. Inverting the space/mass relationship of buildings in the computer makes it possible to see spaces as they relate to each other, unobscured by the physical elements of the architecture, and allows for a unique analysis of the spatial treatment. It is also important to recognise two other important issues cited by Bacon that lie beyond the scope of this book. These are the *continuity of experience*, and *simultaneous continuities*. Movement through space creates a continuity of experiences derived from the nature and form of the spaces through which the movement occurs. It is possible to conceive the essential form of these simultaneous movement systems in three dimensions as an abstract design, from which the design structure emerges. These ideas can then be combined with the more well-understood techniques to form an organic and dynamic view of not only building, but also urban design.

Conveying key design ideas through visualisation techniques such as these means that computers can provide a new way of looking at and evaluating both architectural and urban design proposals. The ability of computers to support visualisations of architectural space, and their abilities to allow users to selectively edit what is seen on the screen, also provides designers with ways in which to evaluate architecture within the context of the surrounding urban environment.

Parametric Expression

Digital design often involves the expression of relationships between interconnected and dependent parts of proposed design schemes. Parts may intersect and overlap, giving rise to a requirement for some form of digital co-ordination. In software terms, such relationships can be represented in terms of parametric expressions between objects. These expressions typically encapsulate mathematical and geometric constraints between objects, which can either be used as functions to check the effects of design changes, or, in their more automated form, to generate new forms by propagating local changes throughout digital models. *Parametric modelling techniques*, therefore, can be used to integrate the development of design schemes, rather than modelling components separately and individually. The parametric framework is substantially different from conventional CAD modelling approaches, requiring less effort on re-modelling and the maintenance of consistency. To achieve such parametric expression, some practices develop design schemes in conjunction with computer programmers, as in the case of Buro-Happold's work on the Great Court roof. The aspiration of these practices is to continue the physicality, and, as much as possible, the immediacy of the design process into the digital environment. Immediacy always implies interaction, however.

A further technologically important lesson that emerges in particular from the Great Court roof project is the value of iterative design, in which design prototypes are successively created and evaluated. *Iterative design techniques* seem to be more valuable as the number of iterations made during a project becomes larger. It is important to iterate quickly in the early part of the design process because that is when radically different ideas can and should be generated and examined. In complex structural forms such as the Great Court roof, the digital modelling process might start from an initial coarse definition of topology, but with some control of surface curvature. The process from then on is one of gradual refinement, increasing mesh densities until sufficient accuracy (millimetre dimensions) for fabrication is reached. During parametric processes, therefore, topologies can change constantly.

NURBS curves and surfaces are increasingly being used for the representation of geometries such as conics and free-form shapes. However, anyone who has modelled with NURBS will be aware that complex forms made up of many NURBS components often have to be fixed to avoid holes and gaps between surfaces. This stymies the expression of parametric relationships between disparate surfaces. Furthermore, digital operations on NURBS objects such composition, intersection and projection do not necessarily result in NURBS objects. All such issues distract from focusing on design interactions in order to resolve technical problems. This is just one example of how digital designers need to maintain a critical outlook whilst keeping an eye on new developments in modelling technology. Generalisations of NURBS such as T-splines and T-NURCCs can potentially overcome some of the problems in this particular case (Sederberg et al., 2003).

A graphically interactive parametric modelling system should support designers in their creation of digital models, as well as in their ability to express constraints between key component parts. To maintain a holistic view of design development, it is important that digital modelling technologies should assist designers in the generation of architectural forms in intuitive and interactive ways.

Environmental Constraints

Architecture is one of the last modes of thought based on the inert. Thanks to computers it can be more complex, constantly mutating to take account of multiple environmental factors in the same way as a ship's sail responds to the wind. Architects should stop thinking about boxes, loosen up and start thinking in terms of more flexible forms like blobs. (Rappolt, 2003).

An important thread throughout the case studies has been the development of CAD models for specific analytical purposes. Some of these were illustrated in the Eden project, for example, in which models were needed for site studies (cut and fill analysis), various structural loading calculations, etc. Many other types of analysis are possible. Significant developments in environmental simulation technology include improved methods of user-interaction, and the realistic simulation of specific environmental phenomena. In design, however, there is a need for improved *integration* not only between various environmental factors, but also between modelling and analysis. The use of environmental analysis and simulation is an increasingly essential feature at both the conceptual and detail design stages. Changes in structural form and topology require corresponding re-evaluations of environmental criteria.

The downfall of all simulation-based methods, however, has always been that users cannot easily design-in desired behaviours. Designers can manipulate the initial specifications of simulations, such as spatial zoning and material properties in energy simulations, for example. The resulting simulations are unpredictable and cannot easily be targeted at desired environmental goals. Evidence is beginning to emerge from computer animation disciplines that control of simulations may indeed be possible (Treuille et al., 2003; Guendelman et al., 2003, James and Fatahalian, 2003). If such techniques can be incorporated into environmental analysis software, then this would enable designers to have interactive control of detailed environmental features at the design stage.

The uses for an animate approach to architecture might be in its conception and design while more conventional tools remain in force for modelling and fabrication. (Lynn, 2001, p. 258)

Contemporary digital models have the capacity to be animate, but if animation is to have meaning that carries through into built form, then this needs to be defined interactively by creative designers rather than through prescribed computational processes in fragmented simulation domains.

While physical form can be defined in terms of static coordinates, the virtual force of the environment in which it is designed should also contribute to its shaping. In this way, topology allows for not just the incorporation of a single moment but rather a multiplicity of vectors and therefore a multiplicity of times, in a single continuous surface. The availability and colonization of architectural design by computer-aided techniques presents the discipline with yet another opportunity to both retool and rethink itself as it did with the advent of stereometric projection and perspective. If there is a single concept that must be engaged owing to the proliferation of topological shapes and computer-aided tools, it is that in their structure as abstract machines, these technologies are animate. (loc. sit.)

Digital Fabrication

In the now-fading industrial era, catalogues of manufactured components and materials have played an indispensable role in architectural practice. Architects spent a lot of their time searching, selecting, and procuring. In the context of CAD/CAM, though, the crucial thing is to know the capabilities and availability of the fabrication facilities offered by various vendors. Then, it becomes possible to design directly for those capabilities – a move that provides a great deal of creative freedom, and involves the architect far more directly in fabrication and construction processes. (Mitchell, 2001, p. 363).

Rapid prototyping technology allows designers to create rough design models through what is essentially a digital sketch modelling process. Digitally produced prototypes can form the basis for later fabrication processes. There is nothing intrinsically new about the desire to build with prefabricated components. Paxton's scheme for the International Exposition of 1851 used industrial fabrication techniques to produce structural components (columns and beams) that could be erected quickly and inexpensively. The structural system on the Eden project was also simple, using hexagonal components as the primary structural elements. Geodesic forms are particularly suited to the fabrication of modular components that map onto their geometries. Projects such as Eden, the Great Court and Gehry's forms differ from Paxton's only in their complexity. This complexity inevitably requires digital support for the development and refinement of the structural system. The continual redevelopment requires analysis of structural and loading characteristics, as well as analysis of relationships between structural materials. The structural analysis calculations in turn are often carried out using finite-element methods. Once a structural solution has been reached, the integrative power of digital modelling technology can simulate the assembly and construction of a multitude of modular components as described in sections **1.3** and **1.4**.

If component parts are more varied in their geometries, and less modular, then once structural and cladding systems have been determined, techniques are needed to ensure that components are capable of being manufactured, and if possible to reduce fabrication costs. Fabricated components often have degrees of complexity that can only be resolved through 3-D digital representation. The decomposition of complex curved surfaces into *developable surfaces*, for example, provides a technique for the digital representation of surfaces such that parts can be fabricated and then joined together to form whole facades. CNC plasma cutting tools can be used to cut curved structural members. Computer-controlled rolling machines can be used to bend steel, and computer-controlled welding machines can assemble steel components. The placement and alignment of parts on site is often carried out with laser positioning and surveying equipment, thereby extending the digital process into the construction process.

What we are beginning to witness is a 'structural turn' within architectural culture. It is clear that a significant number of progressive architects are seeking to step beyond a certain Postmodern sensibility which celebrates scenographic properties and surface effects, and focus instead on the structural integrity of buildings. (Leach, 2004)

Office Organisation

The revolution has been, in part, precipitated by three things: the speed of technological development as described in Moore's Law*; the transmissibility of digital information breaking down traditional boundaries of time and space; and the seemingly infinite forms that information can take. (Lindsey, 2001, p.48)

There is no doubt that the digital representation of design information is playing an increasingly important role in contemporary architectural design practice. The role of digital models may vary between practices, but there is an increasing emphasis on the digital co-ordination of information between the specialist partners involved on any project. For example, digital design models may provide the geometrical source information from which detailed structural models can be produced. They can also be used to detail and co-ordinate services such as electrical, mechanical, heating and ventilation. Geometric information in 3-D digital form is increasingly being provided by architects for use by contractors and manufacturers. Drawings can be derived from 3-D digital models as and when needed, whether for contractual documentation or for other purposes such as presentation. The latter are important for the presentation of design choices to clients, particularly at the briefing and concept design stages.

Digital design also takes place within office and practice contexts in which many other activities occur. These include non-digital design processes such as physical modelling and sketching, interaction with other members of the design team, with engineers and environmental specialists, clients and contractors. The design criteria requiring specialist analysis range from innovative structural and constructional systems through to the many environmental issues that need to be responded to. The reality of everyday interactions in design offices is that they are still essentially people-centred activities. A dynamic design environment requires not only the ability to generate digital design information, therefore, but also the knowledge to organise and apply it to the whole process of design.

The increasing trend towards digital construction processes has implications for responsibility and liability and the roles of professional organisations in general. Other factors such as project management, new procurement practices and competitive tendering are all having an impact on the organisation of office practice and consequently on the role of digital technology. A greater awareness of the design and construction possibilities of digital representations makes it possible for design practices to customise their own interactions with digital technologies without compromising the integrity of individual offices.

*Gordon Moore, co-founder of Intel, observed in 1965 that the number of transistors per square inch on integrated circuits had doubled every year since the invention of the integrated circuit. Moore predicted this trend would continue. Doubling of data density occurs approximately every 18 months, and this is the current definition of Moore's Law.

Digital Expression

Digital technology has reached a level of embeddedness in some architectural practices at which it is possible and feasible for designers to express design intentions directly without being distracted from the design vision of the project. Distractions in the past have been caused by the limitations of digital representations in their capacity to model form, in their prescriptive structuring of design information, and in the deficiencies of the human-computer interface. The use of digital design media to sketch digital expressions representing spatial concepts depends upon the immediacy and transparency of this process in order to communicate intended ideas. The extension of modelling techniques to a wider range of geometries has coincided with improvements in graphical user-interfaces, leading to more expressive digital modelling and visualisation environments. The issue of prescriptiveness has also been addressed. Contemporary digital design processes support user-defined modularity without the need to conform to common, pre-defined model structures. Libraries of prescribed components are as outmoded within CAD systems as they are in fabrication technology.

The downfall of expressionist ambitions in architectural design was that the expressions themselves were detached from techniques of analysis and construction. The ability to express structural forms through design sketches and models was detached from any detailed structural analyses of these forms. When such analyses became possible at a later period of architectural history, this resulted in a greater confidence of architectural expression. The expression of designers' aesthetic intentions in contemporary architectural design projects can now be associated with many kinds of technical requirements. Digital models can be evaluated through digital analysis techniques and simulation software. If the intention is to express movement, for example, then the resulting curvilinear geometries can be structurally and environmentally assessed in the context of cyclical design processes.

Profound change to office practice is beginning to take place as a consequence of the expanding role of digital expression. Those design practices that have an understanding and awareness of current techniques of digital expression, together with some basic understanding of techniques of digital representation, also have the ability to model and analyse complex form, and the potential to exchange digital information with specialist partners, contractors and fabricators. Contemporary digital design processes allow the formulation of design proposals based upon design ideas rather than restricting practitioners into ways of designing determined by the technology itself. Design is paramount. The proof for those that need it can be found by looking at built projects such as the case studies described in this book.

.

Educative Half-Life

We emphasise an interactive way of working throughout, by going into a particular subject in depth, and then designing through a process of documenting, sketching and modelmaking, and the computer equivalent of all of these. (RCA Prospectus 2004-5, p. 36)

A school of design without comprehensive computing facilities should be as inconceivable as the military without satellite navigation or a hospital without CT (computerised tomography) or MRI (magnetic resonance imaging) scanners. Technology such as this makes transparent previously hidden features through three-dimensional visualisations and reconstructions. In the same way, powerful networked computing environments with integrated CAD and analysis software should be available to design students within the context of studio work.

Having a sense of what is technically feasible is as important as developing a feel for what is culturally appropriate. (RCA Prospectus 2004-5, p. 48)

Personal predilections, disciplines and intuitions influence the ways in which students of architecture design, and it is not impossible that a future Gaudi could produce a Sagrada Familia without the use of computers, and perhaps be the better for that, but aspiring architects should be happy that tools now exist to aid and abet their ambitions.

My early work was rectilinear because you take baby steps. (Gehry, 1999, p. 47)

Many great architects reveal their most creative years in middle age. Louis Kahn was in his forties when he designed the Yale University Art and Architecture building (built 1951-53). Mies van der Rohe was forty three when he designed the Barcelona Pavilion in 1929. Frank Gehry was forty eight when he re-adjusted his house in Santa Monica in 1977-8. According to Mildred Friedman:

Frank Gehry is an innovator whose vision reaches beyond the accepted aesthetic and technical constraints of twentieth-century architecture. His singular formal/philosophical stance developed slowly. In the late 1950s and 1960s - the earliest years of his practice - his work was well planned and handsome, and those who knew it regarded him as a genuine talent. But it wasn't until the 1970s that the box began to break apart, and by the end of that decade he had ventured into absolutely unknown territory with his own "dumb little house" - a small, pink Santa Monica bungalow. It became a laboratory in which it was possible to try anything, and he did. (Gehry, 1999, p. 8)

For the hugely talented minority then, it can take time to make connections; how much more so, for the majority. It may be that a greater appreciation of the holistic nature of architecture could be realised at any earlier age if there was constant interaction between sketch pad, models, drawing board and computer from the earliest days of study. This more immediate and more comprehensive awareness of the myriad problems involved in many building projects could shorten the route to what the Germans call *Baukunst*, and perhaps change the design process itself.

Bibliography

Aguilar, G. D.; *Definition of Developable Surfaces with High Level Computer Graphics*, pp. 1–21, in proc. Pacific Northwest Section of Society of Naval Architects and Marine Engineers, January 1987.

Allen, R.; comments pp. 227–230, in *Gehry Talks: architecture + process*, Thames & Hudson, 1999.

Anderson, R.; *The Great Court and the British Museum*, The British Museum Press, 2000.

Andreu, A.; *Analisis de la estabilidad de estructuras de obra de fabrica mediante simulation computational de modelos funiculares*, proyecto de tesis, Universitat Politecnica de Catalunya, Barcelona, Spain, 2003.

Archer, I.; *Nabdam Compounds, Northern Ghana*, in Shelter in Africa, Oliver, P. (ed.), Barrie & Jenkins, 1971.

Bacon, E.N.; *Design of Cities*, Penguin, 1976.

Baker, G.H.; *Design Strategies in Architecture: An approach to the analysis of form*, Van Nostrand Reinhold, 1989.

Balmond, C.; *Almost Famous*, The Guardian, 19th December, 2003.

Barnes, M.; *Form and Stress Modelling of Tension Structures*, pp. 31–39, in Widespan Roof Structures, Thomas Telford Publishing, London, 2000.

Becker, K.-H. and Dorfler, M.; *Dynamical systems and fractals,* Cambridge University Press, 1989.

Bijl, A.; *Computer Discipline and Design Practice: Shaping Our Future*, Edinburgh University Press, 1989.

Boring, E.G.; *Sensation and Perception in the History of Experimental Psychology*, New York, Appleton-Century-Crofts, 1942.

Bosvieux Coilliot G. and Boissier D.; *Gesture Tools for Design*, pp. 31-48, in Revue Sciences et Techniques de la Conception, Vol.1, No.1, 1992, Hermes, Paris.

Bosvieux Coilliot, G., Szalapaj, P.J. and Boissier, D.; *Design Environments with Visual Interaction and Creative Expression*, ICED 95, International Conference on Engineering Design, Prague, August 1995.

Brady. M.; *The Theory of Computer Science: A Programming Approach*, Chapman and Hall, London, 1977.

Brady, M.; *The Forms of Knowledge Mobilised in Some Machine Vision Systems*, pp. 1241–1248, in Phil. Trans. Roy. Soc. London B 352, no. 1358, 1997.

Brady. M.; *Historical Overview of AI Vision Research*, Department of Engineering Science, University of Oxford, UK, 1999.

Brand, S.; *How Buildings Learn: What happens after they're built*, Viking, 1994.

Bray, T., Paoli, J., Sperberg-McQueen, C.M., Maler, E., Yergeau, F. and Cowan, J.; *Extensible Markup Language (XML) 1.1*, W3C Recommendation, February 2004, edited April 2004.

Brown, S.; *Engineering The British Museum Great Court Roof*, pp. 283–286, in Widespan Roof Structures, Thomas Telford Publishing, London, 2000.

Brown, S. and Cook, M.; *The Design and Manufacture of the British Museum Great Court Roof*, Buro Happold, 2001.

Buckminster Fuller, R.; *Synergetics: Explorations in the Geometry of Thinking*, Macmillan, 1975.

Carlisle, D., Ion, P., Miner, R. and Poppelier, N. (eds); *Mathematical Markup Language (MathML)*, Version 2.0 (Second Edition), W3C Recommendation, October, 2003.

Chee, Y.M. and Froumentin, M.; *Ink Markup Language*, W3C Working Draft, September, 2004.

Ching, F.D.K.; *Architecture: Form, Space and Order*, Van Nostrand Reinhold, 1996.

Conrads, U. and Sperlich, H.G.; *Fantastic Architecture*, The Architectural Press, 1960.

Clark, R.H. and Pause, M.; *Precedents in Architecture*, Van Nostrand Reinhold, 1985.

Clarke, J.A.; *Energy Simulation in Building Design*, 2nd edition, Butterworth-Heinemann, 2002.

Collingwood, R.G.; *The Principles of Art*, Oxford University Press, 1938.

Cook, M..; *Digital Tectonics: Historical Perspective – Future Prospect*, pp. 41–49, in Digital Tectonics, Leach, N. et al. (eds), Wiley, 2004.

Cook, P. , Fournier, C.; *A Friendly Alien: Ein Kunsthaus fur Graz*, Hatje Cantz Publishers, 2004

Cook, P. , Fournier, C. and Kada, K.; *curves and spikes*, Aedes, Berlin, 2003.

Cooper, K., Williams, G. and Salvail, P. ; *Evaluating RP Methods: NASA's Side-by-Side Comparison*, pp. 28–30, Modern Casting, Feb. 2002, in proc. SME Rapid Prototyping & Manufacturing Conference.

DataKustik GmbH; *Cadna – software for noise calculation*, Greifenberg, Germany, 2004.

Davies, C.; *High Tech Architecture*, Thames and Hudson, 1988.

DETR; *Our Towns and Cities: the Future*, The Stationery Office, London, 2000.

DeCarlo, D.; Finkelstein, A., Rusinkiewicz, S. and Santella, A.; *Suggestive Contours for Conveying Shape*, pp. 848–855, in ACM Transactions on Graphics, Vol.22, No.3, July 2003.

Di Christina, G.; *Architecture and Science*, Wiley-Academy, London, 2001.

DTI; *Our Competitive Future: Building the Knowledge Driven Economy,* CM 4176, London, HMSO, 1998.

DTI; *Excellence and Opportunity: a science and innovation policy for the 21st century*, London, HMSO, 2000.

Duffy, F.; *The New Office*, Conran Octopus, London, 1997.

Egan, Sir J.; *Rethinking Construction*, DETR, London, 1998.

Evans, R.; *The Projective Cast: Architecture and its three geometries*, MIT Press, Cambridge, Mass., 1995.

Faux, I.D. and Pratt, M.J.; *Computational Geometry for Design and Manufacture*, Ellis Horwood, 1979.

Gann, D. and Salter, A.; *Innovation in Project-based, Service-enhanced Firms: the construction of complex products and systems*, pp. 955–972, in Research Policy 29 (7–8), 2000.

Gehry, F.; *Gehry Talks: architecture + process*, Thames & Hudson, 1999.

Gilbert-Rolfe, J. and Gehry, F.; *Frank Gehry: The City and Music*, Routledge, 2001.

Glancey, J.; *Mud, glorious mud*, The Guardian, 10th November 2003.

Glasgow, J.; Narayanan, N.H.; Chandrasekaran, B. (eds); *Diagrammatic Reasoning: Cognitive and Computational Perspectives*, MIT press, 1995.

Glenn, J. and Littler, G.; *A Dictionary of Mathematics*, Harper & Row, 1984.

Golay, F. and Seppecher, p. ; *Locking materials and the topology of optimal shapes*, pp. 631–644, Eur. J. Mech. A/Solids 20, 2001.

Green, A.E. and Zerna, W.; *Theoretical Elasticity*, Clarendon Press, Oxford, 1968.

Goldberger, p. ; *On the Rise : Architecture and Design in a Post Modern Age*; Times Books, January 1983.

Guendelman, E., Bridson, R. and Fedkiw, R.; *Nonconvex Rigid Bodies with Stacking*, pp. 871–878, in ACM Transactions on Graphics, Vol.22, No.3, July 2003.

Guilford, J.; *The Nature of Human Intelligence*, McGraw-Hill, 1967.

Hambidge, J.; *The Elements of Dynamic Symmetry*, Dover, 1926.

Hamlyn, D.W.; *The Psychology of Perception*, Routledge & Kegan Paul, 1957.

Harbison, R.; *Reflections on Baroque*, Reaktion Books, 2000.

Harth, E.; *The Creative Loop: How the brain makes a mind*, Addison-Wesley, New York, 1993.

Henderson, L.D.; *Fourth Dimension and Non-Euclidean Geometry in Modern Art*, Princeton University Press, 1983.

Hockney, D.; *Secret Knowledge*, Thames & Hudson, 2001.

Hubner, P. and Lassen, V.; *Kirche mal ganz anders: Eine Gemeinde baut ihre Kirche selbst.....*,

Jackson, M.; *Eden: the first book*, St. Ives, Roche, 2000.

Jackson, M.; *Eden: the second book*, Eden Project Books, 2002.

James, D.L.; and Fatahalian, K.; *Precomputing Interactive Dynamic Deformable Scenes*, pp. 879–887, in ACM Transactions on Graphics, Vol.22, No.3, July 2003.

Jay, M.; *Scopic Regimes of Modernity*, in Visual Culture Reader, N. Mirzoeff (ed.) Routledge, 1998.

Jencks, C.; *Modern Movements in Architecture*, Penguin Books, 1973.

Jones, A.C; *Civil and Structural Design of the Eden Project*, pp. 89–99, in Widespan Roof Structures, Thomas Telford Publishing, London, 2000.

Jones, A., Hamilton, M., and Jones, M.; *The Design and Construction of the Eden Project*, Anthony Hunt Associates Ltd., Cirencester, UK.

Kane, A.; *Doing the Knowledge*, pp. 44–46, in The Architects' Journal, 22nd May, 2003

Kenner, H.; *Geodesic Math and How To Use It*, UCLA press, 1976.

Kermode, A.C.; *Flight Without Formulae*, Pitman Publishing Limited, 1970.

Khemlani, L.; *Architectural CAD: A Look Across the Spectrum*, Cadence, January, 2002.

Khoury, P.S.; *http://web.mit.edu/buildings/statacenter/comments.htm*, 1999.

Kloft, H.; *Structural Engineering in the Digital Workflow*, a-matter, Germany, 2000.

Knight, C.; Essay in *Frank O. Gehry: The Architect's Studio* catalog, The Henry Art Gallery, Seattle, Washington, August 2000.

Konesky; B. E.; *Computer Aided Design of Developable Surfaces*, MASc Thesis, 1993.

Krauss, R.; *The Optical Unconscious,* MIT Press, 1993.

Krishnamurti, R.; *The Arithmetic of Shapes*, pp. 463–484, in Planning and Design: Environment and Planning B, Volume 7, 1980.

Latham, Sir M.; *Constructing the Team: Final report of the Government/Industry Review of Procurement and Contractual Arrangements in the UK Construction Industry*, The Stationery Office, 1994.

Leach, N., Turnbull, D. and Williams, C.; *Digital Tectonics*, Wiley, 2004.

Lee, K.; *Principles of CAD/CAM/CAE Systems*, Addison-Wesley, 1999.

Lindsey, B.; *Digital Gehry*, Birkhauser, 2001.

Lyall, J.; *Close encounter: Peter Cook and Colin Fournier in Graz*, Architecture Today, no. 144, January 2004.

Lyall, S.; *Masters of Structure: Engineering Today's Innovative Buildings*, Laurence King Publishing, 2002.

Lyons, J.; *Chomsky*, Fontana/Collins, 1970.

Lynn, G.; *Animate Form*, Princeton Architectural Press, New York, 1999.

Lynn, G.; *Form*, in Archilab: Radical experiments in global architecture, Thames & Hudson, Orleans, France, 2001.

Mackenzie, I. S., Sellen, A. and Buxton, W.; *A comparison of input devices in elemental pointing and dragging tasks*, pp. 161–166, in proc. CHI '91 Conference on Human Factors in Computing Systems, 1991.

Macrae-Gibson, G.; *The Secret Life of Buildings: An American Mythology for Modern Architecture*, MIT Press, 1985

Mandelbrot, B.B.; *The Fractal Geometry of Nature*, W. H. Freeman, New York, 1977.

March, L. and Steadman, P. ; *The geometry of environment: An introduction to spatial organization in design*, RIBA Publications Limited, 1971.

Markley, R.; *Boundaries: Mathematics, Alienation, and the metaphysics of Cyberspace*, in Virtual Realities and Their Discontents, Markley, R. (ed.), John Hopkins University Press, 1996.

Marr, D.; *Vision*, W.H. Freeman, 1982.

Marsh, A.J.; *Performance Analysis and Conceptual Design*, Ph.D. Thesis, School of Architecture, University of Western Australia, December, 1997.

McKim, R.H.; *Thinking Visually*, Lifetime Learning Publications, Belmont, California, 1980.

Mendelsohn, E.; *Ideas about the New Architecture*, 1914–17.

Mendelsohn, E.; *The International Conformity of the New Architecture or Dynamics and Function*, lecture delivered at the Architectura et Amicitia of Amsterdam, at Mannheim and at The Hague, 1923.

Merrick, J.; *Metal Guru*, pp. 2–4, in The Independent Arts & Books Review, 24th October, 2003.

Migayrou, F.; *Generic Architectures*, pp. 6–9, in Archilab: Radical Experiments in Global Architecture, Thames & Hudson, Orleans, France, 2001.

Miles, L.D.; *Techniques of Value Analysis and Engineering*, McGraw Hill, New York, 1961.

Mitchell, W.J.; *Roll Over Euclid: How Frank Gehry Designs and Builds*, in Frank Gehry, Architect, J.F. Ragheb (ed.), Solomon Guggenheim Foundation, New York, 2001.

Morris, J. and Blier, S.P. ; *Butabu: Adobe Architecture of West Africa*, Princeton Architectural Press, 2003.

Nolan, T.J.; *Computer-Aided Design of Developable Hull Surfaces*, pp. 233–242, in Marine Technology, 1971.

Novak, M.; *Next Babylon, Soft Babylon: (trans)Architecture is an Algorithm to Play in*, pp. 20–29, in Architects in Cyberspace II, Architectural Design, Vol.68, No.11/12, 1998.

Novak, M.; *Marcus Novak*, pp. 314–321, in Archilab: Radical Experiments in Global Architecture, Thames & Hudson, Orleans, France, 2001.

Novitski, B.J.; *Gehry Forges New Computer Links*, in Architecture, August, 1992.

Otto, F., (ed.); *Tensile structures; design, structure, and calculation of buildings of cables, nets, and membranes*, Cambridge, Massachusetts: MIT Press, 1973.

Oud, J.J.P. ; *letter to Adolf Behne*, Rotterdam, 17th September, 1921.

Padovan, R.; *Dom Hans Van Der Laan: Modern Primitive*, Architectura & Natura Press, 1994.

Padovan, R.; *Proportion: Science, Philosophy, Architecture*, E & FN Spon, 1999.

Pawley, M.; *Norman Foster: A Global Architecture*, Universe Publishing, 1999.

Pearson, D.; *New Organic Architecture: The Breaking Wave*, The University of California Press, 2001.

Perella, S.; *Hypersurface Architecture*, 2nd Doors of Perception conference, the Netherlands Design Institute, Amsterdam, The Netherlands, in Mediamatic Vol.8, No.2/3, 1994.

Peters, T.; *Building the Nineteenth Century*, MIT Press, 1996.

Popovic Larsen, O. and Tyas, A.; *Conceptual Structural Design: Bridging the gap between architects and engineers*, Thomas Telford, 2003.

Poynton, C.A.; *High Definition Television and Desktop Computing*, pp. 383–402, in Multimedia Systems, J.F. Koegel Buford (ed.), ACM Press, 1994.

Rappolt, M.; Article on Greg Lynn, Icon Magazine, September 2003.

RCA Prospectus 2004-5, Royal College of Art, London.

Robbin, T; *Engineering a New Architecture*, Yale University Press, 1996.

Salvadori, M.; *Why Buildings Stand Up: The Strength of Architecture*, W.W. Norton & Co., 1980.

Sebestyen, G; *New Architecture and Technology*, Architectural Press, 2003.

Sederberg, T.W., Zheng, J., Bakenov, A. and Nasri, A.; *T-splines and T-NURCCs*, in ACM Transactions on Graphics, Vol.22, No.3, July 2003.

Shaw, J; *Jeffrey Shaw – a user's manual: From Expanded Cinema to Virtual Reality*, ZKM Karlsruhe, Germany, 1997.

Schkolne, S., Pruett, M. and Schroeder, P.; *Surface Drawing: Creating Organic 3D Shapes with the Hand and Tangible Tools*, pp. 261–268, in proc. SIGCHI Conference on Human Factors in Computing Systems, ACM Press, 2001.

Schon, D.A.; *The Reflective Practitioner: How professionals think in action*, London, Temple Smith, 1983.

Schmal, P. C.; *Kunsthaus Graz... Archigram, the Original Blobmeister*, a-matter, Germany, 2004.

Shannon, C. E. and Weaver, W.; *The Mathematical Theory of Communications*, University of Illinois Press, Urbana, 1949.

Sischka, J., *Engineering the Construction of the Great Court Roof for the British Museum*, pp. 199–207, in Widespan Roof Structures, Thomas Telford Publishing, London, 2000.

Smit, T.; *eden*, Corgi, 2001.

Smith, G.D.; *Numerical Solution of Partial Differential Equations*, Oxford University Press, 1965.

Smith, H.; *The implications of the Latham, Egan and Urban Task Force reports for interdisciplinary working*, Heriot Watt University, Edinburgh, UK, 2001.

Sorkin, M..; *Frozen Light*, pp. 27–36, in *Gehry Talks: architecture + process*, Thames & Hudson, 1999.

Sowa, J.; *Conceptual Structures: Information Processing in Mind and Machine*, Addison-Wesley, 1984.

Steele, J.; *architecture and computers: action and reaction in the digital design revolution*, Laurence King, 2001.

Steiner, D.M., Pirker, S. and Ritter, K.; *Stronger Opponents Wanted*, Birkhauser, 2001.

Stiny, G.; *Pictorial and Formal Aspects of Shape Grammars and Aesthetic Systems*, Ph.D. Thesis, System Science, UCLA, 1975.

Strawn, J.; *Digital Audio Representation and Processing*, pp. 65–107, in Multimedia Systems, J.F. Koegel Buford (ed.), ACM Press, 1994.

Sutherland, I.; *Sketchpad, a man-machine graphical communication system*, PhD thesis, MIT, Dept. of Electrical Engineering, 1963.

Synge, J.L. and Schild, A.; *Tensor Calculus*, Dover, Toronto, 1949.

Sweeney, J.J. and Sert, J.L.; *Antoni Gaudi*, Architectural Press, London, 1960.

Szalapaj, P.J.; *CAD Principles for Architectural Design*, Architectural Press, Butterworth-Heinemann, 2001.

Szalapaj, P.J.; *The Representation of Contextual Place for Urban and Rural Planning*, EIA9 E-Activities in Building Design and Construction (9th EuropIA International Conference on the Applications/Implications of Computer Networking in Architecture, Construction, Design, Civil Engineering and Urban Planning), Istanbul Technical University, Istanbul, Turkey, October, 2003.

Szalapaj, P.J. and Kane, A.; *Computationally Assisted Design Formulation*, pp. 285–293, in Advanced Technologies, proc. Europia '93 (4th European Conference on the Applications of Artificial Intelligence and Robotics to Architecture), Delft, The Netherlands, June 1993.

Tietz, J.; T*he Story of Architecture of the 20th Century*, Konemann Verlagsgesellschaft mbH, Cologne, 1999.

Treuille, A., McNamara, A., Popovic, Z. And Stam, J.; *Keyframe Control of Smoke Simulations*, pp. 716–723, in ACM Transactions on Graphics, Vol.22, No.3, July 2003.

van Bruggen, C.; *Frank O. Gehry: Guggenheim Museum Bilbao,* The Solomon R. Guggenheim Foundation, New York, 1997.

Vile, A. and Polovina, S.; *Thinking of or Thinking Through Diagrams? The Case of Conceptual Graphs*, in proc. Thinking with Diagrams '98 conference Aberystwyth, UK August, 1998.

Vygotsky, L.S.; *Thought and Language*, MIT press, 1962.

Ward, G.J.; *The RADIANCE Lighting Simulation and Rendering System*, pp. 459–72, in Computer Graphics, proc. SIGGRAPH '94 conference, July 1994.

Waters, J.K.; *Blobitecture: Waveform Architecture and Digital Design*, Rockport, 2003.

Whalley, A.; *The Eden Project, Glass Houses, World Environments*, pp. 75–84, in Widespan Roof Structures, Thomas Telford Publishing, London, 2000.

Whittick, A.; *Erich Mendelsohn*, 2nd edition, Leonard Hill, London, 1956.

Williams, C.J.K.; *The Definition of Curved Geometry for Widespan Structures*, pp. 41–49, in Widespan Roof Structures, Thomas Telford Publishing, London, 2000.

Williams, C.J.K.; *Design by Algorithm*, pp. 79–85, in Digital Tectonics, Leach, N. et al. (eds), Wiley, 2004.

Williams, W.O.; *A Primer on the Mechanics of Tensegrity Structures*, Carnegie Mellon University, 2003.

Winograd, T.; Interview, pp. 53–54, in Human-Computer Interaction, J. Preece, Addison-Wesley, 1994

Winston, P. H.; *Artificial Intelligence*, Addison-Wesley, 1984.

Wooley, B.; *Virtual Worlds*, Blackwell, Oxford, 1992.

Worsley, G.; *How to Build the New World*, Daily Telegraph, London, UK, March, 2000.

Zaera, A.; *Frank Gehry 1991-5, Conversations with Frank O. Gehry*, in El Croquis, No. 74–5, 1995.

Index

Archigram   87, 109
architectural education   265
architecture   27
    contemporary   3, 9, 13, 42
    expressionist   13
    liquid   4
    magazine   208
    naval   248, 252
    organic   47, 50
    virtual   4
artificial intelligence (AI)   215-217
Arup, Ove   19, 159, 179

Baukunst   265
Bezier   87
    curve   212, 246
biome   161, 167-169
BIX media facade   103-109
blob   87
Bollinger and Grollman   89
Bolyai, Janos   87
B-spline
    curve   212
    surface modelling   87
Behnisch, Gunter   61
briefing   121, 138, 232
bubble diagram   233
Buckminster-Fuller   202
Buro-Happold   5, 60, 72, 77, 260

CAD   87, 240, 242
    3-D models   240
    models   91, 223, 226-231, 251, 257, 261
    modelling   258, 260
    modelling software   88
    modelling techniques   35
    sketch model   50, 211, 236
    systems   47, 56
CAD/CAM   29, 198, 205, 234-235, 249, 252-253, 262
    technology   198
CAPP   29
CATIA   208, 212, 234-237
CFD   190-191
Chomsky, Noam   219
circulation   136-137
cladding
    cushions   182

    design   182
    frame   188
    model   183
    panels   99
clients   113, 118-121, 130
CNC   29, 210, 213, 218, 254
compression   72, 74
cognitive science   219
computer
    animation   261
    vision   217-218
computational linguistics   219
concept design   121, 140-145
connected bigraph   203
consistency   260
constraints   74, 244
    circumferential   61
    design   59, 74
    drawing   55
    physical   74
    topological   62
construction   71-72, 77, 79, 82-83, 85, 97, 100, 103
contour model   98
contractors   192, 207-208, 234, 263-264
control points   32, 87
    parametric   89
controlled
    conditions   159
    environment   162, 172, 191
Cook, Peter   87
CPI   119
CSCW   241
curved forms   30, 55-56, 87
curves
    catenary   56
curvilinearity   210-211
cyberspace   4
cyclical design   6-7, 115, 255

design
    stages   120-121
    variables   62
developability   85, 250
developable surfaces   225-252
diagrams   222
digital
    expression   6
    information chain   83
    integration   6, 17

models	209, 213, 225, 232, 255, 257, 260-261, 263-264	
modelling	109, 213, 239, 260, 262	
organisation	6	
representation	242	
sketching	243-245	
technology	207, 264	
terrain modelling (DTM)	160-163, 169-71, 173, 180	
digitisation	32, 213, 242, 255	
directrix	249	
DNC	218	
DOE/2	8	
doubly curved		
facade	103	
form	96	
geometry	87	
drawing	37	
drawings		
2-D	8, 210, 257	
3-D	9	
CAD-generated	50	
dynamic symmetry	52-54	
ECOTECT	8	
Eden project	159-205	
EFTE		
cushions	61, 182	
Egan report	113, 117-118	
engineering	59-60, 83, 207, 209, 211, 217, 231, 235, 237	
environmental		
analysis	146-147	
loads	186	
services	153	
ESP-r	8	
ETC	7	
expression		
developmental	113	
exploratory	113	
fabrication	82-83, 207-209, 225, 234-239, 254-255, 257, 260-262	
FaulknerBrowns	113-157	
Finsterlin, Hermann	12	
Fitts' Law	244	
Foster, Norman	18-19, 60, 74, 77	

Fournier, Colin	87	
fractal	48	
frequency subdivision	166	
funicular model	56	
Gaussian		
analysis	225, 255	
curvature	85	
Gehry, Frank	207-240, 255, 257-258, 262-265	
generalised cylinders	217	
genetic algorithms	4	
geodesic		
dome	173, 200-202	
geometry	166, 172	
line	200	
sphere	160, 201-202	
structures	161, 202, 205	
geometry		
non-Euclidean	87	
trans-Euclidean	106	
gesture	211, 242, 244-245, 258	
Glymph, Jim	208-210, 234-239	
graphical input device	213, 240-246, 258	
great circle	200	
Great Court roof	60-85	
Grimshaw, Nicholas	159, 168, 174, 198	
Hambidge, Jay	49, 52, 54	
hex-tri-hex	174-178, 185	
HTB	166, 168, 179, 180, 198	
HTB2	8	
HTML	245	
Hubner, Peter	47, 50-51	
human-computer interaction	216, 242-243	
Hunt, Anthony	159, 174	
hyperspace	85	
hypersurface	85, 109	
ideation		
fluent	113	
graphic	222	
InfoLab 21	113–157	
InkML	245	
interaction		
3-D	241	
interface		
wimp	217	
interpolation	212	
isoparm	30	

iteration	67, 260	multi-parametric	
		capture	243
Kahn, Louis	17	stylus	244
KBE	26	MULTICS	216
keder	184		
kit-of-parts	19-20	natural language processing	218
knowledge		Nemetschek	50
economy	116	NC	218
engineering	241	non-Euclidean geometry	87
Kunsthaus, Graz	87–109	nonlinear systems	218
		NUBUS	216
Latham report	24-27, 113, 119-120	numerical analysis	
		NURBS	
LCS	216	curves	260
LIDS	218	surfaces	21, 30, 87, 247, 249-251, 260
linear approximation	218		
linguistics	215, 219		
LIMA	8	object-oriented	
Lobachevsky, Nicolai	87	programming	216, 245
Lofting	250	standards	245
logarithmic spiral	49-51	office	
LOM	254	layout	126, 156
LT	8	organisation	263
luff	184, 207	organic geometry	47
		Otto, Frei	61
machine tools	218		
MathML	245	paracube	106
Mendelsohn, Eric	12-16	parameterisation	62
Membrane theory	180	parametric	
Mero	166, 172, 174 185, 198	control	61
		design	235
Microstation	162	expressions	59, 260
MIT	207, 213, 215-239	geometry	55, 64-65
Mithra	8	modelling techniques	55
models		PDM	238
block	213	Perella, Stephen	109
check	213	phantom	
design process	213	points	249
funicular	56-57	surfaces	249-251
massing	148-149	philosophy	215, 219
physical	207, 209-210, 212-213, 220-222, 234, 255, 258	phyllotaxis	49
		planning	232-233
		PLM	238
volumetric	228-229	prefabrication	262
world	217	project managers	113, 117-119, 131
modelling		proportion	50, 54
aircraft	207, 248, 251		
physical	213, 263	RADIANCE	8
ship's hull	248, 250-253	rapid prototyping	29, 213, 254-255, 262
Moore's Law	263		
mouse	217, 242-243, 245	reflection-in-action	37, 240
		reflection-on-action	42

relaxation	66	model	264
Riemann, G.F.B.	87	pricing	234
robotic manufacture	77, 82	syntactic	219
ruled surface	248	stylus device	243-246, 258
rulings	248	Styrofoam	209-210, 254
		surface	
Shannon's theorem 17	244	complex curved	59
shape optimisation	72	curved	61
simulation		developable	201
acoustics	8	doubly curved	60-61
energy	8	models	210, 225
environmental	261	patches	30
lighting	8	Szyskowitz-Kowalski	35-45
software	8		
ventilation	8	tension	60, 78
single chine hull	250, 253	tensegrity	202-203
sintering	254	tensor	84
site analysis	134	T-NURCC	260
site work	164	tolerances	82, 225
sketch		topological	
2 1/2-D	217	shapes	261
design	209, 255, 257-258	structure	108
modelling	148, 257-258, 262	topology	108
primal	217	transformational grammar	219
sketching	37, 94, 211-214	T-spline	260
SLS	254		
Smit, Tim	159	unfolding	201
soap bubbles	61	UNIX	216
SoundPLAN	8	user-definable	87
space programming	232	user-defined objects	240
spaceballs	245		
spline	212	value engineering	224, 255
stair-stepping	254	value management	130, 139
Stata Center	215-235, 237	variables	
stereolithography	213, 254	design process	244
strain	84	dynamic	243-244
stress	62, 84	variational geometry	55
structural		vector	249, 261
analysis	152, 179-180, 262, 264	Vectorworks	233
		virtual	
characteristics	262	environments	258, 261
components	262	model	255
elements	262	reality	4
form	172, 260-261, 264	visual cues	217
loading	261	visualisation	35, 45
materials	262	VR walkthroughs	240
model	230-231, 263		
modelling	152	Walt Disney Concert Hall	207-208, 220, 236
optimisation	55	wind tunnel tests	187
structures		WTB	166, 168, 179, 198
equilibrated	56		
language	219	XML	245